How We Talk about Language

The most important challenges humans face – identity, life, death, war, peace, the fate of our planet – are manifested and debated through language. This book provides the intellectual and practical tools we need to analyze how people talk about language, how we can participate in those conversations, and what we can learn from them about both language and our society. Along the way, we learn that knowledge about language and its connection to social life is not primarily produced and spread by linguists or sociolinguists, or even language teachers, but through everyday conversations, online arguments, creative insults, music, art, memes, Twitterstorms – any place language grabs people's attention and foments more talk. An essential new aid to the study of the relationship between language, culture, and society, this book provides a vision for language inquiry by turning our gaze to everyday forms of language expertise.

BETSY RYMES is Professor of Educational Linguistics at the University of Pennsylvania's Graduate School of Education.

How We Talk about Language
Exploring Citizen Sociolinguistics

Betsy Rymes
University of Pennsylvania

CAMBRIDGE
UNIVERSITY PRESS

University Printing House, Cambridge CB2 8BS, United Kingdom

One Liberty Plaza, 20th Floor, New York, NY 10006, USA

477 Williamstown Road, Port Melbourne, VIC 3207, Australia

314–321, 3rd Floor, Plot 3, Splendor Forum, Jasola District Centre, New Delhi – 110025, India

79 Anson Road, #06–04/06, Singapore 079906

Cambridge University Press is part of the University of Cambridge.

It furthers the University's mission by disseminating knowledge in the pursuit of education, learning, and research at the highest international levels of excellence.

www.cambridge.org
Information on this title: www.cambridge.org/9781108488310
DOI: 10.1017/9781108770194

© Betsy Rymes 2020

This publication is in copyright. Subject to statutory exception and to the provisions of relevant collective licensing agreements, no reproduction of any part may take place without the written permission of Cambridge University Press.

First published 2020

A catalogue record for this publication is available from the British Library.

ISBN 978-1-108-48831-0 Hardback
ISBN 978-1-108-72596-5 Paperback

Cambridge University Press has no responsibility for the persistence or accuracy of URLs for external or third-party internet websites referred to in this publication and does not guarantee that any content on such websites is, or will remain, accurate or appropriate.

Contents

List of Figures	*page* vi
List of Tables	vii
Preface: Being Meaningful	ix
Introduction: How We Talk about Language – Citizen Sociolinguistics and Its Study	1
1 Citizen's Arrest! The "Citizen" and Citizen Sociolinguistics	29
2 Wonderment: The Spark that Starts Talk about Language	66
3 Doing Citizen Sociolinguistics: The Medium Is the Method	98
4 Fomenting Wonderment and Critique: Feedback Loops	128
5 Citizen Sociolinguistics and Narrative	150
6 Acts of Citizen Sociolinguistics	170
Conclusion: Why We Must Talk about Language	185
References	193
Index	199

Figures

0.1	Everyday expertise	*page* 14
1.1	Angry Pepe	43
2.1	Points of entry into conversations about language: arrest and wonderment	69
2.2	Quackson	72
2.3	Barbuzzo menu featuring the word *gabagool*	73
2.4	Top *gabagool* definition, Urban Dictionary	74
2.5	Chadwick Boseman meme	88
2.6	"Finna" definition	94
2.7	Why is gentrification . . .	97
2.8	Why is gentrification so . . .	97
3.1	Examples of online language quizzes	102
3.2	*Pleez* as an example of eye dialect	118

Tables

4.1	Feedback for language self-portraits	*page* 133
5.1	Web 1.0 phenomena and their Web 2.0 analogues	152
5.2	Metalanguage for 1.0 taxonomy of acoustic features vs. 2.0 folksonomy of social value	153
5.3	What narratives do	155
5.4	Key features of logico-scientific vs. narrative modes	157
5.5	Modes of knowing as analogues to Web 1.0 and Web 2.0	158
5.6	Sample word list and lexical prompts for the Accent Challenge	161
5.7	Narrative components of thethugyone's introduction	162
5.8	Narrative components of LifeTracking's introduction	163

Preface
Being Meaningful

> Meaning may not be a precondition of humanity as much as a by-product of it.
> Douglas Rushkoff (2006, p. 8)

Very few will argue with the proposition that "meaning" is important. But what actually is "meaning" and how do we find it? In this book, I propose one way: by looking at talk about language. Talking about something as seemingly abstract as language (as opposed to something more palpable like life and death) might give the impression we are engaged in something meaningless: "That's just talk." But, while alive, *just talk* is our primary way of communicating our experiences. We consider the realities of "life" and "death" and make sense of all the events in between by labeling them with words and having a discussion – often about those very labels. *Meaning* results from these discussions. In this way, as Douglas Rushkoff remarks in the quote above, meaning emerges as a "by-product" of humanity rather than a "precondition" for it. How we talk about the world creates it in a way that is meaningful for us.

Exactly *how* we label and discuss our world can be an object both of critique and of wonderment. All animals die, but only humans can talk about it, and we have many different ways of doing so. The way we discuss the inevitability that we will all one day "kick the bucket," "keel over," "bite the dust," "go gentle into that good night," or modestly "pass away" can spark both criticism and awe. Someone might be accused of insensitivity for using the phrase "keel over" in one context, or of being overly oblique for using "pass away" in another. Like such moments of language critique, moments of wonderment – a blend of admiration and awe, maybe mixed with a little fear – can also lead us into talk about language: "Did you just say *kick the bucket*? Is that really how you describe someone's death? Why? Who said that around you? Who still says that?" Such moments of wonderment and of critique can lead to conversations about language, about how we label and navigate (make sense of) our world. Whatever foments this talk about talk, be it the sting of critique or the spark of wonderment, these conversations map out our own uniquely human journey of talking meaning into being.

Talking about each other's language can be painful too, especially if such talk reveals deep-seated differences and brings out harsh judgments. Sometimes, feeling shame or confusion in the face of critique, we avoid talking about our language, or even thinking about it. We may even use language in certain ways to deliberately ward off critique. This raises an ever-present tension between *talk as a shield* that keeps us from meaningfully engaging with perspectives other than our own and *talk as an invitation*, an opening for communication. Most people don't want to use language, ostensibly a tool of communication and creative expression, in ways that drain it of meaning, alienate people around them, or build barriers. However, much of our socialization as humans forces us to develop a way of using language that does just that. Often, as we learn to be part of a community, we build ourselves a cocoon of locally standardized language that encases us in familiarity. As we grow and develop as part of a specific social group with set purposes, our language potentially becomes even more standardized and specialized.

Paradoxically, this socialization into standardized ways of speaking, a process that facilitates mutual intelligibility, can also function to build language barriers around people who view "correct" or even "meaningful" language in different ways. An embrace of standardized or otherwise isolating ways of speaking and thinking can be a warning sign of looming closed-mindedness. When standardized ways of speaking and other rigid notions about how language should and should not be used dominate a conversation or go unquestioned, other voices, new languages and ways of speaking, locally relevant, original and zesty, disappear, and the most standardized of speakers will continue to cultivate their own isolation from those voices.

Reactions to language like critique and wonderment, however, can function as invitations to construct meaning together in new ways. The sting of critique or a spark of wonderment can bring on conversations about language that take down barriers between groups of speakers by raising awareness about how language builds meaning differently in different contexts. Talk about language provides a means for *resistance to standardization* – resistance to the idea that there is some standardized form of expression that counts more than others. This resistance to the standardization of language, communication, and meaning-making does not in any way necessitate the rejection of clarity and insight of people who are well-spoken, or even those who might come off as pretentious or who self-righteously weaponize language. These voices contribute to an eternally morphing collection of perspectives best considered together. While we can use language as a shield from others, a way to build boundaries between all our tiny demographic comfort zones, talk *about* language opens up a way to engage meaningfully with other viewpoints and in the process develop shared understandings.

Discerning readers will certainly be wondering: What about those who talk about language in hateful and discouraging ways? What about those situations where talk about language entrenches discrimination and narrow-mindedness? Undeniably, people talk about language in ignorant ways that build barriers, stereotype other people, and close down conversations. This book will investigate those narrow, stereotyping, and potentially cruel remarks about language too – as well as the ways that everyday people extend those conversations rather than close them down. Carrying on these conversations about language provides one pathway to understanding the everyday, ramifying nature of our ideological differences.

The purpose of this book is to illustrate the various ways people enter into conversations about language and to suggest ways of promoting the everyday deliberation that can come from considering multiple perspectives and where they come from. This talk *about talk*, though it sounds so abstract and meta, may be the most real, down-to-earth, and uniquely human thing we do. This everyday talk about language comprises what I am calling *citizen sociolinguistics*, an approach to language that differs both from the standardized prescriptions you could get from a grammar book or style guide and the systematic description of language change that a trained sociolinguist might provide. Both standardized prescription and systematic description illuminate ways we humans make meaning through talk about language, but they represent only a tiny pinprick percentage of the infinite variety of conversations about language going on every day. Standardized prescriptions for how language should work, or systematized descriptions of how language changes, are rarely the goal of the everyday conversations about language that are the focus of this book. Instead, citizen sociolinguistic dialogue usually emerges from moments of critique or wonderment, when language appears to lack precision or systematicity, when we discover its inherent idiosyncrasy or unexpected nuttiness, or the way it leads to ruptures in understanding – all this makes us start talking about how language works in our lives for us and the people around us, expanding our awareness of language difference and social distinction in the process. In what follows, I hope to guide readers along on this collaborative production of meaning that can be sparked when we talk about language. The production of meaning never stops and everyday talk about language will not end on the last page of this book. But I hope, as you journey through these pages, you'll accept this invitation to think in new ways about *How We Talk about Language*, and its role in making meaning.

Introduction
How We Talk about Language – Citizen Sociolinguistics and Its Study

> No matter how smart you are, no one is smart enough to see the whole world. There's always a picture too big to see.
>
> Chang-rae Lee, *Native Speaker* (1995, p. 46)

In 2015, a 51-year-old software engineer and Wikipedia editor named Bryan Henderson (username Giraffedata) was revealed to have been systematically removing the phrase "comprised of" from all Wikipedia entries. He considered "comprised of" an offense – a violation of English grammar rules. Between 2010 and 2015 he had eliminated more than 47,000 occurrences of this phrase, replacing it with one he believed to be more correct: "composed of." When the story broke, many weighed in to praise his efforts, or, in opposition, to support "comprised of" as a legitimate and grammatically correct expression. Others were more ambivalent. Jimmy Wales, the founder and overall mastermind of Wikipedia did not shut him down, acquiescing as Giraffedata continued to comb through Wikipedia on his *comprised-of*-eliminating mission. Geoffrey Nunberg, National Public Radio's language correspondent, wrote regarding the ordeal, "It doesn't matter if you consider a word to be correct English. If some sticklers insist that it's an error, the dictionaries and style manuals are going to counsel you to steer clear of it to avoid bringing down their wrath" (Nunberg, 2015).

As soon as I heard the *comprised of* story, I shared it with students and friends, eager for their opinions, and inevitably, after chuckling about the obsessed quality of this Wikipedia grammar shark, circling the encyclopedic waters for a stray "comprised of," people would ask me to contribute my own expertise to the discussion. As someone holding a Ph.D. in Applied Linguistics, friends often look to me as the last word – not only on the "comprised of" issue, but on all language controversies. But even with that Ph.D., I'm afraid I rarely provide that singular answer people are looking for. Because I know that expertise in language use – the ability to diagnose any language "problem" as Giraffedata did – comes from experiences with that language in context. Limited (like all of us) to my own experiences of language, I'm usually not entirely familiar with the context in which whatever expression under question

1

has been used. Unlike Giraffedata, who, at least when it comes to "comprised of," stands cocked and loaded with an assessment and a correction, I'm usually not able to offer up fast and effective solutions to questions about language. Instead, I annoyingly demur: I don't mind "comprised of," but if people around you don't like that phrase, and you have something you want to say to them, just choose a different expression.

People will ask me questions that range far beyond "comprised of," but my answers are equally wishy-washy. What does "Eyebrows on Fleek" mean? To be honest, I'm not exactly sure. "Woke"? I am definitely not the expert on that one! Should "literally" ever be used figuratively? How should we pronounce "croissant"? Well, that depends who you ask! I know these wishy-washy answers are frustrating. But providing a definitive answer to most language questions usually requires more knowledge than any one person can provide – even a very adamant and active language correction maven like Giraffedata. If that's the case, where does language expertise come from? Who should we ask?

My usual answer to that question is: Ask the person who just used that word! What does it mean to them? Why did they use it? Then, ask a few more people. Look around, listen, and observe how people talk about language. Then compare your answers. These suggestions can lead people on an important journey – something like the journey this book will take you through. Rather than offering up stand-alone answers to questions about language, or a theory that explains it all, or a series of myth-busting reveals, I hope to offer a guide for exploring *How we talk about language* – because this everyday talk often provides the best answers to questions about how language works in people's lives. The knowledge you accumulate by listening to everyday conversations about language ultimately may be more useful than any standardized dictionary entry.

This humble suggestion to simply listen to what everyday people say about language differs dramatically from the kind of expertise people are seeking when they consult a grammar book, a style guide, or a professor. I'm providing a process to explore social norms, not a statement of top-down language standards to be adhered to in all cases. Instead of looking to experts in the field of Linguistics for definitive diagnoses of language issues, I am suggesting that these institutionally centered voices are just one of many different interesting and personally invested views on language. We see many more views and realities once we start investigating the everyday knowledge of people who explore language around them and share that information freely – on the street, in conversation, in YouTube videos, in Facebook posts, on Wikipedia or Urban Dictionary, or other media. Bryan Henderson, aka Giraffedata, is one of those voices. We can see many other perspectives out there once we stop looking for the one "right" and authoritative answer and, instead, pay attention to *how people talk about language*. I call this practice of talking about language *citizen sociolinguistics*.

Citizen Science

Citizen sociolinguistics has its roots in a broader concept, *citizen science*, which throughout its over 100-year history, has reconfigured expertise, led to new knowledge, pushed the scientific community to rethink concepts, and generated information that has potential to influence arguments about pressing political issues including environmental conservation and global warming.

A look at the tradition of citizen science – and its power both to inform professional science and to challenge its assumptions – begins to illustrate the new lens on language, the new forms of knowledge, that citizen sociolinguistics might provide. Citizen science uses the intelligence, time, and know-how of laypeople (not professional scientists) to contribute to scientific research. This practice has been going on for hundreds of years: Birds, possums, butterflies, and flowers have been researched by ordinary people. The citizen science collectivity has often given voice to alternative perspectives, adding insight, and soliciting wider community engagement in the commitments of more obscure professional scientists or the seemingly random obsessions of individual thinkers. In the early 1800s, Henry David Thoreau kept meticulous notes on "first flowering dates, first leaf-out dates, and the first arrival dates of migratory birds in Concord, Massachusetts" (Knight, 2012). These careful diaries of flora and fauna were considered pointlessly idiosyncratic in his time, and led his peer and fellow transcendentalist, Ralph Waldo Emerson, to mention in his eulogy for Thoreau that he "had no ambition ... Instead of engineering for all America, he was the captain of a huckleberry party" (Walls, 2017, p. 308).

He may not have been obviously ambitious, but as a meticulously observant citizen scientist, Thoreau was probably more influential as "captain of a huckleberry party" than he would have had he been "engineering for all America." His careful, minutely descriptive diary entries captured what others could not see as important in his time, but which have become a model for climate-change trackers. Following Thoreau's model, citizen scientists continued to monitor flowers, plants, and birds in Concord, and today this body of information, a longitudinal record begun by Henry David Thoreau over 150 years ago and continued by citizen scientists, has been used by contemporary horticulturalists to track climate change and its jarring effects (Nijhuis, 2007). According to some reports, of the 600 flowering plants described in Thoreau's diaries, only 400 have been found today. While the record-keeping by Thoreau began as an idiosyncrasy (and originally had nothing to do with long-term climate monitoring), its embrace by a line of like-minded citizen horticulturalists turned those idiosyncratic musings into a collective project and led to more broadly useful findings about habitat destruction and global warming.

Research on the migration of monarch butterflies tells another story of how an individual obsession developed into collective engagement. The flight patterns of monarch butterflies were an abiding mystery that captivated the mind of Dr. Fred Urquhart who, even as a child, wondered to himself where all the monarchs in Toronto went in the winter. None of the specialists, nor any of the books he consulted, had an answer. Urquhart, who had become a Professor of Zoology at the University of Toronto by the 1930s, devised a way to find an answer: By developing a user-friendly method of tagging monarch butterflies, he was able to enlist thousands of volunteers to tag the monarch butterflies they spotted. After nearly 40 years of carefully plotting the paths of monarch butterflies by pinning to a giant map the thousands of labels returned (via US mail) by citizen scientists, Urquhart found an answer to his question: In January 1975, he received a phone call from hikers on Mexico's Neovolcanic Plateau saying that they had come across millions of monarch butterflies. A documentary about his methods and discovery, *Flight of the Butterflies* (Slee, 2012), features the work of both Urquhart and the citizen scientists who helped him follow the monarchs.

To this day, websites like monarchwatch.org continue to engage everyday butterfly enthusiasts not only in tracking butterflies, but also in facilitating their journey and preserving their habitat – one threatened by modern development. In backyards and schoolyards, citizen scientists now sustain dwindling monarch habitats by planting gardens of milkweed, the one food needed to support very hungry monarch caterpillars, to fuel their transformation into butterflies and ultimately their long journey to their overwintering spot in Mexico. Citizen participation in Urquhart's project not only solved his original mystery, but this collective work has also fostered new mindsets about habitat reclamation and the need for environmental conservation.

Citizen engagement also has the potential to upend assumptions within the scientific community that originally prompt investigation. In 2008, professors at the University of South Australia set out to do a large-scale study of possum behavior in Australia in order to manage the potential nuisance to people, their homes, their pets, and their gardens. Using citizen science strategies, they sent surveys out across the country asking Australians to describe their relationships with possums around them. To the researchers' surprise, the stories told in the surveys largely featured possums as endearing characters (with names like Percy, Mrs. Fatbum, and Jabba the Hutt) and details about unique and even lovable possum behavior. These observations by ordinary folk were collected into a book, *The Possum-Tail Tree*, and, by challenging the scientists' original assumptions about possums' role in Australian agriculture, changed Australian possum management strategy and its public relations approach (Daniels and Roetman, 2009).

All of these projects have drawn on the careful observations and geographical distribution of laypeople – "citizen scientists" – to compile detailed information that could never be attained by a single professional scientist working solo (even with a team of graduate students). Moreover, these three citizen science collaborations not only depended on citizens to gather data, but also fostered scientists' engagement with a community that shared their concerns about a particular feature of the environment: plants, flowers, butterflies, or possums. In all these projects, laypeople were not only crucial data collectors, but they also brought new perspectives to the scientific object of study and engaged a wider array of everyday people, increasing the social value of any scientific findings. Thoreau's notes might have represented nothing but a meaningless "huckleberry party" had they not been taken up by a chain of other citizens concerned with the documentation of Massachusetts flora and fauna. Dr. Urquhart's potentially idiosyncratic and obscure question ("Where do all the butterflies go?") may never have gained recognition were it not for the cadres of everyday people who voluntarily joined in his mission to find the answer – and whose stories make up the now even more widely distributed documentary about monarchs. And possums in Australia may never have been recognized for their non-nuisancey, endearing status had the zoologists studying them not included the voices of citizen scientists.

Citizen Sociolinguistics and Citizen Science

Citizen science is the study of the world by the people who live in it and, as such, have devised ways to understand it that may be more relevant than the ways that highly specialized professionals have developed or have the capacity to carry out. *Citizen sociolinguistics*, by analogy, is the study of the world of language and communication by the people who use it and, as such, have devised ways to understand it that may be more relevant than the ways professional sociolinguists have developed. Citizen sociolinguists, just like citizen scientists, hold an important, yet often overlooked form of expertise: Because they are using language every day, and in most cases need language to make it through each day, their conversations about language and how it works *for them* illuminate the nuanced social value that people put on certain ways of speaking. Just as citizen scientists see things that professionals might not – butterflies and caterpillars on low-hanging branches, details of flora and fauna over decades and centuries, endearing possum behavior – citizen sociolinguists see details and nuance in language use that professionals may not have access to, or just never notice or seriously consider.

Just as citizen scientists increase the awareness of scientific inquiry by being involved in it, citizen sociolinguists create social value around language by broadening participation in conversations about language. Any statement about the proper use of a certain word or pronunciation, say, "*Literally* should not be used figuratively" or "*Sandy* is a man's name" or "*Aunt* is NOT pronounced *ant*," potentially contributes to the social valuation of certain ways of speaking within a given social context. Whether you agree with these statements or not, they are being voiced, and as such, they will have an impact – even readers at this moment may be considering whether they agree with those language claims about *Literally*, *Sandy*, and *Aunt*. These statements about language foment conversations about language, which generate more conversations about language, and conversations about those conversations, and then these conversations accumulate, and the debates roll on, indefinitely. In this way everyday conversations about language both reflect and reproduce the process of social valuation of certain linguistic forms – including the dynamic and ever-changing quality of that social valuation.

These everyday conversations about language are not only a rich resource (some might call it "data") for professionals to analyze, but they are also sources of important and overlooked language expertise. Since we usually look to institutions and credentialed individuals as experts, positing everyday conversation as a source of expertise may seem like a step backwards. If citizen sociolinguistics involves no formal, institutionally granted expertise, how does it have any authority? And what good does it do? I will be illustrating how expertise within citizen sociolinguistics comes from being part of a community – not above it. Throughout this book, I'll be returning to two critical points which are also a foundation of citizen science in general: Everyday discussions about language (1) reconfigure what counts as expertise, expanding awareness of local nuance, and (2) potentially foment grassroots-motivated social action and change. In the same way that citizen science has been able to make visible important aspects of our environment, fueling arguments for environmental conservation and resistance to habitat destruction, everyday acts of citizen sociolinguistics make visible otherwise unseen aspects of language and communication, building expanded awareness of language diversity and change, and its role in society.

Citizen Sociolinguistics on the Street: Greenwich, Moyamensing, and Passyunk

Our journey into citizen sociolinguistics begins now, at street level, in my favorite city and hotbed of everyday conversation about language, Philadelphia. If you want to know how to pronounce a Philadelphia street name like *Greenwich Street*, the people who live there are the best source for you. Readers might be surprised to hear something that sounds like *Green Witch Street* as the preferred pronunciation presented by Philadelphia residents.

This may grate on the ears of someone accustomed to the *Grin-itch* pronunciation of Greenwich Village in Manhattan, Greenwich, London, or Greenwich mean time. You will find opinionated people who insist there is one and only one proper pronunciation for this word, historical linguists able to trace the transformation in this pronunciation through the years, and phonologists who will explain how these sounds change over time. Those responses tell us something about the people offering them up and the types of expertise valued in their own institutional context, but they have less to tell us about how people say *Greenwich Street* in Philadelphia. Neither the strongest opinion nor the most well-documented historical or phonological research will have much impact on how people who live on Greenwich Street say that name every day.

But just using language every day does not qualify as citizen sociolinguistics – there must be dialogue. Citizen sociolinguistics happens when people have conversations about language and share their street-level expertise with a wider community – through this process, citizen sociolinguists gain authority and, by sparking more conversations among new people, foster locally sourced, grassroots-level social awareness. Examples of this type of citizen sociolinguistic *talk-about-language* unfurls in the comment threads under YouTube videos and, for example, under one discussing street names in Philadelphia (including Greenwich St.), where one comment asks anyone out there reading how to pronounce another tricky Philadelphia street name, "Moyamensing":

COMMENT (A): Just show me how to say 'Moyamensing' and I'm good . . .
REPLY (B): Moy-Men-Sing (I'm from south philly so trust me) (1 Thumb up)

Responder B has a ready answer for Commenter A about "Moyamensing" – and justifies that answer with neither opinionated rhetoric nor scholarly grounding, but with personal history as a local: "I'm from south philly so trust me." Instead of relying on institutionally credentialed expertise to explain language around them, citizen sociolinguists like Responder B use the knowledge located in their language community and in their experiences with language in that context to speak authoritatively. And, by asking the question, by joining an internet comment thread, Commenter A has expanded their social network, which now includes local knowledge they might not otherwise be privy to.

On its own, this isolated exchange does not make a great case for the power of citizen sociolinguistic dialogue. Nor would one butterfly observation from an Ohio backyard, or a page from Henry David Thoreau's diary have much real influence on climate-change discussions. But, bit by bit, those flower and butterfly observations and local insights have created a collective shift in the way science understands climate and habitat destruction. Similarly, while one conversation about the pronunciation of one street name will not tilt the scales of language awareness, an accumulation of such conversations builds collective expertise. This type of everyday, local knowledge, distributed among citizen sociolinguists, can collectively push back against the expertise claimed by outsiders. These everyday conversations become acts of citizen sociolinguistics, bit by bit making local knowledge about language visible and, often, contesting outsider involvement and interference.

This story from the South Philadelphia online news site, *The Passyunk Post*, illustrates how discussions of language entwine with issues of local control. The headline, "Zillow predicts Point Breeze and 'Greenwich' to be Philly's new hottest neighborhoods," and certain details in the article draw fire from some readers.

Commenters, like Commenter A below, are quick to take issue with Zillow's mapping of the neighborhood, contesting the claim that this area is or has ever been called "Greenwich":

COMMENTER A: Yeah, you know that neighborhood "Greenwich" that is nowhere near Greenwich St? Or anything associated with that name? This town needs more areas that are watered down New York neighborhood names.

Commenter A's sarcastic reference to Philadelphia's need for more "watered down New York" names, alluding, it seems, to Greenwich Village, implicates Philadelphia locals' distinct *Green-witch* pronunciation as well. Whether Commenter A had that in mind or not, a subsequent comment picks up on this comparison, reminding *Passyunk Post* readers that Philadelphia residents have a special way of saying *Greenwich Street*:

COMMENTER B: It's pronounced Green-Witch in South Philly.

These observations may seem like arcane, trivial details about South Philly, made more trivial by their appearance in a local, online news source. Although they are highly localized details, they are not trivial – their local specificity gives them power, something which *The Passyunk Post*'s editors seem to understand. The *Passyunk Post* covers news for a relatively small section of Philadelphia and insists that contributors be from South Philadelphia if they want their articles published. It actively resists including outside voices, especially real-estate professionals, as stated on their contributors' page. If you would like to write for *The Passyunk Post* ...

You *must* live or work in South Philly and you should know the subjects we already cover ... You should also be a curious, self-motivated person who has plenty of ideas on what to write about. Also, no real-estate pros, sorry. (Passyunk Post, n.d., emphasis in original)

Clearly, *The Passyunk Post* prioritizes local knowledge, and it seems the editorial policy is to actively resist the intrusion of "real-estate pros" (and, they probably hope, their "watered down" neighborhood labels). However, this local paper has a readership that goes far beyond South Philly. According to their home page, there are over one million unique readers per year, far more people than live in South Philly. *The Passyunk Post* potentially provides a site where local voices gain currency, where their expertise *as locals* matters, not only to fellow locals, but also to an expanding readership, which they are educating about South Philly ways. Importantly, this readership may be learning not only from articles posted on the site, but also – maybe even primarily – from the comment threads beneath those articles.

For citizen sociolinguists like those commenters excerpted above, who are engaged in conversations about language in their lives and neighborhoods, local knowledge counts as language expertise, interaction expands the reach and extent of that local expertise, and those sites of interaction around language potentially become a medium for grassroots activism or resistance to outsiders and top-down imposition of more standardized language. Citizen sociolinguistic discussion becomes a means through which everyone learns a bit more about local language and its impact.

Up to this point, we have seen champions of the local pronunciation: the unquestioned advice on how to say *Moy-men-sing*, and the sarcastic reference to those outsiders who pronounce *Green-witch street* like *Greenwich Village*. We haven't seen critics of these unique ways of speaking. But even as some Philadelphia locals speak out in favor of their special ways, some may also express, at times, a wry recognition of the idiosyncratic nature of these ways – solidarity and pride in something outsiders may see as "wrong," but a simultaneous recognition that local knowledge can have blind spots. This complex form of local pride comes through in a blog site called *Ghost of South Philly*, in which the author, Tantris, raises the topic of Green-Witch street, but also parenthetically mentions the "Anglo Saxon" pronunciation of "Greenwich."

Greenwich Street, or *Green Witch* as they say in South Philly (just for the record in the Anglo Saxon language known as *English* Greenwich is pronounced *gren-itch* so remember that when ordering a Cheesesteak at Geno's). Greenwich is a small side street that runs east-west between Dickenson and Tasker. (Tantris, 2006)

Readers not from Philadelphia may find this parenthetical aside baffling. Geno's? Why are we suddenly talking about ordering a cheesesteak? With this remark, Tantris is making an ironic connection to another infamous language debate in South Philly. For years, Geno's, a destination cheesesteak purveyor in the heart of South Philadelphia, had a sign in its window commanding that customers (in Green-Witch-pronouncing South Philly) speak English when ordering their food. The sign, which used to be placed prominently in the window where customers place their cheesesteak orders was illustrated with a billowing American flag and majestic Bald Eagle head, and read as follows (quotation marks in the original):

This is AMERICA.
WHEN ORDERING "SPEAK ENGLISH"

With his mention of the "Anglo Saxon" quality lacking from some South Philadelphia "English" expressions, Tantris is making the wry point that the range of what counts as speaking "English" may be very wide, with arbitrary boundaries. However, the prefatory comment on Geno's sign, "This is America," implies that those who are not from Geno's "America" and who may speak another language, like Spanish, are not welcome. So Tantris's "Greenwich" comment seems to be suggesting that Geno's demand for "English" is not only obnoxious, but also hypocritical – coming as it is from a South Philly resident who speaks nothing like standardized English, someone who probably says "Green-witch Street" in a non "Anglo Saxon" manner. Since Geno himself speaks nothing like the Queen (and, I might add, also uses quotation marks idiosyncratically), his demands for "English" from his customers seem to be (barely) masking other forms of discrimination. Not incidentally, many others have sounded Tantris's critique of Geno's language signs and, after years of protests and controversy about Geno's demands, the recognition that they were hypocritical and even xenophobic became widely acknowledged, and the signs did eventually come down.

Not just anyone can tell Geno to take down his sign and have an impact. But a local who draws on the expertise only a local can have – expertise embedded in an appreciation of local language generally – can level critiques that may have more impact. Though Tantris clearly holds a reverence for South Philly idiosyncrasy, he also pokes some fun at South Philly *Green-witch* holdouts by pointedly criticizing the bigotry of Geno's sign. Despite the criticism embedded in Tantris's parenthetical observation, that insight about the pronunciation of *Greenwich* also endows his critique with local flair, affection, and authority. His lighthearted criticism illustrates the power of expertise that comes from fine-grained knowledge of local language. Embedding his critique in local language lore implies that he is not an outsider gentrifier coming in and telling Geno to be politically correct. Instead, he is locally entitled to raise the issue.

Even as expertise becomes more finely tuned and localized, seemingly exclusive and narrow, its circulation on the Web and across social groups expands the network of those who share this nuanced knowledge. With this expanded awareness of local perspectives, through incremental acts of citizen sociolinguistics, comes the potential for bottom-up social action. As the Geno insult suggests, this locally sourced authority may also be more effective at resisting local forms of bigotry than top-down approaches. (No wonder dictators and fascists try to quell everyday conversation about even the most seemingly trivial topics – as it's through these locally shared points of reference that people build their own collective power).

By now, it should be becoming clear that a number of people in Philadelphia have strong opinions about street names (and other language points). And we have not even come to Passyunk Avenue yet! While taking in the South Philly local newspaper's name, *The Passyunk Post*, readers may have been subvocalizing this as "Passy-unk Post." Or possibly "Pash-unk Post." Or you may not have been subvocalizing at all – just wondering how locals might pronounce that word. There's no easy answer. It's controversial. And, on Philadelphia's City Data Forum there is an entire thread designated to the discussion of "Street Name Pronunciation" in which the pronunciation of "Passyunk Ave" is taken up. The comments below illustrate the extent of deliberation around "Passyunk Ave." which appears on page one, in September 2012, and continues to be debated over three days and three pages, and then revived on page five, nearly four years later, in August 2016 (initials used to anonymize contributors):

MG: Pass-shunk, never passy-yunk.
DC: Pass-yunk.
People who pronounce it the illiterate way usually say Pah-shunk.
MG: It's pass-shunk or, if you prefer, pah-shunk to all the natives I've ever talked to.
EA: My "Souf Filly" grandparents were partial to the latter pronunciation.
MG: I actually think it's charming. I bought some tulip tables off a Souf Filly Italian guy (with a gold chain) last weekend, and he was at "16th and Pas-shunk."
AV: We pronounce Passyunk just like it's spelled – maybe I'm not hanging with the right crowd.
RW: Passhunk is Passhunk.
ROW: I hate to break it to you guys that seem dead set on pronouncing it Pass-shunk for some reason but it is "Pass-yunk" . . . . just like "Mana-yunk" [Manayunk is a Philly neighborhood]
MG: No one says Passyunk like Manayunk, except for transplants from the suburbs.
ROW: Sorry I like to pronounce things the way they are actually pronounced . . . I don't like sounding illiterate. It's very clearly Pass-yunk. Passhunk?! WTH? [acronym for "What The Hell?"]
EA: It's a generational divide more than anything else. I say Passayunk too, although some of my older relatives have "corrected" me. 😉
And aren't you from Ridley Park, MG? Last time I checked, that's a suburb . . .
SG: Yea, the only people I've ever heard pronounce it "Passhunk" are a bit older.
DC: I hear lots of kids in their 20s who grew up in the neighborhood say "passhunk". But then people in SP have crazy ways of pronouncing all kinds of words that have nothing to do with how it's spelled – "Dickerson" for Dickinson, Booveer for Bouvier, gabagool for capocollo (misspelled in the US as capicolla), rihGUT for ricotta, etc, etc.
. . . *four years later* . . .

AJ: I'm really surprised to see any debate on Passyunk. Everything I've read points to Passhunk. It's an old native american word meaning "in the valley." I hear Passhunk by a lot of people and live very close to where DC used to (near Dickinson or "Dickerson" as he mentioned ... haha).

In this dialogue, two camps emerge, and there are strong voices on either side. MG is firmly on the side of "pashunk." He voices this explicitly ("Pass-shunk, never passy-yunk") and repeatedly. He also bolsters his argument with an appeal to "natives" ("It's pass-shunk or, if you prefer, pah-shunk to all the natives I've ever talked to"), and with a local anecdote about buying "tulip tables":

MG: I actually think it's charming. I bought some tulip tables off a Souf Filly Italian guy (with a gold chain) last weekend, and he was at "16th and Pas-shunk."

RW ("Passhunk is Passhunk") falls in line with MG. But ROW is firmly opposed, preferring Passyunk to the "illiterate" way, and EA comes down in between. EA also appeals to local roots, drawing on the expertise of "souf filly" grandparents (who would say "pah-shunk"), but admits to saying "Passayunk" at times. Finally, AJ comes in, four years later, on the side of "Passhunk," bolstering that argument with a completely new contention about the historical roots of the word: "Everything I've read points to Passhunk. It's an old native american word meaning 'in the valley'."

While this thread includes differences of opinion, the discussion stays on topic, and gratuitous insults are kept to a minimum (DC's insinuation that Pahshunk pronouncers are "illiterate" sticks out to me as the most egregious). Collectively, the dialogue provides a range of justifications for either perspective, the possibility of generational differences, the dubious authority of someone from the "suburbs," and the status of "Ridley Park" as a suburb in this regard. It's unlikely that the 2012 participants have seen AJ's 2016 contribution about the Native American origins (and pronunciation) of Passyunk – and nobody else is joining the conversation at this point, but AJ's perspective has been registered and awaits discussion (and now this author and you, my readers, have seen it!).

AJ's post uniquely brings up the Native American origins of Passyunk, but also stealthily embeds them in comradery around other local South Philly ways. In this way it is similar to Tantris's parenthetical remark about Geno's. Just as Tantris was pointing out the hypocrisy of Geno's anti-immigrant sign, AJ is bringing in potentially 'politically correct' information about the original residents of South Philadelphia, Native Americans. This seems like an abrupt departure from the earlier discussion, in which "Souf Filly grandparents," not being from the suburbs, and a gold-chained Italian were key talking points. But AJ also includes important local information and location, and even a nod to the local pronunciation of yet another controversial street name mentioned in the conversation ("Dickerson ... haha!"). While nobody has responded to AJ on this forum (as of this writing), the contribution, like Tantris's comment about Geno's, illustrates how even a simple discussion of street names can allude to a language debate with more wide-ranging social impact – multilingualism and immigration in the United States or the displacement of Native Americans and their languages. In these conversations, the expertise invoked to discuss wide-ranging social issues does not come from outsiders or external, standardized sources, but from the ability of the speaker to embed their new information in a more nuanced ongoing conversation about local language.

This City Data forum dialogue, combined with the previous discussion of Greenwich Street and Moyamensing, provide us with a snapshot of conversation on street name pronunciation in various social media – an example of how we, everyday people, talk about language. In these conversations, citizen sociolinguists, by voicing their views on language, whether by talking on the street in their neighborhoods, writing a personal blog, contributing to YouTube comment sections, or adding to government-hosted data forums, are reconfiguring traditional forms of language expertise.

From these street name discussions, we haven't made momentous discoveries like those citizen scientific revelations about monarch butterfly migration or the effects of climate change. But we can make a few preliminary generalizations about how expertise in these citizen sociolinguistic debates differs from institutionally sourced language expertise we might find in textbooks, atlases, encyclopedias, dictionaries, or professors: Rather than isolating one centralized source for answers, the Internet provides a space where multiple voices add to the discussion. While certain perspectives may be contested, they are still voiced and often defended by other participants. These views include detailed descriptions of the context surrounding contested language – specifics about the street they grew up on, local history about an infamous cheesesteak purveyor, and personal stories about, for example, buying tulip tables on "Pashunk" from an Italian guy with a gold chain, or of grandparents "correcting" one's pronunciation of "Passyunk Ave." They illustrate the always-changing, dynamic character of language – so we can see that what once may have been widely recognized as a *Native American* word now counts to some south Philly residents as a "native" South Philly word. Perhaps most importantly, throughout these discussions, expertise is not granted by institution or credential, but interactionally, and often through claims of local affiliation. If someone is an "outsider" – a Zillow real-estate professional, or a Philly suburbanite – their expertise comes into question. Through this interactional negotiation, *a process that can continue indefinitely*, connections and even communities (though perhaps ephemeral) develop among people who may differ in infinite ways but who have this in common: They want to talk about specific facets of language they use.

I emphasize these points about the multi-voiced, local, fine-grained, dynamic, and negotiated nature of citizen sociolinguistic expertise (see Figure 0.1) because, while the discussion of street names may seem trivial, the process itself, its perpetually ongoing character, and the inclusivity it makes possible are not. As these street name discussions begin to illustrate, and as I will show repeatedly throughout this book, by giving voice to largely unrecognized and diverse views on language, *everyday talk about language counterbalances exclusive, unilateral, and standardized depictions of what counts as legitimate language knowledge.*

As the social network of those who are aware of nuanced local perspectives expands, this locally sourced language awareness gains power, and the potential for social change grows. Those who demand that customers "order in English" may think twice about how they define "English" when they realize that their own pronunciation of many "English" words may also be highly contested. Those who say "Pashunk" may feel solidarity when they hear about the story of the gold-chained Italian, critics of the "ignorant" pronunciation of "Passyunk" may gain some perspective on its historical roots, and "natives" of South Philadelphia may be more reflective about calling themselves "natives" when they hear the view that street names like "Passyunk" are originally *Native American* names. The airing of multiple perspectives may or may not lead to these imagined shifts in awareness, but everyday conversations about language do not stop. And each conversation provides the potential for more locally sourced awareness, grassroots acts of citizen sociolinguistics, and resistance to outsiders' imposition of a different status quo. All this can happen when people talk about language: that is, when they are acting as *citizen sociolinguists*.

Standardized Citizen Sociolinguistics Is Not Citizen Sociolinguistics

Words of caution: Citizen Sociolinguists, as described so far, offer up and valorize highly localized versions of language expertise – expertise most

---

Citizen Sociolinguistic Expertise

1. Multi-voiced, inclusive representation of many perspectives
2. Local, fine-grained descriptions, often embedded in personal stories
3. Always changing, dynamic representations of language
4. Interactionally negotiated indefinitely

Figure 0.1 Everyday expertise

relevant to language users themselves. As will be discussed throughout this book, these depictions of local language and, often, racialized personality types (e.g., "How to talk like a White Girl," "How to Speak like a Singlishman") can themselves turn into standardized, even offensive, stereotypes of social types and communities. The same funny and insightful shortcuts to insider knowledge about localized social types and the subtleties about language and communication associated with them can, instead of liberating speakers from overly regimented speech expectations, become standardized themselves, and turned into fodder for nefarious ends.

This standardization of citizen sociolinguistic knowledge generates recipes for easily recognizable social types, and as such, can be used to profit from alienated human labor. Lorente (2018), for example, in her research on Pilipino domestic workers, describes the "scripts of servitude," or the specific forms of English (or other languages) taught to Pilipinos to market their services to different parts of the world. Specific language classes designed to build a labor force guide these women to learn specific phrases and forms of self-presentation that will produce recognizable social types to be shipped off to work for wealthy families around the world. Similarly, call centers run by global corporations rely on scripts and flowcharts that standardize 'casual' and 'friendly' speech in various languages, creating a simulacrum of everyday sociality – but all in service of efficiency and profit for multinational companies.

Heller and Duchêne (2012) have called this efficient packaging of local language knowledge, "Linguistic Taylorism," invoking the specter of assembly-line style linguistic production, efficiently manufacturing target-language-speakers designed for maximum profitability. This type of linguistic packaging, they argue (as does Lorente, 2018), further isolates workers from other forms of human sociality in the communities within which they are working. In this way, packaging recognizable emblematic features of language as profitable persona types – either as call center operators or as domestic workers in homes around the globe – isolates them as labor, alienating them from participating in other forms of sociality in their new languages.

While citizen-sociolinguistically generated portraits of language users may veer vexingly close to standardizing descriptions of social types, and even provide recipes for linguistic performances like "How to sound like you're from South Philly" or "How to talk Texan," citizen sociolinguists are, by definition, not participating in that labor economy in which language is decoupled from the context of its use. As described above (and see Figure 0.1), citizen sociolinguistic commentary generates multi-voiced discussion, layered portraits of language use, and, often, idiosyncratic resistance to such standardization, as displayed in negotiation about language form, structure, use, and domain, that persists indefinitely. As examples throughout this volume will illustrate, and as Chapter 6, Acts of Citizen Sociolinguistics, will address head on, some of these acts of citizen sociolinguistics are offensive or ill-advised, but, like other types of human creativity, they project a force of rupture, countering systems of standardization, often working to decenter expertise, and most importantly, sparking further talk about language.

Citizen Science, Citizen Sociolinguistics, and the Internet

As the examples so far illustrate, internet-circulated social media – blog posts, YouTube posts, online news sources, city data forums, and all their associated comment threads – provide a mushrooming array of everyday conversations about language. As you may be gathering, many of our everyday conversations about language take place online. Citizen science has now also joined the world of social media and internet connectivity. The social networking capacity of the Web has made the connections between scientists and non-scientists even more important than in the days of Thoreau's meticulously detailed journals, or the stamped letters arriving to Professor Urquhart's office about tagged monarch butterfly discoveries. As Xue (2014) writes:

> The Internet and mobile phones now connect more people than ever before, changing how scientists and citizens interact. Today's Citizen Science is born from and reinforces other shifts in the digital world – "big data," open access, and mobile-phone technology foremost among them – and borrows heavily from aspects of Internet culture: forums, gaming, and social media, to name just a few.

Internet connectivity now pervades citizen science. All of the original citizen science projects described above – the detailed accounting of flora and fauna started in Thoreau's diaries, the butterfly tracking begun by Professor Urquhart, and the possum stories collected by Australian researchers – now have active internet-circulated social media offshoots: Since 2007, Budburst, (budburst .org), following the inspiration of Thoreau's Concord flower trackers, has been enlisting people of all ages and backgrounds to gather information about flowering dates of plants in North America. Dozens of monarch butterfly tracking, milkweed planting websites now exist, as do sites for tracking many more varieties of butterflies and birds. Cell phone apps offer easy on-the-go butterfly tracking and uploading. In the spirit of the original citizen science, everyday people are contributing more than professional scientists could on their own, in larger quantities than ever. While Operation Possum is now over, it is catalogued on a website, Citizen Science Central, hosted by Cornell University and funded by the National Science Foundation. This website digitally mediates dozens of other citizen science projects that track spiders, invasive insects, beetles, lost ladybug species, among other living things, and uses Facebook, image recognition technology, gaming, and cell phone apps to engage everyday people and to facilitate the science.

While many of the citizen science sites focus on bringing children into the fold through games and curricular materials for teachers, the Internet has also afforded the development of more sophisticated technologies for citizen scientific data gathering from both young people and adults. For example, FoldIt (https://fold.it/portal/info/about) uses a Web-based gaming interface to draw on human puzzle-solving skills to understand how proteins, or chains of amino acids, fold up in the most efficient pattern to become biologically viable entities. FoldIt players take on particular protein folding assignments, looking at 3D models of proteins, and find the most efficient fold pattern. Similarly, Galaxy Zoo (www.galaxyzoo.org) draws on citizen scientists to classify galaxies according to their shape, details, and imperfections. As soon as citizens reach consensus on the shape – when 100 percent of them agree that a galaxy is spiral, for example – the professional astronomers will use that consensus as justification to apply for expensive, coveted telescope time to explore that galaxy in detail.

FoldIt and Galaxy Zoo illustrate not only that Citizen Science is highly compatible with internet technologies, but also that humans have capacities that go beyond computers. The FoldIt project counts on human participation so they can take advantage of those uniquely human aspects of perception that contribute to identifying protein shapes – ways-of-looking that computers have not yet been able to learn. In the new, enhanced option on Galaxy Zoo, citizen volunteers now have access to more finely tuned categories of images, selected by machines. This enhanced level of analysis allows the site to combine human "classifications with those of machines, inspired by the idea that the combination of both automatic and human classification may be more powerful than either alone." These sophisticated, cyborgian uses of non-professionals show how the Internet has begun to radically shape the evolution of citizen science.

Some sociolinguistic research has also begun to use the Internet to gather data from everyday language users this way. In the United Kingdom, the linguists Adrian Leemann, Marie-José Kolly, and David Britain recently developed a "language dialect app" which has enabled them to collect reams of dialect data across Great Britain (2018). In the United States, the *New York Times Dialect Quiz* (Katz & Andrews, 2013) published in December 2013 circulated widely across the Internet and on Facebook. This quiz features questions like the following:

What do you call a sweetened carbonated beverage?
(a) soda   (b) pop   (c) coke   (d) tonic (e) soft drink
(f) lemonade (g) cocola (h) fizzy drink (i) dope (j) other

After leading readers through 25 questions like this, the quiz instantly identified "where you're from," pinpointing you on a map of the United States. Based on the Harvard Dialect Survey, part of a linguistics project begun in 2002 by professors Bert Vaux and Scott Golder and adapted from surveys originally developed for rural field research by dialectologists in the 1920s, this repurposing of linguistic data tools in the service of everyday people's curiosity about language illustrates the Internet's potential as a medium for scaling up citizen sociolinguistic inquiry.

Similar to the *New York Times* quiz, but more tailored to scientific inquiry, linguistics researchers are now using "word games" and other language quizzes to lure participants to their research sites. At MIT, for example, Professor Joshua Harshorn and colleagues created a game, verb corner, hosted on the website gameswithwords.org, which uses the game results from participants (an ongoing and increasingly large number of children and adults who play their open-access word games online) to investigate language acquisition and to inform machine learning. And, at the University of Zurich, sociolinguistic researchers have created a website where participants (anyone who lives in Switzerland) play a game in which they identify regional dialects of sound samples, adding to a "heat map" which indicates perceived dialect boundaries.

Crowdsourcing Is Not Citizen Science

Now I need to insert a note of caution. A special alert. A BEWARE sign. The Internet has made it possible to gather huge amounts of data from many people. Highly engaging video platforms, online quizzes about ourselves with instant results, other forms of gamification, and the ever-present *like* button have managed to recruit individuals on a massive scale as free labor in the service of scientific inquiry. But crowdsourcing, this scaled-up use of everyday people (crowds) as mere sources of data is not citizen science. You may have started to feel a little uncomfortable while reading even my brief descriptions of the crowdsourcing platforms FoldIt and Zooniverse: The capacities of human perception may be being called upon, but to what end? Ultimately, it seems, so that humans can be done without. FoldIt, for example, under the heading "Can humans really help computers sort Proteins?" states the following:

> We're collecting data to find out if humans' pattern-recognition and puzzle-solving abilities make them more efficient than existing computer programs at pattern-folding tasks. If this turns out to be true, we can then teach human strategies to computers and fold proteins faster than ever! (FoldIt, n.d.)

It seems that, for FoldIt, human perspectives are only a means to an end: Ultimately computers will be able to handle it – and, "faster than ever!" But computers may not be able to decide on the utility of these new proteins, or the value of a drug used to treat abnormalities within them, or countless other questions in science that require human deliberation. Standardizing human insight is not citizen science. Regarding language more specifically, crowdsourced information about dialects tells us very little about the lived experience of people using the language being recorded. For better and for worse, citizen science – and as we have already seen, citizen sociolinguistics – is idiosyncratic.

Big data may be very useful for some tasks, and it is important to have many people contributing to our big questions, but we also need the occasional "captain of the Huckleberry party" and those who follow that huckleberry jaunt to provide the human and humanly proportioned view of value, of color and shape, variety and idiosyncrasy that make our world delightful and bearable. We may also have to recognize that this huckleberry excursion and whatever we learn from it will occur at a human pace – probably not "faster than ever." As exemplified by the possum project in Australia, citizen science also requires us to step back and take a good look at the basis of our fundamental assumptions about the subject matter we intend to study. Computers simply cannot do this. Worse, the scale at which computers crunch big data makes it possible for an algorithm based on one inaccuracy or false assumption to do vast amounts of damage to even that tiny minority of people or circumstances it fails to account for (O'Neil, 2017). In contrast, small-scale citizen science, ongoing, and engaged with human-level perspectives, transforms the arcane, obscure, idiosyncratic, seemingly academic, and possibly even misguided, into a collective project with recognizable social value.

This distinction at its most extreme could be put this way: Crowdsourcing frames participants as unthinking data sources, disregarding idiosyncrasy as statistical noise to be cleaned away, while citizen science positions participants as local experts. These two perspectives on the participation of "everyday people" fall into relief when we look at unexpected reactions that emerged in response to the *New York Times* accent quiz mentioned above. The vast quantity of *everyday conversations about* the 25-item quiz illuminates some things the quiz never intended to show: While certain words have statistically regional associations, people, no matter where they "are from," have many ways of speaking, and even wider awareness of ways that they and other people speak, and the ability to change the ways they speak depending on their awareness of a given situation. We have become a mobile society and the idea that we have one way of speaking that identifies "where you are from" belies that reality. Many people (my students and my friends for example) took the quiz multiple times, impersonating different versions of themselves, from different periods of their lives. While someone may have grown up in Minnesota, calling a sweet, carbonated beverage "pop," a later self, living on the East Coast, might be a "soda" convert, a move to Georgia might have them asking for a "coke." And, today, that same person could perform any one of those "selves" – or even make up new words, or use different languages! – depending on the situation they found themselves in. What seems more important than "where you are from" is the multiple varieties of language someone has in their communicative repertoire.

Sarah Larson's parody of the same quiz in *The New Yorker Magazine* (2014) also called attention to tacit assumptions behind the quiz, poking fun at the answer choices for each item, and at the ultimate result, a decisive diagnosis of your origin. Her parody mimicked the genre of the quiz, providing very silly possible responses, as in this example:

What do you call the insects that live in your bed and suck your blood?

a. Bedbugs
b. Dream stinkers
c. Blood-yums
d. Mattress assholes
e. No-want-'ems
f. Landlord's tears
g. Nosferatu, Jrs.

After several multiple-choice question like these, readers receive their result, the same for all: "You are from Worcester, Massachusetts."

By spinning out ludicrous, sometimes hilarious responses (Landlord's tears?!), Larson's parody reveals assumptions behind the original *New York Times* quiz. For it to work, the quiz requires that people not use language creatively or thoughtfully, and that they have one and only one consistent response for each question. If quiz takers follow along this way, their answers will yield an inevitable result: their hometown, which the quiz suggests is a place where people only speak one way. In contrast to the creative capacity of people who use language every day and think about its ramifications, the quiz positions people as mindless data sources who unthinkingly emit stereotypical regional dialects. While it may be overstating the point to spend too much time critiquing the assumptions behind a newspaper's admittedly fun language quiz, these assumptions also could be attributed to much of the crowdsourcing of (socio)linguistic data, which relies on unthinking responses of test takers or game players, in some cases even explicitly reminding participants not to think too much (or, as the games-with-words site puts it, "focus on your gut instincts") while answering survey questions or playing a game. This use of people as crowds of anonymous experimental subjects offering up language samples based on "gut instinct" contrasts profoundly with a primary goal of citizen sociolinguistics: to look to people mindfully engaged in everyday conversations about language as sources of local knowledge, expertise, and collaborative deliberation.

Citizen science generates social value because it happens publicly and in conversations that potentially include a range of perspectives. Everyday conversations about language, and the mushrooming range of such conversations, traceable via the Internet, are not simply gathering and storing data for supercomputers to use but creating information and bolstering its relevance through new webs of participation among humans. While some citizen science originates from the questions of trained scientists, the knowledge gained via citizen science is quintessentially connected to the capacities and conversations generated by laypeople. This is not simply free labor or a convenient data source – but knowledge and methods that could only be developed by ordinary people who are neither disciplinary experts nor computers.

Expanding Perspectives on Language

Collaborative deliberation within conversations about language, an ideal for citizen sociolinguistics, isn't always how we might describe conversations on the Internet. Discussion of internet-circulated social media, for many, raises the specter of uniformity of thought, of isolated enclaves where like-minded people gather and reinforce each other's views. But in what we have seen so far in the discussions of South Philadelphia street names, genuine deliberation and different points of view emerge productively. Citizen sociolinguistic discussions on the Web – like the exchange on the pronunciation of *Moy-mensing*, or the controversy over the pronunciation of *Pashunk Avenue* on the City Data Forum – draw together voices who might otherwise not interact, and provide a medium within which people can share their own views on some feature of language and communication. Online discussions about language, unlike those about politics or other social issues, often create community and provoke solidarity – even as people argue or disagree.

Because we all use language, because we all have language idiosyncrasies and recognize them in others, because we all like a good joke, impersonation, or even a funny story about being misunderstood, conversations about language can be fertile ground for shared conviviality, even across very different social types. In his book *Convergence Culture* (2006), the media scholar Henry Jenkins discusses a similar positive quality in discussions about popular culture. A group of strangers with different backgrounds might find difficulty talking to each other about topics like presidential elections or religious convictions, but should the topic change to the latest Marvel blockbuster, or the "final tour" of the Rolling Stones, or the latest Netflix drama, the conversation – and differences of opinion – will likely begin to flow. While the fear of conflict usually steers conversations away from political or religious topics, the same potential for strong opinions and disagreement often fuels discussions of popular culture. The greater the variety of views being shared in a discussion about a movie like *Endgame*, a musical artist, or a new Netflix series, the more interesting the conversation becomes.

As Jenkins puts it, "knowledge cultures" – in whatever media they grow – "depend on the quality and diversity of information people can access. The ability to learn by sharing insights or comparing notes with others is severely diminished when everyone else already shares the same beliefs and knowledge" (2006, p. 249). Of course, this is precisely the lament of media analysts who see the Internet and social media as fomenting ideological enclaves of like-minded people, removed from civic dialogue. But when people come together around shared popular culture, Jenkins argues, the situation changes:

> There does seem to be a much greater diversity of opinion on sites dealing with popular culture than on sites dealing directly with politics. If we want to bridge between red and blue America, we need to find that kind of common ground and expand upon it. We need to create a context where we listen and learn from one another. We need to deliberate together. (2006, p. 250)

I would argue that the same is true of sites that deal with language. When someone posts a video on the pronunciation of Philadelphia street names, tweets a screenshot of a Professor's email banning "Chinese," or provides a tutorial on "gender-neutral pronouns," (the last two examples to be discussed in Chapter 6) a diversity of viewpoints emerges, and disagreements tease out issues of genuine curiosity and concern.

But citizen sociolinguistic dialogue can take dark turns: Once certain linguistic features become stereotyped and widely distributed in the media marketplace, conversations about language can become predictable dead ends, and, at times, layered with bigotry and bile. Even highly localized views and initially open, deliberative conversations about the local flavor of South Philadelphia speech, for example, can become commodified, packaged, and sold as a stereotype ready for mass-market consumption. When conversations circulate around mass-mediated "hot-button" issues (gender-neutral pronouns have become one such hot topic), internet trolls can lead to comments being disabled or even entire sites being taken down.

Despite irrepressible market forces that hijack and simplify hotly contested issues and debates, closing down more nuanced discussions, citizen sociolinguistics is a renewable resource, and conversation about language can never be closed down everywhere. Someone will inevitably add different information, solicit new feedback, or blast open a tired debate with a dose of humor or a personal anecdote. This insistent creativity of citizen sociolinguistics allows it to spin out of one-dimensional arguments and standardized framings of "good" or "bad" language, "good" or "bad" ways of describing language, and "good" or "bad" ways of being human. Because citizen sociolinguistics is rooted in highly contextualized understandings of language, citizen sociolinguists inevitably create new ways of expressing how language means for them. Citizen sociolinguists insist on conveying details of their individual experiences with language – as when someone validates his preference for *Pashunk* over *Passyunk* by describing his experience selling tulip tables to someone with a gold chain near *"Pashunk* Ave." This typical embedding of talk about language in more detailed portraits of one's lived experience has the potential to expand everyone's view of how language works.

Exploring the everyday creativity of conversations people have about language has the potential to offer new knowledge, combat ignorance, and open minds – not necessarily by way of systematic argumentation, but by uniquely illuminating an alternative perspective on language. In his book on the philosophy of aesthetics, the philosopher Herbert Marcuse (1978) describes the liberating power of aesthetically tuned insights we often associate with the artistic process. Art in any genre, he argues, can knock people's sensibilities out of their one-dimensional perceptions (formed, he would also argue, in service of a capitalist society, trained on mass-marketed products and consumption) by opening their eyes to alternate views of the world. Art of any genre can be liberating because it potentially offers up new ways of seeing and understanding our everyday existence. Artists proffer their unique perspective, incrementally altering more standardized views of the world. In this way, Marcuse argues, artistic expression can indirectly function as a side door leading to liberating social change – not through rational argumentation, but through exposing people to non-standardized perspectives, otherwise unknown. Citizen sociolinguists, similarly, have the potential to act as the artists of language use and discussion, shaking up our pre-packaged notions of good and bad language, and illuminating how language works from the perspective of individuals using it.

The Citizen Sociolinguistic Frontier

Internet technology has opened up a new frontier by providing access to a wealth of everyday talk about language on the Web. However, massive amounts of conversation-about-language is meaningless – it's not even "data" – unless we consider how those conversations work and what they mean. Drawing on the citizen science concept, this book outlines a methodology to make sense of *How we talk about language* in ways that are relevant to those of us (all of us) who use language to communicate. Once we turn our attention to *How we talk about language*, we quickly see how people's ideas and conversations about language entwine with their ability to resist outside control and even foment social change. Like citizen science, citizen sociolinguistics does not preordain questions that ought to be pursued. Rather, the goal is to see how participants gravitate to certain questions. Along the way, the social value placed on certain ways of speaking continuously changes. Following the trail of breadcrumbs left by internet contributors provides us a methodology for studying a dynamic world of language use and its impact.

We live in a fantastically diverse world, and we traverse myriad communities and ways of speaking over the course of every day. Restricting research to reports that circulate back and forth through a professional community is no longer an ideal. Using the power of internet-circulated social media to generate data and participatory engagement, and models of citizen science – rather than entrenched academic questions and methods – to create structures for inquiry, may lift sociolinguistic inquiry into a new world that is continually generating new data, as well as new ways of thinking about it. I intend for this approach to be deployed not only by academics, but also by teachers, students, and everyday people who like language, and to encourage collaboration between all these social types. Engaging in citizen sociolinguistics promises to change sociolinguistic research, classroom interactions, and everyday encounters, making them more exploratory, creative, and nonjudgmental.

As language scholars, we could always go back to valorizing only the sociolinguistic findings published in academic journals, go on using the Internet as simply a source of raw language data, reserving the title of *expert* for ourselves, the professionals. This could generate reams of articles with titles like "The Combative Language of Blogs" or "Discourses of Twitter" – endless collections of language systematized and critiqued on our own scholarly terms. Unless we shift our perspective, our research will have very little relevance. It will illuminate nothing but a small pocket of stale inquiry. Instead we need to take up the promise of citizens' distributed expertise, and the Internet's invitation to look more carefully at talk about language that does not originate from scholars, but from everyone using language and talking about it. It seems irresponsible, even unethical, to treat the Internet as some expanse of "unmonitored" talk for we specialists to name and to put in order. Instead, I am proposing a new form of inquiry that recognizes everyday conversations about language as not only an area of inquiry, but also a locus of expertise and a means of sharing knowledge.

Outline of the Book

The rest of this book begins to take readers into the world of citizen sociolinguistics by first illustrating two common pathways into everyday conversations about language. In Chapter 1, Citizen's Arrest: The "Citizen" and Citizen Sociolinguistics, I focus on one speech act that can lead to important citizen sociolinguistic deliberation, the "citizen sociolinguist's arrest," that moment when someone gets called out and critiqued for their language use. By following a trail of questions set off by a "citizen sociolinguist's arrest," I elaborate how such speech acts can lead to important deliberation over any word, phrase, or way of speaking, and, in the process, raise awareness and ownership of those words and how they mean. This chapter concludes by distinguishing the study of "Citizen Sociolinguistics" from other fields of study and approaches to language research, explicitly tracing points of influence and departure from Ethnomethodology and Interactional Sociolinguistics, Linguistic Anthropology, Folk Linguistics, and Cognitive Linguistics.

While Chapter 1 focuses on how critique in the form of the "citizen sociolinguist's arrest" often pushes us into conversations about language, Chapter 2, Wonderment: The Spark that Starts Talk about Language, focuses on a more positive entrée into such conversations: those moments when we experience a sense of awe and curiosity about any unique and quirky aspect of language. This chapter investigates objects of wonderment: words, phrases, or ways of speaking that magnify our curiosity about language, provoking endless cycles of dialogue. Then we'll look at the types of people, YouTubers and their followers, for example, who expose and revel in language wonderment, and finally, the way everyday conversations about language spring from wonderment about specific situations of language use, as in memes about "that feeling when . . ." or Twitter accounts like "Shit Academics Say." We'll also look more carefully at the methods for gathering and interpreting experiences with language that are used within all these conversations. Chapter 3, Doing Citizen Sociolinguistics: The Medium Is the Method, explicitly details the means we use to explore citizen sociolinguistic conversations once our curiosity has been piqued (by arrest or wonderment). As the chapter title indicates, unlike traditional social science, in which researchers design methods specific to their research questions, in citizen sociolinguistics the medium creates the method for inquiry. Learning about how we talk about language involves settling into the medium in which people are doing just that – whether that means following up, face-to-face, on a conversational gambit about a funny expression, turning to Urban Dictionary, following the comments section on a YouTube video, or even adding to your data set by creating a Twitter poll. This chapter concludes with a ready-to-use detailed roadmap for engaging in citizen sociolinguistic inquiry across these realms. Chapter 4, Fomenting Arrest and Wonderment: Citizen Sociolinguistic Feedback Loops, investigates how certain points of view create their own reality through viral internet dissemination. Because Citizen expertise is local, anecdotal, narrative-based, and often personal, it generates its own form of expertise – expert knowledge that is highly relevant and in fact crucial to the lives of other language users in any given social circle. This type of authority, while local, has the power to become globally circulated, largely through internet mechanisms. And this feedback loop provides added authority to local knowledge by extending its reach – potentially providing means for grassroots social change. We will consider the role of positive feedback loops created by "retweets," likes, and extended comment threads. Then we will examine the negative aspects of feedback loops – their potential to create digital enclaves of like-minded language users, raising the potential for *tone-deaf* interactions, in which people speak past each other or use language offensively, unaware of how words, phrases, and certain speech acts take on different meanings and give off unexpected impressions in different situations. While citizen sociolinguistic dialogue at times is a medium for tone-deaf and hurtful comments, it also has the potential to disrupt feedback loops that create and reproduce status quo perspectives on language. To exemplify both institutional enclaves of opinion that get reinforced through isolated feedback loops, and the disruption of such institutions, we will look at one controversy about the use of Chinese in American universities. This case in point illustrates the power of viral internet movements to change perspectives on language by disrupting the usual institutionalized feedback (and silencing) mechanisms. Chapter 5, Citizen Sociolinguistics and Narrative, details one means of gaining authority through everyday conversations about language: the personal narrative. I contrast narrative and anecdotal ways of providing answers to language questions to more typically scholarly rhetoric of authority that involves impersonal statements of fact and the accumulation of vast quantities of "data" from anonymous sources that preferably do not talk back or ever read what has been written about them.

While the first five chapters invite readers to join with citizen sociolinguists to understand their motivations and intrinsic drive as language users to understand and critique the language around them, the final two chapters look more closely at the consequences of citizen sociolinguistic inquiry. Chapter 6, Acts of Citizen Sociolinguistics, returns to our discussion of *citizenship* to explore how the simple act of talking about language constitutes someone as a citizen sociolinguist. Single *acts of citizen sociolinguistics* do not, on their own, reconfigure systemic relations, ethics, or spoken language, any more than an "act of kindness" or an "act of violence" might. However, they raise our awareness of our humanity and relatedness – our Bakhtinian "answerability" – and the role of language in it, in ways that can provoke further talk and have a societal impact. After discussing and exemplifying acts of citizen sociolinguistics, I'll contrast them with what Deborah Cameron has called "language policing." We'll see how the concept of "language policing" and related concepts like "undoing appropriateness" describe a more systematic imposition of a perceived order on everyday language, and the need for resistance to that order. This portrayal of language debates is existentially distinct from both those acts of wonderment discussed in Chapter 2 and the more jarring acts of arrest discussed in Chapter 1. These acts of wonderment or arrest – acts of citizen sociolinguistics – provoke new perspectives on language and society and, as such, are acts of citizen sociolinguistics that constitute their own chaotic and potentially transformative moments outside of top-down systems of control.

In the Conclusion, Why We Must Talk about Language, I turn most explicitly to the potential role of citizen sociolinguistics in language education. Contemporary schools are continuously under stress regarding the role of language and multilingualism. In the United States, bullying, and particularly *verbal* bullying, and *discussions of* verbal bullying have been proliferating for the last decade. School systems face lawsuits about how people use single words and multiple languages on their campuses. At the same time, the Language Arts curriculum in schools changes slowly. In language classrooms, conversations tend to focus on standardized genres – rarely do Language Arts lessons address new words used by kids, different ways of speaking, and multiple languages used in and out of schools and across different peer groups. But conversations about language can be inviting and inclusive pathways into discussions about difference and distinction in our classrooms and society, and these more inclusive conversations need to be part of the Language Arts curriculum. Through discussions about language, we develop the habitual language awareness needed to respect the language of others who use language differently and will inevitably be part of our future.

In the spirit of deliberation, this concluding chapter will also keep the door to inquiry wide open. Just as Thoreau had no idea that his ornate descriptions of birds and flowers might contribute to arguments for environmental conservation, sometimes (usually!) people do not know what movement their acts of citizen sociolinguistics are contributing to. For this reason, I argue that talk-about-language, as an act in and of itself, must be recognized as important activity, in schools, on the street, in church, on Facebook, in YouTube videos, on the bus, everywhere. I conclude by discussing the power of Citizen Sociolinguistics and everyday conversation more generally to serve as a continuous and liberating counterbalance to the institutional need for control and containment of human diversity and knowledge.

Traditional disciplinary sociolinguistics has developed sophisticated analytic tools to make discoveries that might illuminate and even confront social problems related to sociolinguistic distinction, but these findings have not had the impact one might expect. Citizen sociolinguistics offers a means to explore alternative sociolinguistic knowledge: everyday opinion about language, how it functions in context, and how it is created and disseminated. By learning to follow this path of citizen sociolinguistic knowledge, we may be able to explore the impact it has. *We can best learn about society by looking at the way we talk about our words.* Throughout this volume, what I'm suggesting is very simple: Pay attention to how people talk about language. In the chapters that follow I model and describe ways to go about doing this.

1 Citizen's Arrest!
The "Citizen" and Citizen Sociolinguistics

> If, however, two persons find themselves at cross-purposes, it is necessary to dig up and compare the presuppositions, the implied context, upon the basis of which each is speaking.
>
> John Dewey, *How We Think* (1910, p. 214)

"This is a citizen's arrest!" Have you ever faced those words or uttered them as a witness to a crime? It's doubtful any readers of this book have ever been engaged in a citizen's arrest. But presumably it does happen: A citizen's arrest potentially occurs when someone witnesses an obvious crime and no official authorities are around to make an arrest or put a stop to the situation. Any person can step in to do the right thing. Usually there is no need for legal citizenship – in fact the act is officially called an "any person arrest" in the United Kingdom. You may have seen something like a citizen's arrest in a scene from *Batman* or *Spiderman* – fictional superheroes probably perform this act most often, because they are courageous, morally upstanding, and they have superpowers. "Any person" may find it harder. But it persists as a fantasy, and a genuine possibility – and as a useful metaphor. If we see something wrong, we shouldn't have to rely on the presence of a uniformed officer (or costumed superhero) to correct that. We have legal authority to say something – and do something.

Metaphorically, a more common form of the "citizen's arrest" is "calling someone out" – explicitly drawing attention to someone for acting in a way perceived to be inappropriate or antisocial. The arresting citizen might say something like, "Hey, pick up your trash!" "Sorry, there's no smoking allowed here," or even, to someone staring for too long, "Do I know you?" We all may have participated in this type of event – either as a perpetrator or as the arresting person. A common sub-genre of this metaphorical citizen's arrest might be called the "citizen sociolinguist's arrest" – the act of calling someone out for their use of language, maybe with a hint of moral censure. An arresting citizen sociolinguist might be heard saying, "Don't speak Spanish!" "*You* are not allowed to use the 'n-word' in any context," or simply, "Watch your language!"

In over 20 years of teaching and conducting research in schools, recording lessons and conversations, and talking with students about language use, I've witnessed my share of these citizen sociolinguistic arrests. In Los Angeles, where I first taught English as a Second Language (ESL) at a junior high school and at night to adults, and later conducted my dissertation research in an alternative high school, I heard many stories involving the command, "Don't talk Spanish!" or variations of it (Rymes, 1997). Here, an 18-year-old high school student recounts riding the bus with her mother and facing that citizen sociolinguistic arrest:

"Don't Talk Spanish"

SYLVIA: I was on the bus like five years ago. And I was talking to my mom in Spanish, this [girl] says, "Shut up don't talk Spanish."
And I turn around like—
And we kept talking because we were talking.
She goes, "Didn't you hear me don't talk Spanish!"
And I got up and I started saying you know what? You don't tell me to stop talking in Spanish because that's my language you know and then—
So we ended up in a fight on the bus.
She got arrested. I didn't get arrested. I was just strong enough to get on that same bus and ride it again.
Because it wasn't my fault. I was minding my business, she was-
She got on the bus and started saying, "Don't talk Spanish."

In this case, the citizen doing the "sociolinguistic arrest" was herself arrested. But the arresting (and subsequently arrested) girl was voicing a sentiment that had been widely circulating via policy initiatives and general anti-immigrant sentiment in Los Angeles at the time, the mid-1990s. This sentiment crystalized politically when Proposition 187 was passed by voters in 1994. This was a statewide ballot initiative nicknamed "SOS" for "Save Our State," and it proposed that any immigrant without legal permission to be in the state would be ineligible for public social services, public health care services, and public education at elementary, secondary, and post-secondary levels. Moreover, it required providers of these services – like teachers and doctors – to report persons suspected of not having legal permission to be in the state. The ballot measure passed; however, it was held up in the courts and ultimately ruled unconstitutional. But it did fan the flames of anti-immigrant sentiment, and the controversy targeted primarily Spanish speakers from Mexico and Central America. This was the overall climate in Los Angeles in the 1990s that also fomented citizen sociolinguistic arrests like the one Sylvia faced on the bus: "Don't talk Spanish." But, as Sylvia's story also illustrates, citizen sociolinguistic arrests, even those ventriloquating widely circulating sentiments, can be followed by *counter*-citizen-sociolinguistic arrests, in which citizen sociolinguists like Sylvia stand up for their right to speak their own way. As Sylvia put it, "you know what? You don't tell me to stop talking in Spanish because that's my language."

Citizen sociolinguistic arrests may involve confronting others on what language to use, or what words to say or not say, or how to speak, and even what topics to talk about. Often, as Sylvia's story exemplifies, they can have their origins in widely circulating prejudices about languages and their speakers, and what we should or should not say, to whom, when, and how. A few years later when I was working in Georgia, while sitting with and recording second and third graders in reading circles with their teacher, I witnessed similar "citizen sociolinguistic arrests" by much younger children. Often, these young children would, like the girl speaking to Sylvia on the bus, voice their own versions of widely circulating and frequently modeled societal mandates about language. When a student mentioned the race of characters in a picture book, for example, other children in the reading group might call them out with, "Don't be talking about that!" Similar arrests would be made – not by the teachers, but by fellow students, when words like "gay" came up: Don't be talking about that. This is not something we should discuss. Change the topic. Unlike Sylvia's story, these comments usually controlled people's behavior, and the topics of race and sexuality were swiftly silenced in classroom discussion.

Like most of us, I've also been directly involved on both the arresting and the perpetrating ends of citizen sociolinguist arrests. Those instances in which I have been called out as a perpetrator of some language offense have stayed with me most vividly. A searing memory of conversation at a conference I attended as a junior scholar involves just such an incident. In 2002, I gave a paper about my research in Georgia, focusing on how the children socialized each other into norms for speaking in reading groups. One of my examples was their censoring and near-phobic avoidance of the word "gay" because of its implied sense, "homosexual." At the conference, during discussion of one such interaction, I used the phrase *sexual preference* (instead of the more acceptable term *sexual orientation*) to describe the "gay" persona the kids were alluding to. The moment the phrase came out of my mouth I knew I had misspoken. And the intuition was made much more explicit, when, after my session ended, a well-known and openly gay scholar approached me.

In the kindest and most fair way, she citizen-sociolinguistically arrested me, explaining (as I remember it), "You should probably know this, Betsy: Generally, the phrase *sexual preference* has fallen out of favor. It suggests that gay individuals simply *prefer* a certain type of sexuality. It's generally understood that those who identify as gay do so not as a matter of *preference* but as a function of their innate biological orientation. That's why *sexual orientation* is the acceptable phrase." I was mortified at my own ignorance. I thought I was presenting something cutting-edge and insightful from my original research, but my language choice had made me sound outdated at best, and possibly totally misguided, out of touch, and homophobic. I was shamed, embarrassed, even momentarily defensive. My mind raced with defensive counter-arrest questions: How dare she confront me? Didn't she know I probably just misspoke? What's the big deal? Fortunately, I kept these internal responses to myself. To this day, I am grateful for that 2002 citizen sociolinguistic arrest, and I still pause and very consciously consider my word choice whenever I discuss homosexuality in any context.

In each of these examples discussed above, for better or worse, citizen sociolinguistic arrests led to immediate action around language use: Sylvia stood up for Spanish on the bus ("it's my language!), the kids in Georgia never discussed race or sexuality, and I immediately and permanently changed my own word choice. But none of these cases (until now) led to much extended discussion about language. Imagine if, instead, each arrest led to more talk about language beyond the act of arrest (or in the first case, counter-arrest). Why only English on a public bus? Why only English in school for that matter? Why don't we talk about race when we are reading books about differently racialized protagonists and differently racialized people are reading the book together? Why not discuss the word "gay" and how its meaning has changed over the years? Why do gay people often directly address language related to sexual orientation? What can we learn from that? Do they all agree? These conversations about language can lead to important conversations about society and highlight what we individual speakers want to stand up for.

Now, many years after that 2002 conference, I continue to be arrested for my language choices occasionally, and while shame and defensiveness often grip me at first, I try to understand these citizen sociolinguistic arrests as not simply correctives for my own bad behavior, but also as opportunities for eye-opening journeys into perspectives and forms of knowledge different from my own. Most recently, on a number of occasions when I've talked about "citizen sociolinguistics," either among friends or in more formal academic settings, the word *citizen* itself has emerged as a point of contention. Someone will inevitably ask: "Why the word *citizen*? It's problematic!" or "Have you reflected on your use of the word *citizen*?" Just like the scholar who called me out in 2002, these arresting citizen sociolinguists have a point: My use of the word probably has blind spots, and people may have sensed that I was unreflectively using the word based on my own unexamined assumptions about its utility, rather than, as a citizen sociolinguist, exploring the many possible circulating meanings of that word. I needed to genuinely explore: What is the role of the word *citizen* in citizen sociolinguistics?

This chapter models how we can learn from citizen sociolinguistic arrests by not necessarily immediately presuming ourselves guilty or innocent, but by allowing the moment to launch us on a pathway of inquiry – or, to stay with the legal analogy, a "discovery phase." I will model this inquiry approach – this *doing* of citizen sociolinguistics by exploring the multiple contexts of meaning for that very word I have been arrested for using: *citizen*. The following investigation approaches the word *citizen* as a citizen sociolinguist might, by seeking out conversations about the word *citizen*, face-to-face, in the research literature, and on internet-circulated social media. I will stay focused on the kind of expertise that comes from conversations (and disagreements) about language – specifically in this case about the word *citizen*. This chapter details the work of these *citizen sociolinguists* by exploring a range of highly contested assumptions behind the word *citizen*, and the blurring distinctions between different invocations of the word: as a *legal* citizen, an *idealistic and participatory* citizen, a *sarcastic and cynical* citizen, a *deliberative* citizen, and, finally, the potential transformation of all these stances on citizenry into the *censored* citizen. Each of these portraits of the *citizen* runs at cross purposes to the others, so we will, in the words of John Dewey that begin this chapter, "dig up and compare the presuppositions, the implied context, upon the basis of which each is speaking" (1910). This tour through the dramatic differences in how people talk about the word *citizen* illustrates an important interplay not only among assumptions underpinning different understandings of the word *citizen*, but also about the "implied contexts" that afford and perpetuate those assumptions. Each of these views of the world offers a slice of situated expertise.

Given the contested nature of the word *citizen* – and, as we will see, the disturbing nature of some of those slices of situated expertise – it might seem stupidly stubborn to stick with "*citizen* sociolinguistics" as a term for how everyday people talk about language. Why not just call it *any person sociolinguistics*, *everyday sociolinguistics*, or simply, *how we talk about language*? This chapter begins to explore why. (Chapter 6, Acts of Citizen Sociolinguistics, extends the discussion). Following where these discussions have led me, I'll illustrate how the word *citizen* in citizen sociolinguistics calls forth a number of views, worthy of our deliberation, and calls attention to the power of that collectivity of opinion, offering more than simply one institutionalized authority or one individual's everyday perspective. This exploration of the word *citizen* will also illustrate that the nature of citizen sociolinguistic expertise lies not in one or another of these views, but in the interplay between them and the resulting aggregated wisdom.

The modifier *citizen* also distinguishes the participants, materials, methods, and goals of citizen sociolinguistics from the work of other language researchers like folk linguists, traditional sociolinguists, linguistic ethnographers, and linguistic anthropologists. All of these perspectives, as well as those of everyday people talking about language, come with assumptions, often unstated, about what words and ways of speaking mean and do in context. Both a simple citizen sociolinguistic arrest like "Don't talk Spanish!" and a research article on the systematicity of sound shift in the Northeastern United States build on presupposed knowledge and assumptions about what is worth saying about people's speech. How we talk about language, whether as sociolinguists, linguistic anthropologists, political candidates, artists, journalists, grammarians, realtors, teachers, or parents, inevitably implicates our larger-scale understandings and beliefs about our place in society. So, I'll conclude this chapter by discussing the relationships among these related approaches to language: citizen sociolinguistics, the linguistic anthropological concept of language ideology, and the sociological study of ethnomethodology. But we will begin with a seemingly simple question: How are everyday people talking about the word *citizen*?

Citizen Sociolinguistic Inquiry into the Word *Citizen*

What are the powerful meanings of the word *citizen* circulating out there and how are they affecting people in context? The meaning of that word is so dynamic and context-bound that how you think about it may change from moment to moment – from the last time you turned on the news, had a conversation with a colleague, or overheard a heated argument on the bus. So, let's start by taking a look at the everyday conversations in person, in the research community, and on the Internet to see what we can learn.

Good Citizenship versus US Citizenship

My own social networks were the first to push me to reflect on my use of the word *citizen*. Friends and colleagues have pointed out to me how problematic the word is these days, when immigrants and refugees in desperate life circumstances are trying to enter the United States, but are stopped at the border, sometimes separated from their children, and often treated like criminals with no rights at all, simply because they are not US citizens and have no papers accounting for alternative status. Even if these families do find homes in the United States, their citizenship status remains a point of continuous stress. And often this stress revolves around the very mention of the word *citizenship*.

As Ariana Mangual Figueroa (2011) has shown, the use of this word can negatively shape immigrant families' experiences of school. For nearly two years, she conducted research in Southwestern Pennsylvania, observing in schools and homes, recording classroom talk and family events, and having conversations with mixed-status families, in which some members have documentation of legal citizenship and others do not. This mixed-status situation usually results when families cross the border illegally and have more children once they have settled in the United States. For these families, the younger children are US citizens by birth, but their older siblings and parents are always at risk of deportation. While spending extended time with these families,

Mangual Figueroa came to understand the inherent ambiguity around the word *citizenship* as it is used in schools and between children and their parents. In conversations over report cards from school, for example, the parents' attention fell disproportionately on something called the *citizenship grade*. While the citizenship grade was meant to assess good behavior in class (not immigration status), parents and students in these mixed-status homes made a connection to their own precarious status as immigrants and became nervous when their undocumented child received a poor citizenship grade, making instant connections to the ever-present risk of deportation. One mother, drawing on the ambiguity of the word, told her seven-year-old son (not a US citizen) that if he did not improve his citizenship grade, he would be sent back to Mexico.

An important detail in Mangual Figueroa's article about this research comes at the moment when she talks to one school's ESL director about the problems she has encountered with the citizenship grade. As Mangual Figueroa describes the conversation, the ESL director was concerned, but ultimately framed the *citizenship grade* problem as an issue of English–Spanish translation. He suspected that these families had limited English, so documents like report cards and curricular explanations needed to be more carefully translated into Spanish. While this ESL director certainly wanted to do the right thing and be of service to families, his response seemed misdirected. As the conversations recorded by Mangual Figueroa illustrate, at issue was not simply translation between English and Spanish – parents and children knew the English word *citizenship* all too well. Given experiences of these families coming to the United States, their continuous state of worry about their own legal citizenship status, and the ever-present risk that they could be separated from their children who are US citizens, the line between *good citizenship* in school classrooms and *legal US citizenship* was anxiously blurry.

Eventually, the school district and local community began to address this widely circulating anxiety regarding citizenship, including Mexican immigrant families in activities, giving them more opportunities to be active in the community, and fostering a sense of "cultural citizenship" (2011, p. 277). Pointing to these activities as a locus of a kind of citizenship distinct from both classroom behavior and legal status suggests it may be possible to reclaim this word, even in the situations of precarity described by Mangual Figueroa. Abandoning the term *citizen* because there are schools that use it thoughtlessly and without regard for its powerful impact on mixed-status families seems counterproductive. Instead, efforts to foster and reflect on the meaning of words like *citizenship* in the lives of everyday people may generate shared understandings and build community. An ongoing "citizen sociolinguistic" investigation of the word, as Mangual Figueroa's study has already begun, yields a more robust conversation. There is not one "literal" meaning of citizenship and one "metaphorical" meaning, one "cultural" understanding and one "legal" understanding. There are infinite ways of thinking about this word, and as Mangual Figueroa points out, there is a lot of blurring between the meaning of "good citizenship" and "legal citizenship" across contexts.

As the conversations documented by Mangual Figueroa illustrate, deliberation about words involves entertaining multiple claims that come from different perspectives. Some of these claims may be from locals, others from professors, some may draw on the authority of standardizing norms, some may draw on the authority of elite academic institutions, others may call on the authority of years of ethnographic description, or years of life within a community. Because language choices have real effects on people in specific contexts, each of these claims has value – choosing one as the "best" or most "legitimate" or "accurate" is not the goal of citizen sociolinguistics. Instead, looking carefully at all these claims, collectively, can tell everyone much more about language use in context, and, in the process, about societal relations. In the context of schooling in Southwestern Pennsylvania, this broad perspective on language is important not just so that the families learn that there are different circulating meanings of the words *citizen* and *citizenship*, but also so that the teachers, staff, and administrators have a sense of what this word means within families at their school. For this school's personnel, as much as for the mixed-status families in their school district, there is a pressing need for new perspectives on the word. They need much more than a Spanish translation of their school documents. They need to understand the multiple possible interpretations of words – in any language – that they are using with their community. Within any community, developing greater awareness of these multiple interpretations could start by engaging in open deliberation about the meaning of words like *citizen*.

The Legal Citizen: State Subject, Local Inhabitant

As discussed above, the legal definition of *citizen* holds a prominent place among mixed-status families in Southwestern Pennsylvania. And, despite the school district's use of a more metaphorical understanding implied in the "citizenship grade" and their attempt at more inclusive school events that emphasized "cultural citizenship," a brief tour through the Internet underlines the prevalence of the legal and literal definition. Enter the question, "What is a citizen?" into a google search bar and the legal definition – that subject status of most concern to the families in Mangual Figueroa's study – pops up immediately. The first source to appear (positioned there by Google), from dictionary.com, offers up two distinct entries:

cit-i-zen
noun
- a legally recognized subject or national of a state or commonwealth, either native or naturalized. "a Polish **citizen**" *Synonyms:* subject, national, passport holder, native
- an inhabitant of a particular town or city. "the **citizens** of Los Angeles" *Synonyms:* inhabitant, resident, native, townsman, townswoman, householder, local

The first definition within this entry specifies legal status as part of a nation state, as in, "a Polish citizen," while the second recognizes a more informal use of the word as an "inhabitant" of a particular town or city – as in "the citizens of Los Angeles." All the definitions that appear on the first page of the google search offer more definitions focusing on the legal rights and obligations connected with the role, or, simply inhabitance. The first four definitions are as follows (retrieved June 25, 2019):

an inhabitant of a city or town especially : one entitled to the rights and privileges of a freeman. 2a : a member of a state. b : a native or naturalized person who owes allegiance to a government and is entitled to protection from it. (Merriam-Webster)

a native or naturalized member of a state or nation who owes allegiance to its government and is entitled to its protection (Dictionary.com)

a person who is a member of a particular country and who has rights because of being born there (Cambridge English Dictionary)

If you were born in the United States, you are a U.S citizen. If your parents are U.S. citizens, but you were born in another country, you are also a U.S. citizen. (EdHelper.com)

A search for the definition of *citizenship* instead of *citizen* yields an even more specific and limited definition:

cit-i-zen-ship
noun
the position or status of being a citizen of a particular country "the refugees could be granted dual citizenship"

This pervasive legal and nation-centric understanding of the words *citizen* and *citizenship* further underlines the problematic ambiguity of the "citizenship grade" as described by Mangual Figueroa. It also calls into question the ESL director's suggestion that the "citizenship grade" misunderstanding is a "translation" problem. There are widely circulating preferences for the legal, nation-centric definition, and even among the most fluent of English speakers there is likely to be ambiguity between the "legal" definition and the broader sense of social responsibility entailed in "good citizenship." Most – but not all – of the definitions that fall below this most prominent definition of *citizenship* articulate the legal, nation-centric meaning. The first four pop up as follows – but you may notice that one of these four is conspicuously different:

the status of a person recognized under the custom or law as being a legal member of a sovereign state or belonging to a nation (Wikipedia)

Citizenship involves people working together to make positive differences to the society in which they live – locally, nationally and globally (youngcitizens.org)

relationship between an individual and a state to which the individual owes allegiance and in turn is entitled to its protection. (Britannica.com)

in a legal sense, "citizenship" indicates the relationship between an individual and a nation-state. (Csglobalpartners.com)

Readers have probably identified the one definition above that looks nothing like the others. The second definition, from youngcitizens.org, suggests an alternative perspective. Instead of focusing on either legal or geographical identification, this website provides a hint at the idealism many of us might associate with citizenship: that it involves "people working together to make positive differences." This idealism may also have initially motivated those teachers and school administrators in Mangual Figueroa's study who came up with the idea of a "citizenship grade." Youngcitizens.org offers a more active orientation to citizenship than simply legal status or residency, instead pushing "young citizens" to think much more broadly about what it means to actively and collaboratively embody the citizen role. So, parting ways with the legal citizen subject, let's now consider this role, "the idealistic citizen," and how others take it up.

The Idealistic Citizen: What Does Citizenship Mean to You?

The website youngcitizens.org discusses citizenship as something that "involves people working together to make positive differences to the society in which they live – locally, nationally and globally." This description draws neither on legal definitions and policies nor on local inhabitance, but instead appeals to broad ideals that transcend national boundaries. This definition links to the website for Young Citizens, a non-profit located in England with a mission to provide guidance to those teaching England's mandatory citizenship curriculum. According to the website, citizenship education must be centrally concerned with educating students to be active participants in society:

Citizenship education involves developing the knowledge, skills and confidence to enable people to make their own decisions and to take responsibility for their own lives and communities. And in many countries – where democratic society and its institutions are facing threats   citizenship education is becoming increasingly important.

They insist this process is not only "good for" individuals, but necessary for "safeguarding" democratic society against something – something bad, but which remains unnamed:

This process is good for individuals, and essential for strengthening and safeguarding our society and democratic way of life.

This is a far more idealistic and morally loaded depiction of active citizenship than the more static legal nation-state-oriented definition. And many more versions of this stance pop up when we change our google search from "what is citizenship?" to something more personalized: "What does citizenship mean to you?"

This invitation to a more personal response seems to be the strategy of choice for non-profits interested in promoting a broad definition of citizenship. Posing the question "what does citizenship mean to you" to google yields several video montages of personalized anecdotal accounts of citizenship, portraits of citizenship in the United States, not England, but aligned in tone with the Young Citizens organizational mission. The YouTube page for Define American, a non-profit "media and culture organization ... [that] uses the power of story to transcend politics and shift the conversation about immigrants, identity, and citizenship in a changing America," features this idealistic stance. In a three-minute video produced by this organization, "undocumented Americans" tell their own stories. (www.youtube.com/watch?v=aJlHjBXFH48).

According to the video, Define American "asked undocumented Americans what it means to be a citizen." The personal responses edited together in this video have little to do with nation state membership or obedience to authority described in the depersonalized definitions, and they differ substantively from those responses Mangual Figueroa recorded among undocumented Americans in her study. The first speaker, Justino Moro, who immigrated to the United States from Mexico in 2000, has this to say:

MORO: That's a really good question. My concept of citizenship has changed significantly. Before I saw it as a piece of paper, right? As the key to more opportunities, right? I think my concept of citizenship has changed to "what are you doing for your community? What are you doing to have a positive impact ..."

The video editors have pulled out one phrase in Moro's definition for emphasis: *Positive Impact*. As he speaks, this phrase is displayed in gigantic white letters on the screen. For each of the three subsequent contributors in the video, the editors use the same large text callouts to emphasize similar key phrases:

Pay It Forward
Share Our Ideals
Be the Best that You Can Be

By voicing values that align with community well-being, distinct from any legal status, these catchphrases seem to more solidly align with the "citizenship grade" promoted in the Southwestern Pennsylvania schools in Mangual Figueroa's study. And, because these are undocumented individuals, the video suggests that this idealistic form of citizenship can be practiced by anyone in this country, regardless of their immigration status, by embodying those values.

But there are no comments under this video. No real conversation. Viewers can't easily determine who these people to are talking to, or why. The video as of June 2019 had 10,115 views, 44 thumbs up, and nine thumbs down. But what made people give this a thumbs up? A thumbs down? Who were those people? Where, I want to know, are people really deliberating about the words *citizen* and *citizenship*? Given that they carry such weight, given that over 10,000 people have viewed this video, shouldn't a conversation be happening?

In a search of more wide-ranging dialogue, I found the most evocative set of videos in this genre, from the *Los Angeles Times* (2014). Each video on this site represents one individual responding, in from one to five minutes, to the question about what citizenship means to them. Again, as in the other more idealistic video montages, in the face of such a prompt, it seems highly unlikely that any person would respond exclusively with the legal definition of citizenship – the prompt itself seems to be asking for something more. And that is what each of the 12 videos depicts, from a range of Los Angeles residents of different backgrounds.

For James Fugate, an African American bookseller, citizenship means "you have an obligation and a responsibility as a citizen to look at the Constitution, look at the Bill of Rights and then decide to be involved in making them what they are supposed to stand for." For Damolo Akinola, an IT consultant, citizenship gives him "a chance to participate in the debate." Grace Yoo, Executive Director of the Korean-American Coalition, describes citizenship similarly as "the right to have your voice heard." For Judy Baca, a Chicano Studies professor and artist, citizenship has nothing to do with a legal status, but with active participation. She likes to refer to herself as a "citizen artist," and in that role she has been painting a half-mile long mural for years, a depiction of the American experience, based on memories shared by locals. Citizenship, for Baca, means contributing to a collective, kaleidoscopic memory of what it means to be an American. Hiroshi Motomura, a law professor at UCLA, offers an extended discussion of the relationship between citizen participation and integration of immigrants in the history of the United States. Jeffrey Briggs, a 58-year-old attorney, emphasizes the importance of knowing the constitution, obeying our nation's laws, but being active about making changes to those laws as necessary. He praises immigrants who have gone through the process of naturalization as generally more knowledgeable about the constitution and mindful of their responsibilities for civic engagement than citizens born in the United States. Taken together the 12 voices provide a thoughtful representation of different perspectives on the meaning of *citizenship* in the contemporary United States, during a time when, as Mangual Figueroa's research has shown, even the word itself can be cause for fear and insecurity for many residents.

The range of perspectives on display on the *Los Angeles Times* site opens the door for citizen sociolinguistic investigation into contested words, like *citizen* and *citizenship* and leads us into the very thicket of emotion and confusion faced by students and families as well as the school teachers and administrators that Mangual Figueroa worked with. The text leading up to these videos directly addresses issues of immigration and legal citizenship, and the desire to start a "dialogue" about these issues. But this beautifully made, thoughtful, and provocative set of videos provides no space for comments, no possibility for direct deliberation by readers and viewers. There is no discussion, aside from the carefully curated interviews on display.

The lack of space for commentary on these *Los Angeles Times* videos and the disabled comment space under the Define American video left me longing for even negative commentary on any of the definitions of citizen and citizenship depicted. The problematic contrast between participatory citizenship and civic engagement on one hand and the threat of deportation and family separation on the other, between the ideal and the legal definitions, remained floating in a sea of ambiguity and non-discussion. It was starting to seem that legal hard-liners and idealistic civic-minded people rarely come face-to-face, even in virtual internet spaces.

Continuing to search for some dialogue or contesting voices speaking back to the "idealistic citizen" genre, I did find one video in which the comments section remained open. This one, posted by the non-profit organization pointsoflight.org, splices together quick clips of everyday people, in this case, on the street in three different cities, San Francisco, New York, and Chicago. Like the videos posted on the websites for the *Los Angeles Times* and the non-profit Define American, they all make personal statements in response to the question, "What does it mean to be a citizen?" While their responses range widely, nobody mentions legal status or immigration:

- It means you're part of something basically bigger than yourself.
- Follow the rules
- Being a citizen kind of gives you a voice
- You have to VOTE. There is no such thing as a small election.
- You have to be active
- Be aware of what's happening in your community and really trying to figure out what your community needs
- Being a good neighbor, watching out for each other

- Be as nice as possible
- Decreasing our carbon footprint
- Educating yourself
- Be of service, be of service, be of service
- Go into that community and give your time. Your time is so valuable
- We all need to play a part
- I think a good citizen is someone who ... takes care of the environment and the community ...

Source: www.youtube.com/watch?v=DhAV-Z7thbc

This video has over 40,000 views, 79 thumbs up, and 18 thumbs down. This thumb distribution suggests there are some mixed views. Fortunately, because the comment option under this video remains open, we can get a sense of the content of those differing opinions. The 10 comments there – some directly critical – seem untouched by any consistent editorial voice. One comment insists that all these people are ignorant because they seem unaware of the legal definition of citizenship. (This person ignores the set-up, that these individuals were being asked a personal question, explicitly told to describe what citizenship means *to them*):

COMMENTER 1 : Oh my God we are in trouble so many people ignorant of the law ...

Another laments that citizenship in the United States has become meaningless because there are so many non-citizens here:

COMMENTER 2 : It means absolutely nothing in the US anymore ... Nothing. If you are a US Citizen you are now a second class individual underneath the illegal aliens. We must continue to be taxed to death to support those who do nothing for this Country except for that large sucking sound you hear. ["sucking sound" alluding to the view that immigrants suction money away from the US economy]

And several comments mention (or imply) that this video is simply boring:

COMMENTER 3: cough cough*/yawn
COMMENTER 3: boring
COMMENTER 4: 0__0

Two commenters simply wrote "reee:"

COMMENTER 5: reee
COMMENTER 6: reee

Seeing this response multiple times led me to think it must be coded internet language, and after a quick google search I learned it is a typical expression of frustration used by *Pepe the Frog*, an icon of anti-immigrant, white nationalist, racist sentiment. More specifically, "reeeee" is uttered by a unique version of Pepe the Frog, "Angry Pepe":

Figure 1.1 Angry Pepe

The image of Pepe the Frog has been listed as an icon of hate groups by the Anti-defamation League, and according to the *know your meme* website, '"REEEEEEE" is an onomatopoetic expression of intense rage or frustration typically associated with the Angry Pepe character.

Here we finally see a real clash between the legal and anti-immigrant perspectives voiced in the comments and the more idealistic views of citizenship voiced in the video, but no further dialogue results. Responses like the Angry Pepe call of frustration, "reee," the one-word remark "boring," and the blank stare emoticon (0__0), react to the video, but do not engage with it, and could arguably be classified as "trolling" – negative attention-seeking responses by bad actors, affiliating with like-minded bad actors. These comments also illuminate the presence of negativity – even hatred – circulating around the word *citizen*. And they may explain, at least in part, why many other videos on the same topic have no comment section open. Two comments explicitly praise the video ("this vid is amazing" and "nice vid"), but the remaining eight responses ooze negativity. This video was "boring," frustrating in an Angry Pepe way, an illustration of people's ignorance of the law, or an illustration of how immigrants are taking away the legal privileges of US citizens. Shutting down comment sections like this, which seem to provide forums for largely annoying and negative back talk, was likely an editorial decision on the part of the other video makers and the *Los Angeles Times* site editors.

The Cynical Citizen: Sarcasm, Parody, and Counter-Culture

Comments of anti-immigrant sentiment ("that large sucking sound") and quotations of Angry Pepe the Frog ("reee") suggest there may be a reservoir of much darker opinion about citizenship, built on negative assumptions about immigration and the role of immigration in the United States. This dark turn exemplified in the comments section under the pointsoflight.org video emerges more robustly, through sarcasm and parody, on urbanditionary.com.

Urbandictionary.com, however, works differently than standard on-line dictionaries, the more personalized video montages, or the straight criticism in the viewer commentary below those idealistic videos. To deliver its parodic punch, Urban Dictionary returns us to the universalizing stance of the dictionary genre, but with the editorializing power of parody. It usually gives us sarcastic snarky answers and defines (or even invents) lewd words you might hear around a middle-school lunch table but would not find in Webster's. By mocking the dictionary genre, framing sarcasm and lewdness in an authoritative, dictionary-like way, Urban Dictionary sometimes approaches humor. Most often, it achieves, at best, a revelatory glimpse into the author's perspective: a very personal view, parodically disguised as universal truth. For Urban Dictionary, then, a *citizen* is ...

> ... a subjugated human
> ... one who consents to be governed by others. A human being with an inferiority complex.

These definitions mimic the official, timeless quality required in styling dictionary definitions, but sneak in editorializing with subtle asides, colloquialisms like "inferiority complex," and irreverent examples.

The most popular Urban Dictionary Definition for *citizen* (partially quoted above), falls in line with the straight-up "legal status" definitions, but adds typically ultra-harsh Urban Dictionary sarcasm and an illustrative invented dialogue:

Citizen
A subjugated human that was assigned a serial number at birth.

BERNARD: Without a serial number you are the enemy of every state on the Governed Planet
JOE: I disagree, I was taught that Citizen is a good thing
BERNARD: Yes its good, citizenship is the fundamental fulcrum of governing humans
JOE: GOD is my savior

#peasant

This entry invokes the standard legal status definition of citizen, but it also denigrates that legal status, defining a *citizen* as someone "subjugated." This entry also alludes to the more "idealistic" view of citizens put forth by the non-profits like youngcitizens.org and Define American, voicing that view in the invented dialogue, when Joe says, "I was taught that Citizen is a good thing." When faced with Bernard's response, that citizenship is indeed good, at least for those who are governing the citizens, Joe responds simply, "GOD is my savior," which might suggest Joe is not really thinking critically about citizenship, but merely seeking something to believe in blindly. Joe is a dumb foil for the view of citizenship put forth in the presumably enlightened entry, and the view that citizens are dupes of those who govern them. With the #peasant attached at the end, this entry even invokes feudal forms of government, undermining any democratic or idealistic participatory associations readers might have with the word.

This entry received 387 thumbs up and only five thumbs down – an unusually high positive ratio (77:1!) for Urban Dictionary, or as we will see in Chapter 4, most any internet platform. The positive thumbs-up ratio suggests this definition represents a commonly shared understanding of *citizen*, at least among those who vote on Urban Dictionary entries. Who are these thumbs-uppers? Whose views on citizenship would align with this author's definition? Not the "mixed status" families in Mangual Figueroa's account, who see citizenship as a legal form of security in the United States. This entry mocks legal citizenship. Not those everyday people who voiced the idealistic views of citizenship in those interviews on the *Los Angeles Times* site, or the non-profit organizations Young Citizens, Define American, or Points of Light. Joe's role in the entry's invented dialogue embodies this idealistic perspective as an object of ridicule. This entry seems most aligned with those negative comments on the Points of Light video compilation: "Boring," "reee," and the more elaborated view of the commenter who wrote, presumably from the point of view of a legal citizen, that citizenship "means absolutely nothing in the US anymore ... Nothing. If you are a US Citizen you are now a second class individual underneath the illegal aliens ..." The most popular Urban Dictionary entry for *citizen* invokes this sentiment – parodying idealistic views of citizenship and, with dark humor, pointing out that citizenship means nothing more than that we are subjugated dupes of a government. We can now imagine 387 Angry Pepes out there, giving this entry the thumbs up.

Even though I find this particular entry depressing, I appreciate what Urban Dictionary has done for us here: Even as people close down comment sections underneath more idealistic portraits of citizenship, those in which citizenship is framed as positive participatory "paying it forward" or being "the best that you can be," Urban Dictionary remains a place where the negative sentiment about these views can be aired and made visible to idealistic others who may be unaware of this perspective. This dark view of citizenship, one that may also be anti-immigrant and worse, emerges on Urban Dictionary in a way that might be illuminating to, for example, teachers and administrators who would like, through sheer act of will, to promote "good citizenship" without considering not only the fears this may invoke in the undocumented, but also the bile that discussions of citizenship can call forth in those already inclined to anti-immigrant sentiment. Of the slightly less popular Urban Dictionary definitions that follow this one (there was a total of seven entries), not one includes anything very idealistic about the role of "citizen." Two of these entries, like entry #1, emphasize the subjection to governmental control implied by being a "citizen" and suggest that acting as a citizen does not involve critical awareness at all, but blind consent and mindlessness:

> Entry #2: n., one who consents to be governed by others. A human being with an inferiority complex. Synonyms: patriot, nationalist, statist, soldier of the fatherland/ motherland. A normal. A muggle. (39 thumbs up/23 thumbs down)
>
> Entry #6: Someone who automatically believes everything the government or its agents (e.g. the media) say. A synonym for a **blind patriot**. Someone who's programmed to be **spoonfed** and happily munch on **the government's** bullshit and doesn't know it–in fact, has grown to like it. (21 thumbs up/14 thumbs down).

According to entry #1, without citizenship, "you are the enemy of every state on the governed planet," but, for entry #2, with citizenship, you are, pathetically, "A human being with an inferiority complex . . . A normal. A muggle." Continuing this degrading account of citizenship, #6 adds that a citizen "automatically believes everything the government or its agents (e.g., the media) say . . . Someone who's programmed to be spoonfed and happily munch on the government's bullshit . . ." These three definitions of citizenship identify the word as a legal category, but each definition also contains a critique of more idealistic views of citizenship, framing citizenship as slightly pathetic – not a guarantee of rights and privileges associated with legal citizen status (as mixed-status families in Southwestern Pennsylvania might), but an acquiescence to standardized, brainwashed behavior that comes with pledging allegiance to the State.

These three entries critiquing citizenship come from individuals who seem secure about their own position as bona fide *citizens*, certainly more so than families with genuine concerns about a "citizenship" grade. Unlike residents in the United States who may feel precarious about their status here because they do not have citizenship papers, these Urban Dictionary definition writers seem to feel so confident in their status as legal citizens that they freely sound off against the state and the "government's bullshit," on a public forum. As citizen sociolinguists, they are not displaying citizenship by acting as mindless followers of the state with no ideas of their own, but by actively posting their own ideas, sarcastic and cynical though they may be, about what it means to be a "citizen," on Urban Dictionary. In the process, they have also illuminated some paradoxical dynamics around who is entitled to criticize citizenship and who needs its protections.

In stark contrast to understandings of the word *citizen* among immigrant families, a context that raises the specter of legal action and even deportation, all the Urban Dictionary definitions for *citizen* give off this cynical, even entitled, attitude about the word. Of the four remaining definitions, three identify the word *citizen* as a nickname for different consumer products (Citizens of Humanity Jeans, a type of Haircut ["The Citizen"] you might get if you were appearing in court, or a code word for cocaine, the Schedule II illegal drug). One definition defines *citizen* as "a member of a particular group," offering this example, ""Bill's not gay. He's definitely flying the flag, but he's not a citizen. He's more of a metrosexual." (27 thumbs up, 18 down). Moving from the term *citizen* to *citizenship*, the Urban Dictionary definition for citizenship echoes the tone of disdain in the *citizen* definitions (7 thumbs up, 7 thumbs down):

Citizenship
The act of doing what authority figures tell you to do.
It is part of my citizenship not to go mass murder people.

This author shows no recognition that citizenship may offer protection or a sense of belonging, no sense that it involves responsibilities or privileges. Citizenship is synonymous with obedience, "doing what authority figures tell you to do." The disturbing example sentence even suggests that "citizenship" might be the only thing preventing someone from committing mass murder. With an even seven thumbs up and seven down, this entry might even just cancel itself out in terms of relevance to the world. Still, its consistency with the Urban Dictionary's *citizen* definitions remains.

What can this investigation tell us so far about everyday use of the words *citizen* and *citizenship*? Around these two words at least, the Urban Dictionary community shows a total disconnect from the lack of citizenship that causes persistent anxiety within those mixed-status families Mangual Figueroa writes about. But this is a different kind of disconnect from that of school administrators or others who talk about a "citizenship grade" or the idealistic video montages answering the question "what does citizenship mean to you?" These cynical Urban Dictionary authors seem aware of the potential for broad, non-legalistic views of citizenship, but express disdain for those ideals – seeing these idealistic citizens as, to paraphrase entry #6, happily munching on the government bullshit that is spoon-fed to them. The dramatic nature of this disconnect can't be overstated: At one extreme, mixed-status families live in fear of family separation because of the legalities of citizenship. At the other extreme, YouTube commentary and urban dictionary authors mock legal citizenship as a joke – because we have to blindly do what the government tells us, or because immigrants are making it pointless. In the middle are those who would rather think about citizenship as a form of participation in society that is distinct from the legalities but necessary to sustain our shared humanity.

No matter where your own opinion falls along these extremes of legality, idealism, and cynicism, this cannot be denied: Among people who have different social networks and different goals, the words *citizenship* and *citizen* can work very differently, and those different perspectives emerge in different genres of talk about language. Still, the point of looking at each of these definitions is not to find the "right" one, but to understand how everyday people define *citizen*, how those definitions differ radically across social groups, and how those different circulating assumptions might affect how the word *citizen* operates. Our definitions depend on where we sit – and as such, when we encounter new people, misunderstandings may be inevitable.

The Deliberative Citizen: The Inseparability of Circulating Opinions

Misunderstandings may be inevitable because these different evocations of citizen, the legal, the idealistic, the cynical, all seem to be at cross purposes. But that doesn't mean we can't work to combat the most damaging misunderstandings. Following Dewey's advice, now "it is necessary to dig up and compare the presuppositions, the implied context, upon the basis of which each is speaking." What are the presuppositions and implied contexts behind the concerns about legal citizenship, idealistic citizenship, or cynical citizenship? Mangual Figueroa has unpacked the implied context behind those mixed-status families' understandings of *citizenship*, illustrating their reasons for prioritizing the legal definitions of these words. The presuppositions behind more idealistic views of citizenship seem to a be well-meaning desire for inclusion of all voices, a kaleidoscopic portrait of the citizenry that doesn't rely on legalities for its legitimacy. School administrators in Northeastern Pennsylvania, residents of Los Angeles, teachers of the citizenship curriculum in England, non-profits seeking to provide a path to legal citizenship – all these interested parties have assumptions about the positive values of being part of a community, idealistic views of citizenship that they want to be foregrounded even in the face of more discrete legal realities of immigration status and deportation. The cynical views voiced in commentary that opposes this idealism, suggest that other individuals, though secure in their own legal citizenship nevertheless feel a different kind of threat to their well-being, a sense that they, as citizens, pay their taxes to support those who are not paying or contributing, just taking away their hard-earned money and chipping away at the value of their US citizenship. This sense of the trials of citizenship with no rewards – of being disenfranchised – comes forward in the harshest of the Urban Dictionary entries, those defining citizenship as a burden, borne by those who are powerless or stupid enough to allow themselves to be governed.

Placing these contradictory definitions and presuppositions side by side illustrates deep differences across communities. It follows that in diverse settings – like schools and public internet comment spaces – interactions involving this word will be unpredictable. Some definitions share underlying assumptions, some do not. The presuppositions behind the cynical view of citizenship, put forth by the Urban Dictionary authors, are functionally similar to those of the mixed-status families. For different reasons, neither view can recognize an ideal of citizenship that is divorced from legal requirements: For immigrants, it's their precarity that makes it difficult to see beyond the legal realities of being a *citizen* – be it for a citizenship grade in school, or a citizenship test for the government. The specter of deportation always looms. For the jaded Urban Dictionary authors and critics of the idealized citizenship videos, their sarcasm suggests an analogous disconnect from idealized forms of citizenship, a sense of their own disenfranchisement. These are presumably legal citizens, but they still feel powerless in the face of government authority: They don't see their role as taxpayers as contributing to something larger than themselves – they see it as the government taking their money.

Idealism about being a citizen rings hollow if it does not account for the legalities and the realities of people who feel disenfranchised – both those cynics who feel citizenship has become a joke for them, and those who desperately need to be seen as "legal citizens" to remain connected to their family. Even the best of the idealistic "what does citizenship mean to you" interview videos yield primarily generalizing statements, we might even think of them as "stereotypes" of the "good citizen," circling around the notion that being a "citizen" is about contributing to your community – engaging in service, being informed, putting in time, voting. These views don't account for either the tenuous living conditions of mixed-status families or the cynical underpinnings of the Urban Dictionary perspective.

All these definitions of citizenship illustrate acts of citizen sociolinguists – be they undertaken by undocumented immigrants, idealistic non-profits, or cynical Pepe the Frog followers. These citizen sociolinguists contribute time to talk about their language, to argue, and to respond to others. They are acting as citizens by contributing talk about language. I'll be discussing this active form of *citizen sociolinguistics as citizenship* in more detail in Chapter 6.

The Censored Citizen

While the word *citizen* can generate debate and cruel remarks, and worse, stress within families and schools, avoiding the controversy through blind idealism helps nobody. Censoring comments, even though they may be cruel and disturbing, could be more damaging to public life. And though we see plenty of free-flowing offensive speech on the Internet, even in this brief exploration of the word *citizen* we have also seen censorship: On most of the more idealistic YouTube videos, "comments have been disabled." The *Los Angeles Times* site, which purported to be starting "dialogue" about citizenship, provided no space for reader commentary. This subtle form of censorship – blocking comments from those who might contest an idealized view – threatens to build a censored portrait of what *citizen* means to everyday people, and an incomplete understanding of how the word functions in our society.

In his 1922 book *Public Opinion*, the public philosopher Walter Lippmann wrote that "Without some form of censorship, propaganda in the strict sense of the word is impossible." Slicing through Lippmann's double negation we might paraphrase this as *Censorship makes propaganda possible* – and we have now begun to see how this happens. The idealized presentation of participatory citizenship, the proposition that we all can simply "pay it forward" and contribute to something "bigger than us," regardless of our legal status, when presented without any space for critique or commentary, verges on propaganda. And there are far more cartoonish versions of the idealistic version of "what does citizenship mean to you" posted on the Internet. For example, this montage of children supposedly voicing their own personal views of citizenship painfully illustrates Lippmann's point. In response to the question "what does citizenship mean?" these children, posed in front of a map of the world, an American flag, or large plastic outdoor playground equipment offer responses like these:

- Being honest, helpful, and kind to other people in your community.
- You can learn how to be a good citizen by talking with your parents, your teacher, and maybe even your principal.
- I think people who serve in the coast guard are good citizens.
- I think people who serve in the military are good citizens.
- I think my dad is a good citizen because he serves in the military . . .
- Part of being an American is you're allowed to have life, liberty, and the pursuit of happiness.
- America is different from other countries because of the rights we have like freedom of speech because we get to speak out and protest what we think is wrong and what is right.
- Maybe you're suggesting that the government should do something different? You are allowed to say that instead of being thrown in jail like in other countries.
- I learned to be a good citizen from scouts, my parents, and my school.
- I would learn how to be a good citizen from my teachers and my family and all the people who are important in my life.

Source: www.youtube.com/watch?v=1h2rLQ5YtAk

The joyless demeanor and monotone delivery of these responses runs counter to the freedoms they imply we are enjoying as citizens of the United States, and the parallel structure of many of the responses suggests that some fill-in-the-blank sentence starters may have been provided to help these kids come up with their responses. I imagine a preparatory worksheet with options like these:

You can learn how to be a good citizen by _____.
I think people who _____ are good citizens.
I learned how to be a good citizen from _____.
American citizenship is different from other countries because _____.
One response includes an entire phrase-chunk from the US Declaration of Independence ("life, liberty, and the pursuit of happiness") stated in primary school monotone read-aloud rhythm. Now we can see that the video montage genre itself invites a form of censorship. I suspect an "outtakes" roll, the video clips left on the cutting room floor, would have been illuminating. (See Chapter 3 for an extended discussion of the role of outtakes in citizen sociolinguistics)

It is not surprising that – mercifully – the comments section for this video has been disabled. Given our knowledge of circulating cynicism, of troll comments like "reee" (or far worse) that are likely to come on the heels of idealistic citizenship montages like this, posting these children's videos and leaving them open to that sort of feedback would be cruel. However, to Lippmann's point, it is precisely this ability to block that feedback that makes it possible to post this propaganda-like production. The non-profit involved in this production was the American Enterprise Institute – a conservative think tank whose primary mission is to minimize the role of government in the economy but which also promotes "viewpoint diversity" in the marketplace of ideas. It is unclear what the motivation was behind this video production from 2011. Whatever the motivation, viewpoint diversity seems lacking.

As these idealistic, even saccharine, views on *citizenship* get pitched without feedback, deliberation about citizenship stops. The voices of those immigrants who live in fear of anti-immigrant sentiments, or worse, of being separated from their children because of the legal requirements for citizenship, ostensibly those who most need to be given voice by those idealistic views of citizenship, may never be heard at all. And the voices of anti-immigration movements go underground, surfacing in coded Pepe the Frog language, or thinly veiled with parody in Urban Dictionary entries. These videos would do nothing to influence the values of those disenfranchised Urban Dictionary authors calling "bullshit!" For the deliberative citizen to actually deliberate, these alternative perspectives, situated, always changing, and often in conflict, need to be aired. The fact that those sentiments exist means they have influence. The only person who understands each of these points of view enough to give voice to them – the experts on those perspectives – are the people in those positions. But their views are useless –possibly even dangerous – if we drive them underground and don't know about them. That's why *citizen* sociolinguistics is about everyday conversations about language, but also about how we define expertise within those conversations. No one person owns the word *citizen* or has the right definition. Nobody has enough expertise in all contexts of communication to define words out from under someone else. That is simply an act of brute power. But in exercising their human tendency to notice and talk about language, everyday citizen sociolinguists define their own words and name their world.

Citizen Expertise

Politics of Expertise: Who Defines Our World?

In discussions of the word *citizen* and its meaning, we have seen different types of expertise that appeal to different sources of authority: the freestanding authority of dictionary definition style, the authority of parodying that style in urbandictionary.com entries, the authority of a translator who might be able to clarify the purpose of the citizenship grade to immigrant families, the authority of the legal mandate and the power of the constitution, the authority of stereotypes and widely circulating images like Pepe the Frog or the "sucking sound," and the collective authority of the person-on-the-street or children-in-front-of-a-flag interview compilation. The way citizen sociolinguists achieve expert status relies on very different forms of persuasion and may result in different pathways of action.

Claims to expertise as a citizen sociolinguist may come from their local connections, their family, their friends, the relationships that mean the most to them, their understandings of institutions around them, or infinite other sources. But not every voice gets the same amount of attention – or is heard at all. As illustrated in the foregoing investigation of competing understandings of the word *citizen*, having the power to express oneself or sociolinguistically arrest someone as *any person*, as a *citizen*, is not completely separable from the institutionally granted power of being a legally recognized citizen – someone who won't be reprimanded, or worse, sent across the border and far from home, for saying what they believe in.

So, what good do these variable forms of expertise do us? Who should define the word *citizen*? Or settle any other language matter? Given the wide range of opinion out there, maybe it is best after all to let well-educated professors do it for us, best not to leave language deliberations in the hands of everyday people. Let's consider two opposing takes on that proposition. From one perspective, how-language-works seems too important to leave up in the air, to the random deliberation of any person, someone who might invoke arbitrary authority of media-circulated stereotypes to bolster their arguments – or simply type out trolling comments like "boring" or "reee" that close down deliberation in favor of one perspective. When citizen sociolinguists imply, like one Urban Dictionary author did, that a blind invocation of "citizenship" is the only thing that might be keeping someone from committing mass murder, invoking the word "expertise" seems a stretch. From this point of view, it might be better just to stop using the word *citizen* in any way other than a technical, legal sense. It's too controversial, too saturated with stereotypes that will inevitably lead to confusion among ordinary people. And for that matter, let's keep language matters out of the hands of these fools altogether!

From another point of view, discussions of the word *citizen* – and all other language controversies for that matter–seem too important *not* to leave in the hands of deliberating citizen sociolinguists, those who have the local knowledge to combat top-down generalizations and stereotypical thinking. Even though a citizen sociolinguist may voice something bitter and illogical, at times something we'd rather not pay attention to, their perspective remains relevant – because it reflects how they experience their position relative to others in our society. Citizen expertise is both easy and hard to come by, simple and complex in its expression, and sometimes difficult to comprehend. And, in this respect, the role of citizen voice in democracy has been hotly debated by two critical thinkers in the United States.

Walter Lippmann and John Dewey on Public Opinion

That first perspective voiced above – that people base their understandings on superficial media-circulated stereotypes and are thus not to be taken seriously – has authoritative representation in the writings of Walter Lippmann (1922). Precisely because everyday people call on stereotypes, often conveniently recirculated by the media, to make sense of the world, Lippmann believed it was dangerous to leave the control of society in the hands of the everyday citizen, any person, forming public opinion on the basis of a pervasively "moralized and codified version of the facts." Lippmann pessimistically argued that "the pattern of stereotypes at the center of our codes largely determines what group of facts we shall see, and in what light we shall see them." If we live in the United States, we are likely to interpret words and scenes like "Americans," we will understand our role as "citizens" in an American way; if we live in England, we will inevitably see things differently, in an English way.

Lippmann would probably hate the idea of citizen sociolinguistic deliberation, relying on value as it does from the voices of everyday people, whom he might describe as generally groping to find meaning from a bewildering array of facts at their disposal, calling on stereotypes ("I would ask my scoutmaster, teacher, or principal!") to order their confusion. Lippmann believed that only well-educated professional policy makers would be able to make sense of all the information that we need to take in to make important decisions. In the face of the huge quantity of information circulated today on the Internet, Lippmann would no doubt double down on his commitment to leave the management of that information to the experts – not to the rantings of a resentful taxpayer, the blind idealism of Los Angeles creatives, or small children ventriloquating the views of the American Enterprise Institute.

In our short tour through everyday views on the word *citizen* we found that some people insist on stating idealistic views of citizenship, valuing contributions from all members of our society – while others view citizenship as a joke and see immigrants as sponging off the system, "sucking" away our resources. We also discussed working immigrants in this country who live in well-founded fear of being separated from their children because of their citizenship status. The mess of stereotypical portraits of freedom and oppression combined with the real precarity experienced by immigrant families illustrates precisely the kind of problem Lippmann didn't think democracy was equipped to handle. And, from Lippmann's perspective, paying attention to the perspectives of various citizen sociolinguists would not solve these problems either.

But Lippmann's peer John Dewey (1910) would see this mess of contradiction as a call for democratic action – and education. While Dewey and Lippmann both recognize the tendency for people to rely on shared assumptions, often unquestioned, to build their understandings of the world from an array of bewildering information, they had different ideas about how education could bring people out of this confusion. Lippmann cynically saw educators as building morals and values by eliding critical thinking, providing instead, that "moralized and codified version of the facts"; Dewey saw educators as potentially powerful advocates of critical thinking, pushing students to articulate tacit assumptions, and to work to resolve logical contradictions. Dewey believed in citizens because he felt only everyday people have the capacity to help the elite see beyond stereotypes. Everyday people, connected directly to issues most relevant to their lives, if properly educated, may be best situated to resolve conflicts because they understand localized commitments and concerns. We've seen these localized commitments emerge in discussions about language – like the knowledge of the mixed-status families in Northeastern Pennsylvania, or the local lore of South Philadelphia residents discussed in the Introduction. Even trolls who post comments like "boring" or cynics who write sarcastic Urban Dictionary posts are important to this process of education – not because they (or anyone else) should have the last word, but because, in this case, they reveal the elitism inherent in the more idealistic stance toward citizenship. More generally, this diversity of everyday voices has the capacity to remove blind spots we all have when we don't look beyond our own perspective.

We need some way to deliberate among these different perspectives – they do nothing if they are locked in isolation and speak only to one another. For this reason, Dewey also wrote emphatically that we need all citizens to be educated – and with one another – so that nuanced local concerns could enter into the conversations that support a healthy democracy. As he wrote in *How*

We Think, when we all agree, we do not need to examine our assumptions, but when we disagree, our assumptions come to light and are available for discussion:

> If two persons can converse intelligently with each other, it is because a common experience supplies a background of mutual understanding upon which their respective remarks are projected ... If, however, the two persons find themselves at cross-purposes, it is necessary to dig up and compare the presuppositions, the implied context, upon the basis of which each is speaking. (1910, p. 214)

For John Dewey, bringing different views together is the essence of education, and universal access to education provides citizens connection to and practice in these fruitful everyday acts of inquiry. Dialogue among views can take us away from stereotypes – like the stereotype of the idealistic participatory citizen, or the good citizen who looks to her teachers and parents for answers, or the cowardly conformist muggle citizen we have encountered in Urban Dictionary definitions. Concentrating power, that is, the authority to describe our language and our role as citizens, in the hands of an elite group dooms the majority to live by other people's definitions and standards. Those definitions and standards, if not subject to deliberation, will be rife with blind spots. While Lippmann argues against handing government control over to citizens whose minds are inevitably a muddle of unexamined assumptions and stereotypes, Dewey understands that any group of people who are easily agreeing may be simply out of touch with the lived experience that feeds counterarguments and so, not thinking. Returning to those examples of citizen sociolinguistic arrests that started this chapter, that out-of-touch person could be the one who demanded that Sylvia not "talk Spanish" on the bus; it could be the second-grader who silences any talk about race or use of the word "gay"; it could be me, your humble narrator, blithely and ignorantly using the word "sexual preference" in my discussion of gay sexuality. To promote deliberation over different perspectives, we must hear those different perspectives. Real education, Dewey believed, could provide the context for the airing of and deliberation over those different points of view.

While Lippmann was concerned primarily with public policy, Dewey believed that critical awareness was necessary for everyone in any situation. Any aspect of life might unpredictably become critically relevant as an object of inquiry. As Dewey writes, "No object is so familiar, so obvious, so commonplace that it may not unexpectedly present, in a novel situation, some problem, and thus arouse reflection in order to understand it" (1910, 120). For citizen sociolinguists, language remains such an object of reflection. Often seemingly trivial aspects of language, like the pronunciation of *Greenwich* or *Passyunk* become the objects of reflection. At other times, more obviously critical issues come up, discussions of *English only* or the role of *citizenship* in schools and society. For these discussions to matter, deliberation among different forms of local expertise is crucial. Lippmann's view of the confused masses who rely on stereotypes to make sense of the world could certainly be applied to all the citizen sociolinguistic opinion about the meaning of *citizenship*. But all these views matter – even those most apparently bitter and biased. The fact that stereotyped notions of what counts or should count as a *citizen* pop up so readily whenever the word is mentioned means we should probably talk more about the word – not less. If not, naïve or idealistic portraits of citizenship, or more specifically, as we saw in Mangual Figueroa's research, the unexamined use of the word to promote *good citizenship* in schools, could be damaging to the students it hopes to serve.

In 2002, I let go of my misguided use of the phrase *sexual preference*, because it didn't represent the views I wanted to get across. Now, readers may wonder, why not let go of the potentially misleading word *citizen*? I now hold fast to the word *citizen* in *Citizen Sociolinguistics* because I want to be part of those conversations about the powerful role citizens might have when they talk about their own language. I am not using this word in naïve disregard for its potential meanings and the differing assumptions beneath them, but for its Deweyesque acknowledgment of the importance of local and everyday voices, and because to use the word is also to stay open to deliberation about it, without granting one perspective precedence. The deliberation over just one word, *citizen*, reveals important connections between local conditions and people's opinions about language. This investigative process can be usefully applied to all discussions about language, all citizen sociolinguistic arrests over ways of speaking, choices of language or code, or topics of conversation. In all instances of language debate, the voices of people who use that language are inherently imbued with the expertise of their situated perspective. Ultimately, instead of trying to ascertain the relative expertise of certain definitions or opinions, we need to look at how such conversations get generated, how these conversations build and sustain communities and beliefs about types of speech and the people speaking, and how such assumptions and stereotypes get disrupted and changed.

How Citizen Sociolinguistics Is Distinct from Related Forms of Language Study: A Different Politics of Expertise

As should now be clear, citizen sociolinguistics reconfigures language expertise as multi-voiced, always changing, and context-bound, as located in the deliberation of multiple points of view held by different people in varied situations. As the discussion of *citizen* illustrates, understanding what words mean can't be accomplished by appealing to one source of expertise (which is itself part of a specific set of social conditions), but must turn to the interplay between multiple points of view. In the Introduction, I discussed how citizen sociolinguistics distinguishes itself from simple crowdsourcing or data science – by seeing citizens not simply as sources of language data, but as experts in their own right, given their close encounters with language in context every day. So, citizen sociolinguistics is not data science. But readers may still be wondering at the choice of the word *citizen* at all, especially given the controversy around that word discussed in this chapter. Friends and colleagues have asked, in their own citizen sociolinguist arrests: "Isn't this the same as 'folk linguistics'"? (Preston, 2011) "Haven't other sociolinguistics talked about this in terms of "language mavens" (Pinker, 1994) or "verbal hygiene?" (Cameron, 2012). "Isn't what you're talking about what linguistic anthropologists do already?" Short answer to all of those questions: Not at all. But, before we get on with this book, let's clarify the distinctions. The terms "folk linguistics," "language mavens," and "verbal hygiene" involve discussion of concepts related to what I have begun to outline here as the project of *citizen sociolinguistics*. What I'm talking about is most closely tied to what the field of linguistic anthropology has called "language ideologies." But as will become ever clearer as we go forward, citizen sociolinguists don't simply exemplify a range of language ideologies, they also engage with each other, foment change, complain, argue, savor, and build world views by talking about the role of language in their lives. *Doing citizen sociolinguistics is a way of engaging with society.*

Folk Linguistics

Folk linguistics differs from citizen sociolinguistics in its research questions, in its methods for investigating those questions, in its findings, and in its ways of disseminating those findings. To aid in the contrast, let's first summarize our discussion of citizen sociolinguistics so far. Citizen sociolinguistics is the work people do to make sense of everyday communication and share their sense-making with others. Like any people inquiring into their world, citizen sociolinguists have certain questions, methods for investigating those questions, an accumulation of findings, and typical ways of disseminating those findings (to be discussed in detail in Chapter 3). Citizen sociolinguists' questions are constantly changing. One day, an important question to a particular citizen sociolinguist might be, "How should I say 'Passyunk Ave' in South Philadelphia and who says it that way?" Another day, or to someone else, an important question may be, "What is citizenship and who uses that expression? What would it mean if I used it?" Citizen sociolinguists use just about any means available to explore (and expound on) language and communication. These may include (but are certainly not limited to) YouTube, Word Reference forums, Facebook and any internet-circulated social media, and the comments, likes, or dislikes that unfurl in any of these forums. Since citizen sociolinguistic work often involves using social media and the Internet, citizen sociolinguists' questions and findings constantly and speedily renew, change, and snowball with accumulated features of social context. Like citizen sociolinguistic questions, citizen sociolinguistic findings are ephemeral. Nobody has the last word.

Yet, in a given fleeting moment, the answers are highly relevant to a specific someone at a specific point in time. Inevitably, answers involve more than language: Pronunciation of the word *Greenwich* for example, might include hints of the race/class/gender/age of people who use it, a history of various encounters with the word, highly distinct local differences, and even the relationship between how someone uses that word and the role of gentrification in the changing fabric of a community. These distinctions may be the subject of extended online dialogue, or even new blogs about the word. Similar distinctions would emerge for another street name like *Passyunk*, or the way people greet each other or order a sandwich, because citizen sociolinguistic meaning does not inhere in the words themselves but in the experience of using that expression. Generally, any findings or performances by citizen sociolinguists are spread by other citizen sociolinguists in real life or via social media in a recursive and never-ending process.

In contrast to citizen sociolinguistic questions, which are constantly changing and different for everyone, folk linguistic questions serve the interests of professional sociolinguists and dialectologists, and perhaps by extension, applied linguists working with teachers or language policy makers. Most generally, folk linguists ask, "What are the subconscious cultural models with which folk (defined as all non-linguists) are operating?" (Preston, 2011). Folk linguistics has a range of methods for getting at these subconscious models: Comparing folk-drawn dialect maps with those produced by linguists using statistical analysis and dialect surveys; "matched guise" experiments in which people are asked to listen to ways of speaking (without seeing the speaker) and attribute a range of personality traits to what they hear; and even discourse analysis, in which the linguist identifies tacit folk assumptions as they emerge in interviews or conversation. For example, if a person says, "I don't have a dialect. I happen not to be from the South," the Folk Linguist notes this person's "folk" cultural model for "dialect" – namely, that a "dialect" is something that only people in the South have (Preston, 2011). This assumption – that dialects only happen in the South – is, of course, entirely at odds with an academic folk linguist's perspective. It's *folk knowledge*, not linguistic fact.

But this *folk knowledge*, from a citizen sociolinguistics perspective, is crucial to understanding how language works, because this knowledge, not the folk linguist's *fact*, is what tends to circulate through the community and influence how people act and relate to one another. Findings generated by folk linguistics research, illuminating assumptions "folk" have about language that may or may not match with professional linguistic findings, in contrast, do not circulate within the community of those speakers who are the subject of the research. These "folk" understandings about language may be disseminated to professional communities involved in teaching language or policy and planning. If, for example, folk linguistic studies reveal contradictory local impressions about certain dialect features, policy makers may need to know this before designing any specific curricula or rules about how those features should be discussed, mandated, or taught. These recommendations are based on the findings of the folk linguists, not on discussions with the local citizen sociolinguistics from whom the folk linguists derive local "cultural models."

Folk linguistics, then, has its own cultural model not shared by citizen sociolinguistics. That model presupposes that professional linguists alone can identify the cultural models of the "folk" and that these cultural models may, in the hands of linguists, serve the needs of other linguistics-related professional fields. Citizen sociolinguists, in contrast, are in the business of sharing (with each other) their own cultural models around language and communication – models that are ephemeral, constantly changing, often controversial, and always swathed in situation-specific social cues.

Folk linguists are primarily linguists. Their authority comes from their institutional credential and their research contributions are in service of that institution. Citizen sociolinguists are everyday people and linguists may be among them – but their primary audience is each other, not a professional community of research scholars. Any person becomes a citizen sociolinguist when they engage in the practice of having a conversation with someone about language. Their commentary provokes more discussion. However, their authority does not come from an institutional credential, but is instead achieved in specific contexts, in different ways, according to the interactional norms of those contexts.

Language Mavens

"Language mavens," so-called by Steven Pinker in his book *The Language Instinct* (1994), may also be conflated with people doing what I am calling "citizen sociolinguistics." Pinker compiles an impressive catalogue of readily recognizable and widely circulating opinions about language held by these "mavens," such as "no split infinitives" or "never end a sentence with a preposition." But Pinker does not see these language mavens as conducting citizen sociolinguistic arrests that might be interesting in their own right and in the deliberation they provoke. Instead, Pinker takes on the role of one counter-arresting individual: a linguist and scholar debunking these opinions, returning after each example of language mavenship to his arguments about cognitive mechanisms (not interactional ones), what he calls the *Language Instinct* that drives language change.

While some citizen sociolinguists may fall under the category "language mavens" (Giraffedata, discussed in the Introduction, who removed all instances of "comprised of" from Wikipedia, comes to mind) – the citizen sociolinguistic perspective, that is, the perspective that we need to pay attention to how everyday people talk about language, does not debunk what language mavens like Giraffedata are doing by appealing to some higher-order institutionally sanctioned theory of linguistics. Instead, the citizen sociolinguistic perspective offers ways to investigate the words of all people who talk about language and have strong opinions about it – including so-called "language mavens" – to explore the local context that undergirds their perspective and the interactional effects of their contributions, and to continue the deliberation surrounding their views.

Verbal Hygiene

Deborah Cameron's book *Verbal Hygiene* (2012) also catalogues ways that people police each other's speech, making the critical point that these attempts to clean up language are often proxies for other prejudices or fears about society. I also make similar points about the work of citizen sociolinguistic opinion as it circulates on the Internet, and I am concerned with articulating how prejudices about immigrants, race, or gender masquerade as opinions about language. Like Cameron, I insist on connecting the deliberation about language to what this deliberation can teach us about our position in society. The two are inseparable.

However, *How We Talk about Language* differs from *Verbal Hygiene* in that it accounts for a much wider range of everyday commentary about language, the rapid and exponentially cumulative nature of this opinion when it is circulated via internet-based social media, and the potential for feedback, contestation, and change via those same channels. And, unlike Cameron, I'm also concerned with those most trivial bits of language that spark people's interest – a street name, a local greeting, or a funny pronunciation – not only those language debates that clearly point to prejudice. Citizen sociolinguistics covers anything we talk about when we talk about language – because trivial discussions can illuminate new corners of societal deliberation, concern, and possibly, import. This distinction is crucial to the discussion of "Acts of Citizen Sociolinguistics" and will be elaborated in Chapter 6.

Language Ideology

The import of everyday opinions about language has been discussed in linguistic anthropology and pragmatics as "language ideology," as introduced to the scholarly world in a 1992 special issue volume of *Pragmatics*. My understanding of the role of everyday opinion aligns with the notion of language ideology articulated in this volume and in Silverstein's (1992) postscript to it.

Silverstein describes how the concept of "ideology of language" (what I am calling "everyday opinions about language") functions as a theoretical/methodological tool for understanding the highly specific "semiotic complexities" of language use in context. The chapters in the *Pragmatics* special issue illustrate various examples of opinions about language, and the social formations generated through such ideologies, gathered through traditional linguistic anthropological fieldwork. This book, *How We Talk about Language*, engages with this same theoretical/methodological nexus but looks at a broad range of language ideology through an examination of everyday conversation and internet-based social media and its unfurling of opinion, rather than long-term linguistic anthropological fieldwork within one community.

In sum, citizen sociolinguists come in all forms – they may be creating parodic dictionary entries, they may be acting in the role of "language maven" and eradicating all instances of "comprised of" on Wikipedia, or sounding off about gentrification and the local pronunciation of Philadelphia street names. In online forums and YouTube comment sections, everyday citizen sociolinguistic commentary has a range of ways of accruing "expert" status – a status that usually has nothing to do with institutional designation or conferred degrees. However, sometimes institutionally sanctioned voices offer critiques of this work. In the case of folk linguistics, linguists with PhDs step in to offer explanations for the linguistic inaccuracies of "folk" wisdom. In the case of Stephen Pinker, he calls on the theory of Universal Grammar and what he calls "the language instinct" to debunk the grammar prescriptivism of language mavens. And Deborah Cameron uses her expertise to identify the institutional processes and mechanisms that enforce norms of "verbal hygiene" and to describe the power imbalances that perpetuate language prejudice. Each citizen sociolinguistic community as well as the professional accounts of those communities illustrate that highly localized language ideologies affect how we talk about language. These opinions about language both depend on and comprise social formations. In this way, *How We Talk about Language* is about language ideologies of the type described by Silverstein (1992).

Language Ideological Activism, Ethnomethodology, and the Citizen Sociolinguistic Arrest

Citizen sociolinguistics provides a way to explore the processes through which such ideologies get built, with the added goal of illuminating how everyday participation can further shape those conversations. I am not offering a prescription for how we should do language. Nor am I simply offering a description for its own sake about how people speak and develop community norms. Instead, I am offering a way to fine-tune one's awareness of these conversations, so that we can begin to participate in them more knowingly, the same way we might fine-tune our awareness of our body and what keeps it healthy, so that we can heal ourselves before our body needs a more dramatic intervention from the medical experts. In this way, the modifier "citizen" acknowledges the potential power of any person's voice in everyday conversations about language and its connection to society, or sociolinguistics.

There is no final, authoritative ideological reading of these voices, nor is this a radically relativist project. The moral imperative behind this perspective is simply: keep exploring. Keep noticing language discussions, account for their varied forms of genius, attend to conflicts around language, investigate how they are related to one another and to the societal contexts within which they grow. Follow where the conversation leads. These conversations about language are powerful tools for shaping public opinion and understanding the world around us.

Citizen Sociolinguistics is both a description of what everyday people do when they talk about language, and a call to scholarly action. Acknowledging the expertise of members in any community, in the way we have been practicing in this chapter, has a tradition, if not in linguistics, certainly in sociology. Harold Garfinkel coined the term "ethnomethodology" to describe the new methodology he developed to study the everyday, tacit knowledge of members in a social group. He would devise breaching exercises to illuminate those tacit assumptions, sending students out to violate expectations for space, for example, by standing directly next to another person in an otherwise vacant and spacious elevator, or sitting next to someone on a bus when all the other seats were available. Or he would have students violate interactional expectations by having them respond to the question "How are you?" with something like, "What do you mean exactly? How am I physically? Mentally? Emotionally?" The disturbing responses these actions usually elicited revealed the unspoken rules we all follow: that usually the question "How are you?" functions only as a greeting, that people spread out to take up all the space in the elevator or on a bus and prefer not to snuggle with strangers if the option is available. His students usually found these breaching experiments very uncomfortable to perform, and today they may strike some as unethical. The intense discomfort that resulted from these simple breaches, however, illustrates Garfinkel's point – everyday actions are loaded with tacit, morally loaded assumptions about how people should act.

The metaphor I've been using in this chapter, that of the "citizen sociolinguist's arrest" similarly draws our attention to everyday expectations for language use. I suspect that every reader can recall participating in such a speech act. Everyone has made a claim against someone's use of language or been subject to criticisms of their own ways of speaking. Understanding these acts through the lens of Garfinkel's ethnomethodology illuminates the value of these citizen sociolinguistic arrests: These explicit callouts make visible the tacit knowledge about language and society held by everyday people. Discussions about language – often in the form of harsh opinions or heated arguments that might result from a citizen sociolinguist's arrest – make our assumptions about society visible. Language gives us something to point to – and usually that pointing leads us beyond language.

Sometimes these assumptions differ across groups of people and societies – as we have just illuminated in the discussion of the word *citizen*. These contradictory assumptions can lead to people talking at cross purposes. Drawing on Garfinkel, John Gumperz (2001) recognized a practical problem with the tacit nature of these assumptions: the rampant possibility for misunderstanding. And so, he introduced Garfinkel's ideas to the linguistic domain by studying what he called "cross talk" – precisely those moments in interaction when our tacit assumptions about how language should work do not correspond to those of the people to whom we are speaking. In his classic *Discourse Strategies* (1982), Gumperz foregrounded the process of "conversational inferencing," that is, the unspoken moment-to-moment interpretation of tacit social norms done by people in interaction in real time as they talk to each other. His goal was to understand the everyday discourse strategies that conversationalists call on to make sense of communication. His approach highlighted the everyday working knowledge of speakers (their "discourse strategies") but also illuminated breakdowns of such understandings in contemporary "cross-cultural" interactions. Along the way he also suggested how such an approach would be useful across professions in which situations of "cross talk" occur. In the chapters that follow, I will, like Gumperz, be laying out an approach for understanding the knowledge and processes of knowledge production that everyday communicators deploy as "citizen sociolinguists," illustrating that approach in multiple contexts, and suggesting how the concept of *citizen sociolinguistics* (like the concept of *discourse strategies*) can be useful to understanding and working within the complex communicative environment of many contemporary professional (and non-professional) settings.

As the next chapters unfold, you will also see that everyday conversations often travel through the distribution tendrils of social media, and as such have even more power and influence than the kind Gumperz was describing. Recently scholars have been working to explain the relationship between sociolinguistics and "new media." However, no one has taken an integrated approach like *citizen sociolinguistics* to understanding our new media communicative terrain. Some, as discussed in the Introduction, use social media as a crowdsourcing tool, getting more data than ever before thought possible, but using that "data" to investigate largely institutionally driven questions. Other *new media* researchers focus on sociolinguistics and social theory as *applied* to new media rather than investigating, as we do in this book, how new media are a platform on which everyday people discuss language *themselves and in their own terms*. The coming chapters will illustrate how citizen sociolinguistics is itself a form of inquiry that takes place among citizen sociolinguists largely on the Internet, but also in face-to-face communication.

Post Citizen's Arrest: Judge and Jury, or Eternal Deliberation?

My friends and colleagues made a "citizen sociolinguist's arrest" when they suggested I think more carefully about the word *citizen*. Mangual Figueroa made a "citizen sociolinguist's arrest" when she discovered the problematic use of "citizenship grade" and discussed it with the ESL director. "The Ghost of South Philly" blogger made a (virtual) citizen sociolinguist's arrest when he called attention to Geno's hypocritical "speak English" sign. Comments on a local news site about a neighborhood developer reminded people of the proper pronunciation of "Greenwich Street" in South Philadelphia, distinguishing it from "Greenwich Village." All of these occasions lead from language to discussions of societal relations. And it should be clear by now that legal citizenship is not required to participate in citizen sociolinguistics. Any person can do it and everybody does.

One advantage of an "any person" or "citizen's" arrest over an actual arrest by the authorities is that it not only raises awareness by making an affront explicit but it also provides an opening for deliberation, for everyday people to work things out on our own. We don't need to throw that perpetrator in jail – but in the process of raising their awareness we also let that perpetrator know they are part of a larger world, one in which their actions have consequences. A metaphorical citizen's arrest about language is ideally the beginning of a conversation about language, an opportunity to learn about each other's perspectives rather than subject someone to a standardized "sentence" arrived at by an external judge. While Lippmann might prefer to have the more educated classes in control, to turn over these perpetrators to a trained expert, Dewey would appreciate the deliberation between citizens and the mutual awareness that might come out of those metaphorical citizen's arrests. Dewey would also emphasize that a genuine education sharpens our awareness of differing presuppositions so that we might best participate in this kind of deliberation.

In the next two chapters, I will talk through how we can both learn from and participate in this process of indefinite deliberation over language norms – which are inevitably deliberations about civic life. I will illustrate how we can push our students and ourselves to listen to everyday conversations about language, to talk back to those conversations, and to follow carefully where they go, as a way of learning about language nuance in context and how language controversies – even those that may seem trivial – connect to broader social concerns. Once we develop habits of mind that reconfigure both "expertise" and "standardization" this way, local knowledge gains currency, social networks expand, and new voices enter the conversation – not just as "nonstandard" cultural others, but as experts.

2 Wonderment
The Spark that Starts Talk about Language

> Curiosity is one of the permanent and certain characteristics of a vigorous intellect.
> Samuel Johnson, *The Rambler* (1751)

In Chapter 1, I introduced the term "citizen sociolinguistic arrest" to describe one possible point of entry into conversations about language. The citizen sociolinguistic arrest is a common, easily recognizable speech event that occurs when any person decides they need to step in and correct someone's language, define their words, or advise them on their conduct as communicators. Everyday examples might include commands like, "Speak English!" or "Watch your language at the dinner table!" The critique offered by citizen sociolinguists on such occasions potentially leads to important deliberation about language. This chapter addresses an equally common and recognizable speech event that sparks extended language discussions: wonderment.

Citizen sociolinguistic wonderment is a blend of admiration and awe (sometimes touched with silliness, fear, or skepticism) regarding ways of speaking. This type of wonderment pulls us into conversations about language when, for example we listen to Trevor Noah jokingly discusses new research on "The World's Sexiest Accents" on *The Daily Show* on Comedy Central (www.youtube.com/watch?v=v1UeU7qPs4E). The study Noah lampoons lists the "New Zealand accent" as the sexiest in the world, followed by South African, Irish, Italian, and Australian. As of this writing, the YouTube site for this clip has attracted over one million views, and 24,000 comments. Even if listeners doubt the validity of this research or are skeptical about the presumed descriptions of said "accents," it raises curiosity about different ways of using English. This form of citizen sociolinguistic wonderment tells us nothing about how people really speak in any of these countries or their objective level of sexiness. But, more importantly, this wonderment sparks conversation, deliberation, and discussion not only about language, but also about people's associated understandings of the social characteristics of speakers of these languages, generalizations that may be reinforced or debunked, perpetuated or laid to rest. Trevor Noah's report on the "World's Sexiest Accents" is obviously a joke, but it is reporting on a real survey research project focused on people talking *about* language, perpetuating more talk about language. These "accents" are not inherently sexy, but so much talking about them might make them so – or bring on entirely new dimensions of meaning. The wonderment surrounding the mere idea of "sexy accents" can spark important conversation, expand people's language awareness, and as we will see later, even motivate social action.

In language classrooms, citizen sociolinguistic wonderment also sparks curiosity and engagement. If you want to start a lively discussion in even the sleepiest classroom, among the most disaffected youth, ask about the language they use with each other, outside of school. Then tell them about some language you used in your youth. In Philadelphia, you might challenge them to compare their own pronunciations of street names like "Greenwich" and "Passyunk." Or see if they can define the word "jawn." Wonderment (and high decibel levels) will probably best describe the interactions about language that follow. In the conversation below, for example, I'm talking with four high school boys during their English class about language activities I had been doing with them throughout the semester. Bill has just returned home to suburban Philadelphia after a weekend in New York, where he noticed that people call a sandwich made on a long roll a "hero" instead of using the Philadelphian word, "hoagie." He has been speculating that maybe nobody else, that is, nobody outside of Philadelphia, says "hoagie." This leads to some reflection from everyone about their experiences with language in context:

Completely Different Planet (January, 2015)

TOM: I mean, he is right that there's more people saying *hero* than *hoagie*, prob-I mean, where else do they say *hoagie*, dude?
BILL: Nowhere else=
MARC: =nowhere else=
DEAN: =nowhere else=
TOM: Nowhere else, really? That's sad. HOW?
BILL: I don't know, it's weird to think about
TOM: Say down the shore [the New Jersey oceanside] they say *hoagie*.
BILL: Also they say like, they say *shaved ice* instead of *water ice*. Like-
TOM: Where? Everywhere else?
DEAN: Everywhere else
MARC: Wow, that's-
DEAN: Wait, really? I feel so like, closed
TOM: WHY? It feels really- it's unsettling
BILL: I like it
BETSY: The shaved ice?
MARC: Shaved ice

BEN: Well, no, not the shav- Heh heh- that even in like the few places that are close to us, like Pittsburgh, in the same state. That they have many different words for the things, it's like-
DEAN: It's like a completely different planet.

In this conversation, the five of us are discussing language in context. But not because someone has issued a citizen sociolinguist's arrest. Instead, this discussion was provoked by wonderment about New Yorkers' language and specifically their use of the word *hero* to describe a sandwich that most Philadelphian's would call a *hoagie*. Collectively, the boys savor Bill's suggestion that the word *hoagie* exists "nowhere else," echoing his words, "nowhere else ... nowhere else ... nowhere else." They don't voice any negative judgments about New Yorkers for saying *hero* instead of *hoagie* or insist that New Yorkers change their ways. Instead, this difference sparks the boys' curiosity about other possible differences and distinctions, as more examples continue to enter the discussion: *water ice* versus *shaved ice* and, later in the conversation, *sprinkles* versus *jimmies*. This is a citizen sociolinguistic discussion, that is, everyday people talking about society and language. Their state of wonderment propels them along a happy path to conversation about language and its peculiarities, fueled by a genuine curiosity Samuel Johnson describes above as characteristic of *a vigorous intellect*.

Types of Citizen Sociolinguistics: Words, People, Situations

Like the sting of a citizen sociolinguistic arrest discussed in Chapter 1, the spark of wonderment surrounding a hoagie conversation or a list of "world's sexiest accents" can foment everyday conversations about language (see Figure 2.1).

As this chapter proceeds, we'll continue to follow these sparks, investigating how language becomes an object of everyday discussion and investigation, not as the result of critique, but as the result of wonderment and curiosity about language and its role in everyday life. We will investigate objects of wonderment, like the words and phrases *hoagie* and *water ice*, that draw huge amounts of questions and commentary. Then we'll look at the types of people, YouTubers and their followers for example, who expose and revel in language wonderment, and we'll explore the way everyday conversations about language spring from wonderment about specific situations of language use, as when memes identify recognizable existential states – the world-weariness apparent in market-driven repetition of "Wakanda Forever!" or the human distillation of awe in the ultra-viral YouTube video, "Double rainbow all the way," and the expressive power of combining these situational distillations. Sometimes, however, these situational representations can miss the mark, as when white

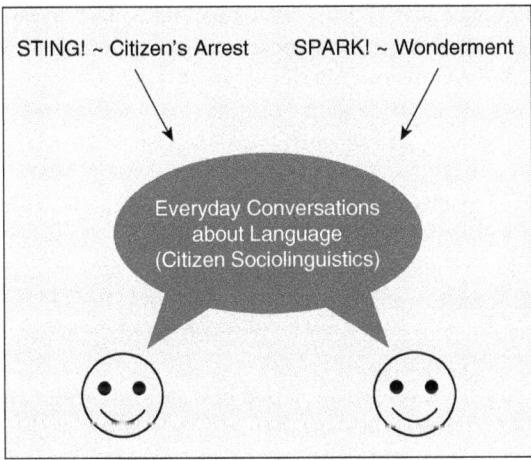

Figure 2.1 Points of entry into conversations about language: arrest and wonderment

suburbanites awkwardly take on the language of hip-hop, or newcomers to a city misuse the local argot. These situations often get noticed and discussed following citizen sociolinguists' arrests, highlighting how language and its meaning can't be pinned down, owned, willed into expressing our intentions. Instead, we always maneuver through a world of others' words – drawing blows and praise, fostering connection and alienation, wonderment and arrest, at every turn.

Words

As we saw in the previous two chapters, single words can act as a fulcrum for wide-ranging controversy that can't be resolved with a simple trip to the dictionary. Sometimes, as in the case of *Passyunk* Avenue, these words are hard to classify, even in terms of a specific named language, say "English" or an unnamed "Native American" language. Instead, citizen sociolinguists offer more locally relevant classifications of these words and how they work in context, as part of a way of life. Whether discussing Passyunk Ave., hoagies, water ice, or the word *citizen*, individuals speak from the unique expertise that comes from seeing things according to their specific context and set of experiences. Citizen sociolinguist exploration can begin when one identifies a word that seems confusing, sparking curiosity and prompting inquiry, and a search for those experts who detail the assumptions circling that word – about how one should pronounce it, who gets to use it, and what it might mean if other people

70   Wonderment

do. By way of illustrating this process of citizen sociolinguistic investigation, in what follows I cover citizen sociolinguistic discussion of the meaning of a few words that have sparked my own curiosity in this way: the practice and pronunciation of the words *croissant* (and how an American should pronounce it), *gabagool* (aka *capicola*), and *succinct* (*suss*-sinkt or *suck*-sinkt?).

Croissant   The pronunciation of the word *croissant* inevitably baffles English speakers. The degree of variation and mode of expression extends far beyond simply knowing or not knowing the French language. Some use a special-sounding French pronunciation like kwuh-SAHN. Others, a more American pronunciation, like kruh SANT. I've even heard the super-American CREscent. Or even CROYscent.

Of course, how you say this word, just like how you talk about *citizenship*, depends on what kind of impression you want to give, where you are, what sort of event you are participating in, and how flexibly aware you are of your language use. To explore the subtle rules behind croissant pronunciation, to gain the awareness necessary to use this word and its myriad possible pronunciations effectively, to avoid a citizen sociolinguist's arrest, requires some everyday citizen sociolinguistic exploration: a trip through several internet sources and questions to friends and colleagues are a good place to start.

A google query, "How should I pronounce 'Croissant'?" leads to a few possibilities. One woman from RachelsEnglish.com confidently explains that if you are speaking American English, you must say kruh SANT (https://rachelsenglish.com/pronounce-croissant-word-week/). Another YouTube video features this same pronunciation, slow repetition of the "American English" rendition, accompanied by a simple picture of the typed word, and a cold and lonely wind blowing in the background for 16 seconds: kruh SANT ... kruh SANT ... kruh SANT (www.youtube.com/watch?v=gcW1mO2xJPw).

But other internet posts carefully explain the truly "French" way to say this word. For example, this response to the question 'How is 'Croissant' pronounced? (posted under the "ethnic food" category on Yahoo Answers) was designated the "Asker's Favorite":

COMMENTER A: Phonetically – 'Kwar-sor' -spoken fast.. Haha, best way I can describe a French accent in type!

So, both the "American" Kruh SANT, and the "French" Kwar-SOR have proponents. To choose between Kruh SANT or Kwar SOR, we still need more nuanced information about using the word *croissant* in context. *KruhSANT* and *KwarSOR* are out there in circulation, but there seem to be no criteria available to inform our choice of the best pronunciation. Why is this such a hard question? Why are some YouTube tutorials or other Web sources so one-sidedly partisan? The distinction between these two pronunciation camps sustains an absurd level of wonderment.

As a citizen sociolinguist, turning to everyday conversation among peers may not offer anything more decisive, but it will definitely yield more stories, more details about context, even more wonderment. I talked to a few students and friends about *croissant* pronunciation, and the usual response was bemusement, some chuckles, and this type of description: I say *kruh SANT*. But my mother uses *Kwuh SAHN* (or *Kwar-SOR*) no matter what the context. One mom from Long Island might say something like this, a rough replication of her daughters' rendition:

MOM: Greab me a cup a caaawwwfeee and a *kwar-SOR*.

Another Mom (from Boston) would say something like this (another rough transcription of her daughter's impersonation):

MOM: I'll take heam and cheese on a *kwar-SOR*. And a cup a cawfee, skim milk, two sweetnuhs.

Now why do these American Moms say this one way, but the YouTube teachers of American English insist on kruh-SANT? What does this tell us about language? Who is the expert?

Still searching for alternatives, I asked my Parisian, Ivy League French instructor friend, "What do you think when an American says, in the midst of a Ham and Cheese type sentence, *kwar-sor* with that super-French pronunciation?" She smiled, "I think it sounds cute." This expert on The French Language, born and raised in Paris, in response to the refined *kwar-sohr* pronunciation of American moms, did not choose to say "exquisite" or "correct" or "c'est magnifique!" but, smilingly, "cute!" And, when my friends discussed their mothers' pronunciation of the word, I sensed them also glowing with positive sentiment for this lovable feature of their mom's repertoire.

So, a little citizen sociolinguistic investigation here reveals nuanced ways with a word, but no absolutes about how we must say it or what counts as "American" or "English" or even "French." Instead, we forge on, learning new ways, and new understandings of languages in conversation with each other, with one another.

Once we start investigating, and sharing our discoveries, we are part of an ongoing citizen sociolinguistic dialogue. After writing about this word in my personal blog, several people mentioned to me they recognized the "mom" types of pronunciation as a feature of their own (American) mother's speech. One mom commented on the blog with a response about her own experiences with croissant pronunciation:

CB (2017): Back in the 1970s, in admittedly very American Chicago, I took French in high school from a native speaker who insisted on perfect French pronunciations (and was VERY withering in her corrections!), so I pronounce croissant with the "kwuh" first syllable – it just comes out that way! I never thought about it all these years until recently, my teenage daughter called me out on it, and she delights in imitating my "affectation" ... I've tried to say "krah," but it just feels super-weird in my mouth, so I think I'll just have to suffer on with a smile ... and maybe add a beret!

CB's candid story about her very strict high school French instruction, the calling-out from her daughter (a light-hearted "citizen sociolinguistic arrest"), her continued use of *kwuh* even in light of her daughter's teasing, and her final decision to "suffer on with a smile ... and maybe add a beret!" exemplify the power of citizen sociolinguistics – not to tell us the correct answer, not to supply standardized expertise one might get from a French text book or even a YouTube tutorial, but to provide the awareness that we have choices. Awareness of those choices gives us the option to add a little flair and personal style to our interactions.

But the croissant story doesn't end there. Shortly after CB posted her comment, Tom Holland, a rising young movie star and the most recent Spiderman actor, used an entirely new croissant pronunciation, transcribed widely on social media as *quackson*. This was just silly and controversial enough to provoke more wonderment – and a series of articles, memes and endless discussions about *quackson* all over the Internet, including several Urban Dictionary definitions, like this most popular entry (See Figure 2.2).

Many people also claimed that Tom Holland never really said, *quackson*, but something less ridiculous, and closer to a proper "French" or even "British English" pronunciation. And another round of conversation about croissant

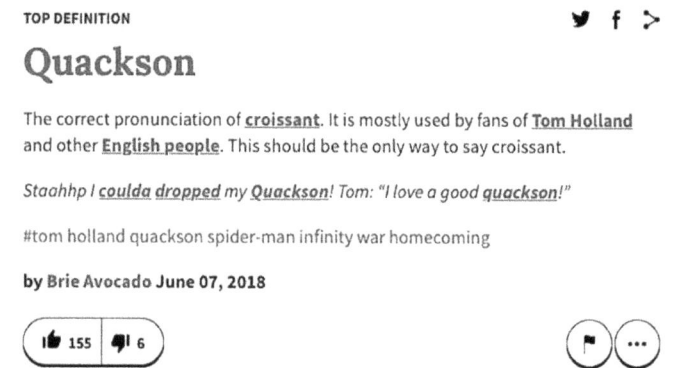

Figure 2.2 Quackson

pronunciation continued, the talk *about talk* far outstripping the relevance of anything Tom Holland may have actually said, illustrating the eternally morphing and always ongoing nature of citizen sociolinguistic expertise.

Gabagool As the *croissant* investigation illustrates, sometimes wonderment and curiosity spark discussions that lead simply to more savoring: a greater appreciation for the cuteness of some moms' *kwar-SOR*, or a love of Tom Holland's *quackson*. Another food word that has led to similar savoring is the elusive *gabagool*. Seeing the word spelled *gabagool* on the menu of a local Philly restaurant sparked my own wonderment (see Figure 2.3). Having lived in Philadelphia for over 10 years, I had the vague feeling this was just an ironic nod to the way people here pronounce the delicious cured meat, capicola (also spelled *capocollo* – another controversy). But, since it was printed out on a real, official menu of an upscale center city restaurant, I thought I might be mistaken. Maybe *gabagool* was just one more variation on Italian meats and cheeses that I didn't know.

I turned to Google, which confirmed my initial impression that *gabagool* is "just" another way of saying *capicola*. The top definition on Urban Dictionary (the first google hit), also supplies a couple useful analogs in the "Napolitan" dialect: *manigot* (for manicotti) and *rigot* (ricotta). (see Figure 2.4).

This Urban Dictionary author also knew a little linguistic detail about voiced consonants (like "g" or "b") and their unvoiced equivalents (like "c" or "p"), and satisfyingly described the "rule in this dialect" that governs pronunciation of these special words: voicing the unvoiced consonants and chopping off the final vowel. So, capicola → *gabagool*.

But despite its elegant clarity, this snappy formula doesn't explain how *gabagool* ended up on a Philly menu, or as an ongoing cultural motif on the *The Sopranos* TV show. That same google search also yielded videos that illustrate a more layered portrait of the usual context surrounding the use of this

for the table to share family style ...

Not Your Mama's Antipasta

gabagool, castelrosso, olives, marinated artichokes, buffalo mozzarella,

roasted peppers, grissini, sweet fennel cracker

Shaved Brussel Sprout Salad

toasted hazelnuts, lemon, olive oil, parsley leaves, parmesan

***

Figure 2.3 Barbuzzo menu featuring the word *gabagool*

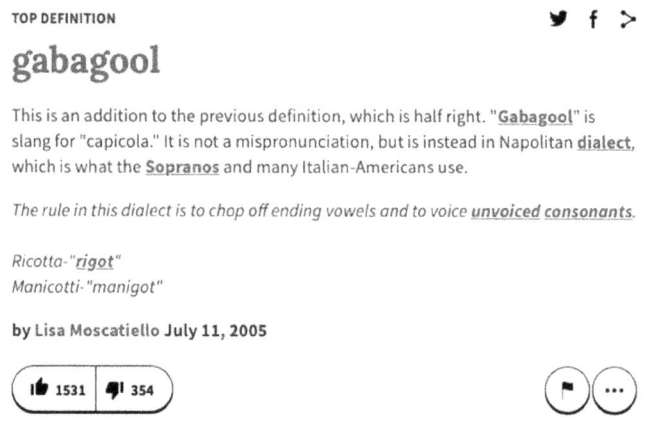

Figure 2.4 Top *gabagool* definition, Urban Dictionary

word. These videos differ significantly from the stark decontextualized prescriptive instruction delivered to viewers on *croissant* pronunciation. Instead, the most popular *gabagool* videos contextualize it by using more nuanced citizen sociolinguistic expertise, detailed explication (by video) of all the elements of a scene that contribute to the meaning-making going on there. These video portraits of a word-in-use exemplify what Clifford Geertz would call "thick description" (1973). *Gababool* is not simply a "Napolitan" way of saying "capicola" with voiced consonants and the end "chopped off," but an invocation of an entire way of life.

In the YouTube *gabagool* videos, this way of life unfolds: we begin to see all the other features of a scene that go into using the word *gabagool* in situ. The most popular video example, by far, is a clip from *The Sopranos* (www.youtube.com/watch?v=kR0OPOMea1Y) in which Silvio Dante, outrageously played by Stephen van Zandt, demands, "Gabagool! Ovah here!" All the details of the Sopranos' milieu, the gilded suburban New Jersey living room, the multiple generations of mobsters, the daughter dutifully serving the gabagool on a platter to the guests of the extended family, contribute to the thick description necessary to understand how the word *gabagool* functions here. Everything in this scene that surrounds Silvio Dante's line, "Gabagool! Ovah here!" illustrates the context of a stereotypical New Jersey Italian American Mob family.

As Meadow Soprano (Jamie-Lynne Sigler) illustrates in her line, "Don't eat gabagool, Grandma, it's nothing but fat and nitrates," there are also other stereotypes in play here. The character Meadow Soprano has grown up in a culture of US health-consciousness, surrounded by healthy cuisine in which gabagool plays no part. But her use of the word illustrates that even speakers of the word *gabagool* who don't know much Italian or feel much reverence for the cuisine, can fluently speak this variation. This pronunciation may have very little to do with any "Napolitana" heritage as the Urban Dictionary entry suggests, but instead be a way of speaking that originates in New Jersey and Philadelphia. According to Atlas Obscura (Nosowitz, 2015), you will not even hear *gabagool* (or *rigot* or *manigot*, for that matter) if you go to Southern Italy, their ostensible original homeland.

Gabagool does not literally originate in the "old country," but serves as an *emblem* for identity and lifestyle of those who share that heritage and who affiliate with one another in today's context. Say "Gabagool, ovah here!" and you are not simply demanding some capicola, you are being a specific type of Italian American, born and raised in the tri-state area, who honors family and tradition. Your fellow speakers will recognize you and savor the word. Even the comments from the *Sopranos* YouTube clip (and another compilation of all the gabagool scenes in the series) zero in on love for just this word:

- Commenter 1: "Gabagool" is one of my favorite words (5 replies)
- Commenter 2: Gabagoohhhhhhhhhhhhhhhhhh (9 replies)
- Commenter 3: ... who ate all the gabagool? (5 replies)
- Commenter 4: CARMELA! WHERES THAT GABAHGOOOOL? (3 replies)

Another YouTube clip illustrates that speakers who only superficially know this word, but would not be able to reproduce the thick description and cultural nuance of the Italian American context that accompanies it, can also seriously misuse the word *gabagool*. In another popular video that came to the top in my google search for gabagool, Michael, from the show *The Office*, tries to use a Soprano's style *gabagool* in a standard business lunch restaurant and makes no sense at all. (www.dailymotion.com/video/x2rwp7b). Michael, in characteristic awkward and transparent brown-nosing fashion, tries to impress their Italian American client at lunch, but instead shows a dramatic misreading of context, using *gabagool* in a setting that is far more like Applebee's than a gathering in the Sopranos' living room. The waitress has no idea what he is talking about, and Michael ends up ordering spaghetti with marinara sauce and a side salad instead.

This brief exploration of the multilayered expertise needed to understand the word *gabagool* epitomizes something both wonderful and cautionary about learning languages: A novice need only know a few words to join in and start speaking. However, using those words effectively requires much more knowledge about who else uses those words, in what settings, and how. In the case of capicola, you must saaaaavor the gabagool – despite the fat and nitrates. The tenuous connection of *gabagool* to Italy also illustrates that words aren't locked into being part of "A Language." Inevitably, communities of speakers develop their own uniquely local communicative flair, and that local flair requires not simply knowledge of a word, or its voiced consonants, but a sense of context. As Michael-from-*The-Office* illustrates, if you don't understand when, where, and how to use one of these emblematic words, you might be better off just not using it. (Or Michael might consider dining at Barbuzzo, where the word is ironically spelled out for him on the menu.)

Succinct Sometimes the savoring and wonderment about language emerges from conversations with friends, conversations about our mothers, or even an ironic Philadelphia menu. Other times, a citizen sociolinguistic arrest can itself provoke wonderment. I'm always surprised when friends of mine mention words they have questions about because they have been apprehended in a citizen sociolinguist arrest. One day, over brunch with friends, for example, one accomplished lawyer in the group mentioned that his boss had corrected his pronunciation of *succinct*. My friend had been saying *suss*-sinkt and his boss had insisted on *suck*-sinkt. My friend immediately changed the way he said it.

The fact that he actually changed his language in response to that citizen sociolinguistic arrest sparked naïve wonderment in me. As a *suss*-sinkt person myself, I was shocked to hear about his prescriptive, *suck*-demanding boss. And even more shocked that my friend – intelligent, sensitive, and perceptive guy that he is – didn't call his boss out for being such a rigid prescriptivist. Later, baffled by this level of rigidity, I told the story to my 19-year-old son, who assured me that my friend's boss must have been just "messing with him." Possible. But my son may have overestimated the subtlety of humor that goes on in law offices. I turned to the Internet to see what other people had to say about *succinct*.

First, I checked with my Twitter feed. A quick poll (*suck*- or *suss*-?) revealed that everyone who cared enough to respond preferred *suck*-sinkt. Moving on, I looked through YouTube tutorials, and found the first several were all firmly *suck*-sinkt-promoting videos, all in the same genre of the "American" *croissant* pronunciation prescriptions. The representative (and the most viewed) example (www.youtube.com/watch?v=zzoAXiJDLjA) simply shows the word SUCCINCT in all caps, while the voice-over calmly and patiently repeats, "Suck-SINKT," a calm incantation that brought me back to the American kruh-SANT . . . kruh-SANT . . . Kruh-SANT tutorial.

I was disappointed by this firmly *suck*-sinkt-sided video, but happy to see that it received 32 thumbs down (i.e., dislikes) and that many comments on this and other similar tutorials contested this rigid prescription. Seeking validation of my own view, my eyes fell on one commenter who had, like me, noticed all the dislikes this video received:

COMMENTER 1: I love all the dislikes, like this isnt how you pronounce it or something LOL (3 thumbs up)

I quickly realized there is some irony in this commenter's "love" for the dislikes. He seems to be mocking those dislikers when he self-assuredly adds, "like this isn't how you pronounce it or something LOL." This sarcastic comment receives three thumbs up, suggesting some following, though small.

Then I saw one self-deprecating comment that hinted at the absurdity of worrying about this word, an expression of wonderment at the existence of such a controversy and its ability to propel viewers, maybe even against their own volition, to this site.

COMMENTER 2: What am I doing here. (11 thumbs up)

With 11 thumbs up, it seems some people recognize and empathize with this existential stance, at least more than with the sarcasm of Commenter 1. Another viewer goofily zeroed in on the isolated *suck* problem with a simple one-word comment:

COMMENTER 3: *Penis*

No thumbs up for this one.

Finally, I found a couple of *suss* demo videos. One video specifically labeled *suss* an "Aussie" pronunciation (www.youtube.com/watch?v=Sz9tPl6dmbM). Another, focused on English language instruction, also described the *suss* pronunciation as a legitimate Aussie way of saying *succinct*, exemplifying it with a real Aussie bureaucrat's speech (https://youglish.com/search/succinct/aus). But this site also advised viewers not to "mix accents" and to focus on just one:

Focus on one accent: mixing multiple accents can get really confusing especially for beginners, so pick one accent (US or UK) and stick to it.

This statement presumes that the Aussie *suss*-sinkt pronunciation aligns with UK pronunciation. Setting aside the fact that Australia is not and never has been part of the United Kingdom, and that even within the United States and United Kingdom people have different ways of saying the word, and that "mixing accents" is probably not that confusing. The idea that one could "pick" an accent seems to suggest that either version of *succinct* would be acceptable to this YouTuber – as long as you pick one and stick with it. The results of this quick internet review suggest that, like the pronunciation of *croissant*, people should pronounce *succinct* in whatever way suits their personal taste or situational needs. And, maybe, if you are in Australia, people will accept either one.

I feel like that review should settle the argument – do what you like! But a post on my personal blog about this *succinct* debate, laying out these very same issues, yielded a range of reasons for choosing one version over the other, with a slight tilt to the *suss* side of the debate. All the *suss*ers, however, also hedged their claims, acknowledging their version may be a regionalism or personal idiosyncrasy, misaligned with dictionary definitions or proper schooling.

A comment on January 9 aligns with the *suss* camp, but not without a little ambivalence:

> COMMENT (1/9/19): I'm 75 years old and have been firmly in the "suss" camp since I first learned the word, whenever that was. But then, I was raised in Oklahoma City.

Despite this commenter's firm claim to be a *suss*er, their afterthought, "but then, I was raised in Oklahoma City," seems to self-deprecatingly qualify their use of *suss* as a regionalism from flyover country.

A commenter on February 11 similarly aligns with the *suss*ers, but hedges her firm commitment with acknowledgment that she's been challenged about it:

> COMMENT (2/11/19): I am a firm advocate for 'suss'inct! I have no memory of this ever having a different pronunciation, or there ever being a debate regarding it. I was challenged on my pronunciation by a colleague. The same one, might I add, that 'sh'ooled me about my pronunciation of "sh"edule vs "sk"edule. What to do? Live and learn

This commenter, like the commenter from Oklahoma City, embraces her "suss" identity and history with the word ("I have no memory of this ever having a different pronunciation"). Given her pronunciation of *sh*edule, she seems to be consistently applying what the YouTuber above called the "UK accent." However, she tells of being ready to "live and learn" from those who have challenged her about it. Both the Oklahoman and this *sh*edule pronouncer modestly acknowledge the presence of both pronunciations, and then hedge their own choice to be "sussers" in light of other language authorities.

The remaining two comments represent the voice of those challengers: Advocates of the *suck* pronunciation. This comment specifically mentions the target of his challenge, his wife:

> COMMENT (12/24/18): It bothers me every time my wife says sussinct. I've asked her why it's not the same as success. That didn't help.

This commenter appeals to Merriam-Webster "and most other dictionaries" to back up his own pronunciation:

> COMMENT (2/25/19): Merriam-Webster – and most other dictionaries – lists suk-sinkt as the first pronunciation and suss-sinkt as the second. So I'm going with what I've used all my life: in a word with two c's in a row, the first has a k sound, the second an s sound: accident, vaccine, eccentric. So, as you unpleasantly write it, suck-sinct.

Neither of these pro-*suck*-sinkt comments hedge or apologize. They speak with confidence that they are correct. The 12/24 commenter's remark, "that didn't help," implies exasperation after his vain attempts to "help" his wife say the word correctly. The 2/25 commenter chooses the first pronunciation listed in Webster's as validation of his own pronunciation. While he acknowledges the second pronunciation listed in Webster's, which allows for *suss*, he debunks that option and firmly stands with "suck-sinct," citing other "two c's in a row" words he knows in which "the first has a k sound, the second an s sound."

Overall, the follow-up commentary on my *succinct* post features two commenters who worry about their language, recognize their own idiosyncrasies, and make mitigating remarks, and two who confidently use language their way, call on sources of authority as backup, and critique those who differ. (A fifth post, on the *suss-* side, struck me as possibly disingenuous and lewd, so I'm not discussing it here.) Simply a sample of five here, but a working hypothesis worth considering, as the citizen sociolinguistic deliberation continues might be this: The *suss*-sinkt pronouncers mitigate their claims to their own language because what they have grown up saying has been flagged by others as non-standardized usage; The *suck*-sinkt commenters, who may have never been challenged in their own language usage, underline the way they speak *as* the standard, reproducing that standardized version of language in the process. These mitigators may go on using *suss*-sinkt, and the confident *suck*-sinkt speakers will continue to insist they are right, creating a self-reinforcing feedback loop with one right answer. These *suck*-sinkt hard-liners are consistent with my friend's *suss*-censoring boss at the law office, but in my quick review, *suss-* also has good representation.

Ultimately, choosing how to say *succinct* or *croissant*, and who can say *gabagool* and in what context, or resolving any other issue of language wonderment has a lot in common with whatever methods were used to choose the "world's sexiest accent" – that study recounted at the beginning of this chapter. Interested parties weigh in on their choices, and those with the firmest conviction probably say more. In this case, no matter what others say, the talkers get their way. Like the man who systematically removed "comprised of" from Wikipedia, and in the process may have curbed its use more generally, those who opinionate most forcefully are likely to have their responses become the status quo. A "new Zealand accent" may not be, in your opinion, sexy at all, but as we talk about it in that context, as more people consider it so, as more movies portraying a hot new Zealander as the male heartthrob permeate the mass media, the "sexy New Zealand accent" will become undeniable. If someone insists on pronouncing *succinct* a certain way, and that person is your boss, that pronunciation will become the correct one in that context. Those who say *suss*-sinkt will be considered less articulate, less educated, maybe even worse at doing their job. This perception of connections between language and social type is talked into being – until someone else talks it out of the running, and that can be the role powerful citizen sociolinguists take up.

People

The hesitation or firm support voiced in comments around word controversies illustrates that people out there wonder about language, think about it, critique it, own it, even create their own versions of "correctness" in how they talk about it. Sometimes, they also advocate for their perspective. Many people take to YouTube to share their own personal thoughts on how they speak – and receive thousands, even millions of views and comments. I have many favorites: Sean Monahan and his advocacy for "Phillytawk" (www.youtube.com/watch?v=l3 lZFiyd_-0), Thethugyone, modestly taking the South Philly Accent Challenge (www.youtube.com/watch?v=TXt1fHZIHtk), KatieMayoxx on "Things Welsh People Say"(www.youtube.com/watch?v=XcHMD0_DVe0), and Amos Yee teaching the world how to speak the Singaporean English, or "Singlish" (his YouTube channel has since been removed for political reasons).

These are all people who, while presenting their own sense of wonderment about how they speak, simultaneously, though not necessarily deliberately, act as advocates for a broader way of viewing language in the world. Their language exemplifies their proud stylistic departure from the prescriptivism of standardization. And, by speaking as individuals, their views also depart from the language description of traditional sociolinguistics, which relies on statistically useful quantity, and discounts or even purposefully tries to negate the awareness of speakers as it traces patterns of language change over decades and centuries. Individual citizen sociolinguists who take the time to make YouTube videos about the way they speak may be initially propelled by a sense of wonderment about the characteristics of their language, but their enthusiasm is multiplied by people responding to them, sparking more dialogue about language. Let's now take a look at two examples of this wonderment and the dialogue it sparks by considering two citizen sociolinguistic personalities, confidently speaking about the way they communicate, and the deliberation they have stirred by doing so.

Kelly and the Konglish Accent Tag Kelly, who usually posts videos about makeup and merch and has over 92,000 followers, took a departure from that genre one day to post a YouTube performance demonstrating her "English" and "Konglish" ways of speaking. To show the world her ways with words, she runs through the Accent Tag inventory – a list of words to pronounce (e.g., caramel, aluminum, mayonnaise, spitting image) and lexical prompts ("How do you address a group of people? What do you call a sweet carbonated drink?") that was developed by dialectologists decades ago. This research tool has since been repurposed under the names "Accent Tag" and "Accent Challenge" as a script and springboard for talking about language on YouTube and other social media sites. (www.youtube.com/watch?v=GWOVL2bUKMI).

While the list of words and lexical prompts could take about 60 seconds to recite, Kelly's video lasts longer than eight minutes because she takes time to contextualize her performance. She mentions that she grew up in North Carolina and Atlanta, Georgia, that she was raised by Korean-speaking parents, and that at the age of 10, "when kids develop that whole language thing," she went to Korea to live. Then she moved to Southern California as a teen. Because of her varied experiences with language, Kelly has a sense of wonderment about her own language practices, compelling her to make her own "accent tag video":

KELLY: I just thought this whole accent tag video was really interesting and it kind of pushed me to actually make a video.

She introduces her unique performance of the Accent Tag both in her "American" accent and as a "Konglish" speaker:

KELLY: So, I'm gonna do it in two versions. My first version is my accent when I'm in America and my second one is my accent when I'm in Korea because I don't like having my American accent when I'm in Korea so I speak like this – they call it Konglish. It's like Korean and English put together and I have this Kong-oh-lish-eh accent. So I'm just gonna do two versions of it.

Her performances that follow, of her American and Korean selves reading through the word lists and prompts, yield stark contrasts. For example, in the American version of the accent tag, she recites "spitting image," in the "Konglish"(or "Kong-oh-lish-eh") version, "spitting-image-ah." She says "remote control" as her American persona, but "re-mo-quan" as her Konglish-speaking Korean self.

Kelly also goes beyond one singular account of her "American" language: While she says she does not (yet) use "y'all" when she addresses a group of people, she has observed Texans say "Hey, how y'all doing," and says she'd "like to pick up on that." Overall, her performance articulates a language awareness and flexibility developed over a life spent living in multiple countries and communities. It seems that the more experiences she has had in different contexts, the more choices she has accumulated about how she will speak – Korean? Texan? Californian? She does not necessarily orient to one standard pronunciation but selects between many possibilities. Kelly has the courage and originality to post a multilingual version of her "accent challenge," to display her flexibility and pragmatism in actively choosing how she will speak according to context.

Despite the liberating aspects of Kelly's performance, she has an apologetic tone throughout the video that echoes the hedging responses of the *succinct pronouncers* described above. She is a survivor, having learned how to use language creatively to fend off others' attacks and to join new communities. But she also describes her own fluid language use more negatively, inserting judgment into her language descriptions, with phrases like *way off, really weird, FOBby,* or *jumbled up*.

Kelly's video exemplifies the ambivalence behind language flair and creativity. Even as wonderment can propel online displays of language flexibility, the fear of "citizen sociolinguist's arrest" remains: The imagined gaze of some standardizing Big Brother reveals its presence in Kelly's mitigating and apologetic hedges about her own facile ways of speaking. Her video illustrates a broader tendency present in many of these everyday accent displays. Sometimes people online speak apologetically about their own language – voicing comments they have heard from other people. Other times, people speak out proudly about the nuanced features of their own language. Usually, the same person does a little bit of both.

In many cases, that ambivalence propels more language wonderment. Many of the over 1,600 comments about Kelly's Konglish Accent Tag encourage the originality and flexibility or her way of speaking, praising the "adorable" quality of Kelly's Konglish, as in this comment:

COMMENT: (2015) your konglishee: simple adorable :3)

Some viewers include more tips about Konglish:

COMMENT: (2014) Wow, you really sounded like Korean when you spoke Konglish. BTW, theater sounds like ssiuhtuh in konglish

Others add comments about other languages and the process of pronouncing borrowed words, like this one about Japanese pronunciation of English words:

COMMENT: (2015) I do the same when I speak Japanese. You just gotta say it in a way that flows with the rest of the sentence. Hence the whole "romanized" or "borrowed" words in Asian languages like Korean and Japanese. For ex, if I were to say sports in English, I'd just pronounce it as sports. But in Japanese, I'd say supotsu something like that.

These descriptions of language use and adjustment across contexts and sound systems have captivated Kelly's viewers, and she has been able to show her thousands of YouTube fans how a transnational life like hers can bring on a heightened awareness and appreciation of language fluidity. Through her Accent Tag video, Kelly has served, if indirectly, as a citizen ambassador of the transnational English/Konglish perspective, sparking conversation about language fluidity by presenting her own wonderment about using language in the multiple contexts that have made up her life.

Nyle DiMarco: Citizen Sociolinguist of the Deaf Community   Nyle DiMarco has also taken on this role as citizen sociolinguistic ambassador, spreading wonderment about language in the deaf community. Most hearing people, unless they have daily and direct connections to people who are deaf, have little interest in sign language. But as kids, wonderment about sign language is common. We may have thought about how amazing it would be to know it: Maybe we happened on the card with the alphabet and learned how to spell our name, or to sign a few top-secret words to friends. But after a first enthusiastic burst, the card gets lost, the signing seems like too much effort. It's hard to stay motivated when you and all your friends are not deaf. Learning all the letters and then spelling every word out gets to seem incredibly laborious. But, in many corners of our world and of the Internet, wonderment about signing persists, and, most recently, super-personality Nyle DiMarco has generated a large share of it.

Before we get to Nyle, however, simply googling "How to use sign language" leads into the sense of wonderment and intimate human connection that may draw hearing people to learn more about signing. The most popular YouTube video features minimal effects, nothing special: a single person signing, in front of a blank background, and what the video has identified as the top 25 most useful signs in American Sign Language (ASL). Even this simple, no-nonsense video has over six million views (www.youtube.com/watch?v=Raa0vBXA8OQ, accessed August 9, 2019). The comments underneath give some sense of what motivates people to come to this site, and it is not to learn a secret language. Most comments mention encounters with deaf people – real or fictional – and the desire to make a visible effort to communicate like them: They have fallen in love with a deaf person. Or they have a regular customer who is deaf. They've tried a little sign and witnessed how gratifying it is to connect through this medium. Many are filled with stories of connection and wonderment in the face of ASL, like this one:

CAWTICO 2 YEARS AGO: i work as a cashier in a grocery store part time after school. A deaf lady regularly comes through my till as im the only one who knows she is deaf. Lately ive been learning how to sign ASL so i can communicate with her better. Last week she came in and as i signed to her, her face just lit up with excitement and joy. It's amazing what you can do for lots of people just by giving a little bit of your spare time to learn ASL. (2.1K thumbs up)

Other comments mention popular movies and TV shows that have given them the spark of wonderment regarding signing. Several comments mention *Koe No Katachi* (A Silent Voice), an anime film about a deaf girl (https://en.wikipedia.org/wiki/A_Silent_Voice_(film). And others say that *Switched at Birth* (www.imdb.com/title/tt1758772/), a TV show about twins, one of whom is deaf, brought them to this instructional site.

And here arrives our Citizen Sociolinguist star: Nyle DiMarco, who plays the deaf heartthrob, Garrett, on that show. Nyle DiMarco emerges as a gorgeous, young, creative, confident, brilliant, and deaf man. He also appeared on *America's Next Top Model* – and won. He competed in *Dancing with the Stars* – and won. He's obviously an extraordinarily gifted human. But what makes him a citizen sociolinguist? In addition to modeling, dancing, and acting, he is continuously explaining, largely through YouTube videos, Twitter, and other social media, how sign language works for him and why. He shows the world the role signing plays in his life – the same way other citizen sociolinguists talk about and act out the everyday role of Singlish, Konglish, or other language varieties.

Nyle talks about and explicitly shows viewers how he signs with his family, with his friends, while flirting, at the movies. He embodies what communication can look like in the hands of a socially gifted, smart, and confident young man – who is also deaf. One of his YouTube videos posts answers to questions people have asked him through Twitter, and his response to one question in particular, "Were you ever bullied?" caught my attention. He replies, "No. Maybe I was made fun of, but I never listened. Because I have always loved being deaf." He points out that being deaf has never been an issue for him – his entire family was deaf, he says, and "they knew what to do."

Educators often talk a lot about how damaging a "deficit perspective" can be for learners. In the case of deafness, if you consider it a deficit, you may never focus on a deaf individual's strengths. Nyle DiMarco embodies the opposite perspective – as he describes himself, he has never seen his deafness as a deficit. He views his own deafness as an asset. He exudes self-respect – and respect for others. In this way, Nyle DiMarco's citizen sociolinguistics is illuminating not only for the Deaf Community, but for all of us, because he is talking about communication and modeling what it looks like in ordinary situations.

Nyle DiMarco also models how to engage in controversies about language. His experiences surrounding the movie *Black Panther* illustrate this attitude in action. The first time he went to the theater to see this movie, full of excited anticipation for the show, the captioning machine the theater provided for him was a disaster, running behind the dialogue and awkwardly blocking subtitles for the fictional Wakandan language spoken by characters in the movie. He tweeted about his experience, including a picture of him with the captioning machine, illustrating how it completely obscured the Wakandan translations. DiMarco also wrote about his experience in *Teen Vogue* (DiMarco, 2018), describing in candid detail how awful his trip to the movie theater was (he left after 10 minutes).

DiMarco made a larger point about the importance of subtitling movies more generally, and the biased views against it:

> I've heard the standard counterargument. Onscreen captions degrade the viewing experience. They're annoying and distracting. I call BS. People don't mind subtitles when they don't understand the language being spoken. (DiMarco, 2018)

Nyle goes on to point out that many popular mainstream shows (*Narcos* on Netflix, for example) include subtitles for those viewers who don't know languages other than English. And, even *Black Panther* included subtitles in English for Wakandan speech. His clarity, and his humble description of his own viewing experiences on Twitter, rallied thousands of Twitter followers in support of his point: Subtitles of all types often improve the movie experience for everyone – why exclude those that are for deaf people?

But if you look up "Nyle DiMarco's Black Panther Controversy" on line, you may find another citizen sociolinguistic controversy, this one with DiMarco on the receiving end of the criticism. He attracted ire from members of the black deaf community when he posted a video announcing his own, self-created ASL sign for "Black Panther," and writing in all caps, "HOW TO SIGN BLACK PANTHER IN ASL." He was criticized for this: As a white, deaf celebrity, he may have overstepped his role as a spokesman for the deaf community. An online news site, *The Moth News*, reported the controversy (Daily Moth, 2018) and elicited this most succinct comment aligning with the negative feedback slamming Nyle's self-appointed role as representative of Black Panther for the deaf community:

> COMMENT: SMH [Shaking My Head] Hate it when deaf "celebrities" think they are representing for many deaf communities but really they put themselves ahead before us to promote themselves in ladder of fame, well done to black deaf communities to "slam" them on the spot ... Ya dig?

How did Nyle respond? This seems like an important test of not only deaf communication, but communication in general. I asked a sign language interpreter friend of mine, who told me, "Nyle did apologize, saying he did not mean to take over and use his fame to overstep boundaries, and I don't think this tainted his overall reception in any way."

I looked around online a bit then, and found that not only did he apologize, he also fully embraced alternatives. Immediately after his Twitter post, many other signs were proposed for "Black Panther," and one black, deaf man posted a different version of an ASL "Black Panther" sign – what is now the widely recognized, cross-armed *Wakanda Forever!* pose. Nyle retweeted the new sign and the post, adding thanks, and unmitigated enthusiasm:

> I SERIOUSLY LOVE THIS ASL FOR BLACK PANTHER BETTER!!! FEELS SUPERHEROIC.

The Twitter feed continued to take up this SUPERHEROIC version of the sign. While a few critics remained, most responses piled on to thank Nyle for his contributions, and even for promoting greater unity among the deaf community.

As a citizen sociolinguistic spokesperson, Nyle DiMarco is constantly talking about language, about being deaf, about using sign and other modalities, and respecting whatever comes back. His points about his own communication – and his reactions to citizen sociolinguists' arrests – are not meant to stand as immutable truths, but to begin a dialogue about communication and human dignity. Along the way, more citizen sociolinguists – like those who coined the ASL "Black Panther" sign that stuck – join in to contribute the expertise that can only come from their unique perspective.

Situations

"Donut stop!" Years ago, my son would blurt out this phrase any time I raced through a yellow-on-the-verge-of-turning-red stoplight (rare occasions, I promise!). Ostensibly to break me of what some might consider reckless driving habits (but also, I suspect, to reward their own donut cravings) my kids would force me to stop for donuts at the next available *Dunkin'* outpost (of which there are many in Philadelphia). The phrase *donut stop!* became a quirky deterrent to my fast and furious driving patterns. Though we rarely stop for donuts anymore, *donut stop!* remains in our family repertoire as a pithy editorial comment – appropriate any time I've floored it through a light or otherwise overly gone on the offensive with my driving style. And now, in this paragraph, *donut stop!* exemplifies how inscrutable language can be if taken out of context. Any time we talk about language, trying to make sense of some unexpected turn of phrase – a strange greeting, or a funny use of first names, or a phrase like *donut stop!* – inevitably someone will invoke the importance of the context in which it is being used to illuminate what was going on. Sure, you can use that word, but only in *this situation*, in which that word has a special meaning – but that word's meaning may also change, depending on how that interaction unfolds, who is talking, or their current mental state. As humans, in a given situation, we have finely tuned, if rarely discussed sensibilities for flexibly making sense and managing it all. Usually, consciousness of our own nuanced attention to human interaction and its situational intricacies hovers beneath the surface, but when someone remarks explicitly on this finely tuned knowledge of the situation, it can lead to ongoing discussion and even a shared sense of wonderment.

The sociologist Erving Goffman pinpoints precisely this fine-grained sensibility in his classic essay, "The Neglected Situation" (1964). According to Goffman, one of the key shortcomings of social scientific inquiry has been its tendency to extract interactional features from the situation, with the goal of scaling up to make correlations between much broader categories (e.g., gender, socioeconomic status) and certain behaviors (posture, gesture, eye contact) to arrive at seemingly scientific conclusions: Women apologize more. Men take up more physical space. These studies may also lead to generalized recommendations and predictions: Stand up straight to command respect, take up more space to appear powerful, don't stand too close in X culture, never make eye contact in Y culture. Research like this, Goffman argues, neglects the intricacies of situations that are most relevant to everyday social actors – momentary actions that shape how we understand what to do and say, and how we take on finely tuned, but often fleeting roles. Correlational social science certainly couldn't account for the effects of a *donut stop!* proclamation in my car, nor most of the intricate interactional detail humans need to negotiate in everyday interaction. These details are often highly creative and entertaining too, and so it happens that citizen sociolinguists often revel in wonderment of the situational details that Goffman identified as critical to understanding human society.

Several internet trends illustrate how precisely people tune in to features of a situation – those features that standard correlational sociolinguistic research attempts to ignore. Twitter sites like "Shit Academics Say" (317,800 followers) and the viral YouTube video "Shit Girls Say" (over 21 million views), for example, illustrate in detail how situationally specific, yet instantly recognizable our mutually shared behaviors are. Consider all the complexity of a typical academic conference discussion encapsulated on this @academicssay Tweet:

If you can't say anything nice, say it as more of a comment than a question (tweeted on 7/9/19, liked 3,703 times, retweeted 883 times as of 8/15/19)

As the enthusiastic response (over 3,000 likes) suggests, the Twitter audience appreciates this observation of the thinly veiled critique that might often follow a remark that begins "This is more of a comment than a question . . ." Anyone who has been to a conference or two, or presented a paper themselves, will recognize this situation, and the moment of dread as we wait to hear what will follow. Of course, what follows might also be a compliment! How such situations unfold is always a matter of specific context. Still, observations like this tweet lay bare those intricacies, making us more aware and even sardonically appreciative of the subtle negotiations happening in such everyday interactions. We are understanding the fine-grained details of a shared socialization into how a recognizable subgroup ("academics") behaves ("shit they say") in certain situations.

Internet-circulated memes of all kinds point to that same recognition of Goffman's neglected situation, the intricate management of the combination of language, context, and demeanor that we often take for granted as we perform differently from moment to moment over the course of each day. As this chapter continues, we will consider the way people use *memes* to share that situational knowledge, and, we will also consider, as a point of contrast, a few examples of what I call *linguistic gentrification*: cases that illustrate awkward misrecognition of the situation, made apparent when someone extracts words from one situation and unthinkingly inserts them in another.

Memification The memification of everyday life illustrates how everyday people express their knowledge of the nuanced types of communication necessary to manage the impression they give in social situations. To illustrate, let's return to the *Wakanda Forever* speech act and pose addressed above in our discussion of Nyle DiMarco. At a later point in the social life of the *Wakanda Forever* speech act, the very same gesture that conveyed solidarity, unity, and empowerment in the film (and for Nyle DiMarco and the deaf community as discussed above) became overused. As time wore on and media appearances piled up, and the star Wakandan, Chadwick Boseman, performed the pose for cameras, likely on demand, again and again, his facial expression began to show signs that Boseman, the actor, was not as committed to Wakanda as the fictional Wakandan character his fans expected him to embody. Recognizing this subtle fade in enthusiasm, everyday citizen sociolinguists began to make visual jokes about it through memes. Below, for example:

This meme illustrates the creator's fine-grained perspective on what it takes to perform adequately in incrementally different social situations. In the case of the *Wakanda Forever* speech event, it is not enough to look great, be a movie

Figure 2.5 Chadwick Boseman meme

star, and make the requisite pose; our face must also display a finely tuned expression that shows we are *into it*. In the process, this meme-maker also invokes another situation that non-movie stars might easily relate to – the boredom associated with the fading of that idealism one initially has after getting a new job.

This recognition of the details needed to enact the right role in a situation is precisely what Goffman (1964) was discussing in his point about the "neglected situation," and Goffman's mentor, Harold Garfinkel (1976) referred to that tacit knowledge everyday people have of these details as "members' meanings." As members of a society, we recognize not only the pose and the phrase that accompanies it, but also the subtleties of facial expression and posture that this movie star must embody when taking on that role. We also recognize the idealistic energy common on the first day at work – as well as the understandably faded enthusiasm as fatigue sets in. Even though we go through life relying on this knowledge, we usually do not articulate it. As members of a society we know things that we have never been taught explicitly: Don't sit next to a stranger on the bus when all the other seats are vacant, don't offer a catalogue of personal details when someone asks "How are you?," face forward when you ride on an elevator. Because these are lessons learned through life, we know how to perform "normally," even though we might not be able to give an outsider – say, a visitor from another planet – a set of well-articulated rules to follow. Nobody would ever say, "To be normal, you should look a little drained and unenthusiastic after your first two weeks at a new job" or even tell Chadwick Boseman, "You need to fire up that Wakanda pose so people don't see you as just an ordinary worker like them." But when those expectations are violated – as when Chadwick Boseman does not consistently embody superhero levels of energy while performing his *Wakanda Forever* pose, we notice. This noticing can generate a spark of wonderment, a shared recognition of a common human condition: Life is hard – even for superhero actors.

Memes and fantastically viral YouTube videos rely on these "members' meanings" the tacit knowledge about nuanced situational expectations. While the *Wakanda Forever* meme-maker was drawn to the humor of a superhero's fading of enthusiasm, other situations become notable for too much enthusiasm – a level of excitement that far exceeds situational norms. In a department store or car dealership, the driven enthusiasm of the "hard sell" can send customers scurrying out the door. A parent showing excessive enthusiasm over a new "healthy" dessert may likely end up the only one eating it (been there). There seems to be a finely calibrated sense of how much enthusiasm each situation or object or set of relationships calls for. We recognize a faded enthusiasm (like Chad Boseman's), we flee from artificial or seemingly forced enthusiasm, but we may also be sucked into a contagious enthusiasm every once in a while. As adults, a blast of genuine enthusiasm can even feel like a return to the innocence of childhood, a feeling of experiencing something for the very first time. Genuine enthusiasm may be hard to capture in a way that can be shared – and as adults, it's hard to trust it when we see it. While "enthusiasm" is supposedly an internally generated, almost visceral emotion, we are wary of it. The "members meanings" that gauge our expressions of enthusiasm or responses to enthusiasm from others are very finely tuned.

We may not know how finely tuned our expectations are for requisite levels of affect relative to a given situation until we see them violated. Just as Garfinkel illustrated our expectations for "How are you?" responses by having students robustly violate them, one might test members' meanings for enthusiasm by violating ordinary expectations for enthusiasm. If we see some people overly enthusiastically greeting each other, for example, we might instantly decide their friendship is superficial. A scene from the super-viral "Shit Girls Say," when two girls greet each other in a public place with ecstatic screaming, hugging, and jumping up and down, illustrates this untrustworthy level of enthusiasm.(https://www.youtube.com/watch?v=u-yLGIH7W9Y.)

Another memified video, however, illustrates that on rare occasions even adults can be drawn to the childlike wonderment embodied in genuine enthusiasm. The simultaneous oddness and wonderment of unbridled, genuine, un-self-interested enthusiasm in a grown human became memified after the super-viral circulation of one of the most popular YouTube videos ever: the double rainbow video. (www.youtube.com/watch?v=OQSNhk5ICTI). I encourage readers who have never seen this to join over 46 million other YouTube viewers and watch this video. In it, one man (YouTuber Yosemitebear62) reacts with genuinely *uncanny* levels of enthusiasm to the sight of a double rainbow. The video, over three minutes long, has no music, no special effects, just the voice-over of one man hysterically laughing, crying, and exclaiming in a nirvana-like state of enthusiasm. Here is a rough transcription:

YOSEMITEBEAR62: Whoa, that's a full rainbow. All the way. Double rainbow. Oh my god. All the way. It's a double rainbow all the way. Whoa. So intense. Whoa. Man. Aww. Whoa. Whoa!!! My God!!! Oh my god! Hahaha oh my god! Woooo! Oh Wow! WOOO! YEAH!!! Oh my, oh my, oh my god look at that. It's starting to look like a triple rainbow. Oh my god. It's full. Double rainbow all the way across the sky. Oh my god. (laughing and crying). Oh god. Oh my god. Oh god. What does this mean? OH! Oh my God. Oh! Oh GOD. It's so bright. Oh my God it's so bright and vivid. Oh. Oh. Oh. It's so beautiful (sobbing and laugh-crying and sobbing and laugh-crying). Oh my God. Oh my God. Oh my god. Oh my god it's a double complete rainbow. Right in my front yard. Ha, ha, ha, ha, ha hahahahah!! Oh my god. Hehehehe. Oh my god, what does this mean? Tell me! It's too much. I don't know what it means. Oh my god. ((Laughing, crying, breathing deeply)) It's so intense. OH. ((sighing deeply)). Oh my God.

The non-normal extremity of this reaction creates nearly as much wonderment in viewers as the sight and video of the double rainbow did for the original YouTube contributor, Yosemitebear62. To this day, the YouTube video continues to draw comments on the nuance of his voice-over, from savoring echo ("wHaT dOeS tHiS mEaN?!??) to the funny one-liner ("a triple rainbow would kill this guy"), to the affiliative ("Just saw a double rainbow today and immediately thought of you"), to the reverent ("This guy found so much beauty and peace in nature he started crying. That's when you know you've found a higher understanding of life and the world around you. Still love this video"). The double rainbow video and its popularity illustrate the shared recognition of a rare situation: a moment of genuine, adult enthusiasm. But this video also illustrates how adult enthusiasm seems odd when it falls outside our finely calibrated expectations. Three minutes of solid wonderment extends far beyond any usual human capacity for enthusiasm. Laughing, crying, and exclaiming with no ulterior motive other than expression of his own pure sense of awe can make a viewer uncomfortable. The outbreak of cynical takes on the video illustrates how the responsibilities of adult life make the three-minute gusher of enthusiasm and existential wonder seem absurd. One meme, for example, excerpts these words from the original double rainbow post: DOUBLE RAINBOW ALL THE WAY. WHAT DOES IT MEAN? and provides this cynical response: IT MEANS YOUR TIMECARD IS INCOMPLETE.

But despite cynical responses, the norm-breaking of Yosemitebear62's extended display of enthusiasm draws people to wonderment and continues, years later, to spawn follow-up stories, songs, videos, and of course more memes.

Memes in Combination This memified recognition of the essence of situations – the nuance of human behavior, language, and context – has ramifying effects when different situations combine, providing the basis for an internet-based poetics. Combinations of viral videos, phrases, and fonts, the hallmark of today's internet memes, can reveal how finely tuned everyday people are to the nuance of situations. Consider the following meme texts, for example:
Double rainbow all the way!!
Ain't nobody got time for that.
Eyebrows on fleek
All your base are belong to us
One does not simply . . . walk into Mordor
Cash me ousside howbow dah?
My guess is that most readers can identify several of these phrases as common internet memes: phrases that drop from seemingly nowhere and are

suddenly said everywhere. (If you don't recognize any of these, google a few and you will soon discover a new world.)

Why do these exist? You may be thinking now, "Who knows?" "Who cares?" Or even "This stuff is a disease, a pox. There's a reason it's called *viral* circulation!" But all these phrases both illuminate and build a common culture, a shared, modern-day poetics capable of spreading ideas, laughter, joy, idiocy, and general being-together-ness – "members' meanings" – the same way adages ("A stitch in time saves nine," "Early to bed, early to rise ...," "Haste makes waste"), poetry, folktales, or fables provide a medium for sharing ideas among a social group. Like poetry, memes lose their thrust when paraphrased or translated literally word for word. Memes get meaning not from individual words, but from the way words (and images, fonts, sound, music) are put together. As an astute student of mine pointed out, the expressive power of "Ain't nobody got time for that" does not come through in a translation like, "Nobody has sufficient time to do that." Similarly, "Double rainbow all the way!" would lose its essence as an expression of enthusiasm and awe were we to instead use Wikipedia's description, "a meteorological phenomenon that is caused by reflection, refraction and dispersion of light in water droplets resulting in a spectrum of light appearing in the sky."

Because they capture the subtleties of communication, the tacit knowledge we need to navigate social interaction, and because they often rely on freestanding chunks of words and expressions, memes are a citizen sociolinguistic way of illuminating how we use language as a creative tool of situational expression – extending language far beyond the realms of representation and standardization. Memes do not reproduce a standardized, rule-bound way of constructing meaning. Often, as soon as one seems to become overly standardized in its form and meaning, it morphs, combining with other recognizable memes, building new forms of language awareness. The arid diction of "One simply does not walk into Mordor" and the earthy "Ain't nobody got time for that" provoke renewed sense of wonderment about language, because they illustrate our shared tacit knowledge about the distinctiveness of language use in each of these situations. The fantastical "I'll get you, my pretty" from *The Wizard of Oz* lends an extra hint of evil when it is layered onto a more contemporary political rivalry. And the memified chunk "Double rainbow all the way! What does it mean???" accentuates the awe and unbridled enthusiasm of Yosemitebear62 when combined with the ordinariness of the response, "it means your timecard is incomplete."

Constantly recombining language chunks from different situations, memes provide the medium for continued snowballing of expression. In the same way "donut stop!" resurfaces from time to time as I'm driving through town with my kids, phrases from memes return to everyday conversation, subtly weaving their shared imagery with situational nuance. My kids' guitar teacher has even been known to say, "Double rainbow all the way!" when a sublime piece of music-making occurs. Expressing ourselves can be more effective, creative, joyous, and *communicative* when we combine words/languages/gestures and images so freely; when "Ain't nobody got time for that" can be used in the same sentence as "the quadratic equation"; when "Double rainbow all the way" is used during music lessons; or when phrases from Spanish, French, Tagalog, and English can rally one another in new, yet recognizable, combinations.

Every day we face this cross-situational negotiation, as we work with people who bring different situational knowledge and "members' meanings" into new situations. In the world of memes, this can have wonderfully creative effects. In the world of everyday communication, people constantly negotiate the boundaries of situations and the way language can and should be used within them. Crossing boundaries happens continuously, and the effects vary infinitely.

Linguistic Gentrification

Memes and the everyday ability to combine and recombine them reveal how finely tuned citizen sociolinguistic sensibilities are to the intricacies of situations. Inevitably, those combinations can be miscalculated. Instead of sensitively accounting for context and calibrating language use accordingly, sometimes citizen sociolinguists awkwardly appropriate language from different situations and import it into their own world without any sensitivity to that nuance. I call this *linguistic gentrification*.

Most people recognize the process of neighborhood gentrification: A once affordable neighborhood with history and architectural character becomes transformed by wealth into a place that the very people who nurtured the character of that place can't afford to live in anymore (or don't even want to). With a moment of thought, you can probably think of a few examples of *linguistic gentrification* too: Everyday, lowbrow, maligned, "non-standard," or scandalous language gets repackaged as cool, trendy, and even standardized – so much so that the original users may no longer want to use it.

When neighborhood gentrification strikes, features of old run-down structures originally organic to a way of life – like a breezy front stoop or an original ice box – get repurposed as signs of sophistication. Likewise, linguistic gentrification: Features of language originally part of a way of life – and some looked down on in schools or marked as "non-standard" – become markers of sophistication, local knowledge, or social cachet. Often these gentrified features originally come from speech typified as "African American." Those very features deemed "non-standard" resurface as expressively powerful and get used by white people. To illustrate, consider conversations about "double negatives" in English. While most white people and English teachers will decry the use of a "double negative" as grammatically incorrect, privileged

Figure 2.6 "Finna" definition

students in an Ivy League University will use the phrase, "Ain't nobody got time for that!" strategically and to great effect. Similarly, the word "finna" has gained popularity these days in suburban Honors English classes I've been working in, and it even appeared in a collective slang word cloud they have been creating each semester to document youth language at their school.

"Finna" also appears on the Internet in this dictionary.com entry (the very first hit for a google search) (See figure 2.6).

"Shawty," "salty," "jawn," "no cap," and the ubiquitous "bruh" are other words gentrified by suburban Honors English 11th graders. But when asked about "finna," "salty," or "shawty," few students can provide a sense of the social history of the situational expectations and members' meanings associated with the use of these words aside from their own personal contact with them. Most assume they just were part of auto-tuned YouTube songs or videos that somehow went viral. A few mention Kanye West lyrics as a good source of these expressions. In conversation, one student mentioned that "finna" might come from "fixing to," a "Southern" phrase. But others had no idea that "finna" might be parsed that way.

To their credit, these kids are developing their own "members' meanings" around the use of these words. But using new words this way with little recognition of other contexts of their meaning has the potential to offend people who have different members' meanings associated with those words and their situated use. Recently, for example, I came across a Facebook post complaining about a pun using the word "jawn." The author's complaint simultaneously pointed out linguistic gentrification in the context of literal neighborhood gentrification. The offending "jawn" appeared on a blackboard tent outside a coffee shop in an upscale part of Philadelphia and read, in colorful capital letters: The Facebooker posted a picture of the sign and remarked as follows:

JAWN
IN
ON THE
FUN
HERE IN
OLD CITY

EO: Gentrification in #Philly be like ... let's incorrectly use the word "jawn" by trying to "jawn" in on the fun ...

He also added his own caption: "Get Y'all people, K?!"EO's remark to "Get Y'all People, K?!" implies this use of "jawn" is a form of appropriation by one group of people from another – shifting from wonderment in the use of shared language and recognition of our common approach to situations, to citizen's arrest: calling out white, well-heeled folks for taking over someone else's language and using it awkwardly, without regarding the subtleties of the situation and members' meanings.

Just as neighborhood gentrifiers vary in their knowledge of the history of the city they occupy, linguistic gentrifiers have varying levels of awareness of the historical foundation for these words, phrases or features of pronunciation. And newcomers to words and phrases like "jawn," "Ain't nobody got time for that," or "finna" use them with wide-ranging degrees of awareness and finesse. Some gentrifiers – of cities and language – surely recognize underlying character and build on that. Others might lack that sensitivity, driving away residents and speakers, losing generations of history and life ways that built the original character that drew us to those places and expressions.

A World of Others' Words   As the use of "jawn" on the coffee shop blackboard illustrates, the line between wonderment and arrest can be a fine one. I felt like I had potentially done my own bit of linguistic gentrification when my own use of that very word *gentrification* with respect to language drew some critique. After using the word in a blog post to describe how sometimes wealthy, privileged, white people use phrases taken from the life ways of non-wealthy, less privileged, black and brown people without knowing the deeper story of that language, I wanted to suggest that, just like neighborhoods, our words have had previous residents. Ironically, and perhaps too late, I realized the word *gentrification* itself has its own vivid history, of which I am only a partial witness. As the literary theorist Michael Bakhtin has stated, "We live in "a world of other's words" (1981, p. 143). And this certainly became clear when I used the term *gentrification*. One reader responded this way, on Twitter:

TWEET 1: Sorry, @brymes, I find "gentrification" a really problematic term; applying it to language only muddies the waters

But another came to my defense with this formulation:

TWEET 2: It seems very different to acknowledge its complexity than to completely dismiss as a viable concept.

But others joined in with the perspective voiced in Tweet 1, suggesting I simply not use the word gentrification *at all:*

TWEET 3: The dehumanizing and scapegoating is so woven into the frame, I can't see how you'd extricate it.

Any word I use, to quote Michael Bakhtin again, comes already "populated – overpopulated – with the intentions of others" (1981, p. 294). And, clearly, I had blithely used the word "gentrification," not knowing the previous intentions of others using it. I hubristically thought I could, in a 500-word blog post, populate it with my own intentions: a useful analogy for a citizen sociolinguistics. Not so?

Ironically, these responses suggesting I ditch the word *gentrification* illustrate the point I was trying to make: As it turns out, I was gentrifying the word *gentrification*, attempting to people it with my own intentions, the same way newcomers attempt to take over neighborhoods with theirs. But in that short exchange, we also began illustrating the positive potential in such a process by constructing a new social life for the word *gentrification*. And we began to use it as a way to think about language too. As a character in Chang-Rae Lee's novel, *Native Speaker* puts it:

No matter smart you are, no one is smart enough to see the whole world. There's always a picture too big to see. (Lee, 1995, p. 46)

No one person has a god's-eye view. No expert could compile the infinite possible situational meanings of *gentrification*, or *Double rainbow all the way*, or even the word *citizenship*. We can't possibly know all the situational nuances these words and phrases might hold in other contexts. But, as we talk about language together – as we deliberate on *gentrification* or *citizenship*, as we explore different perspectives and learn about more situations and contexts and their combinations, we assemble a bigger picture of language, communication, and humanity.

As the complaints about my use of the word suggest, the very act of using a certain word, like *gentrification*, whatever it might be referring to, can be offensive. Those Twitter responses suggest that people out there have a negative sense not of the practice of gentrification, but of the use of the word *gentrification*. These responses took issue with my metaphorical use of the word. It didn't seem to matter that I was not a gentrifier, or a developer, or whether I was revitalizing neighborhoods and preserving their original character via anti-capitalist, non-profit philanthropy. They did not like that I was using the word.

To get a blanket impression of how people see the word *gentrification*, just how "loaded" that word is, how peopled it is with the intentions of others, even when disconnected from its literal action on communities, I googled the phrase, "Why is gentrification ..." and waited for the autofill to happen. Without regard

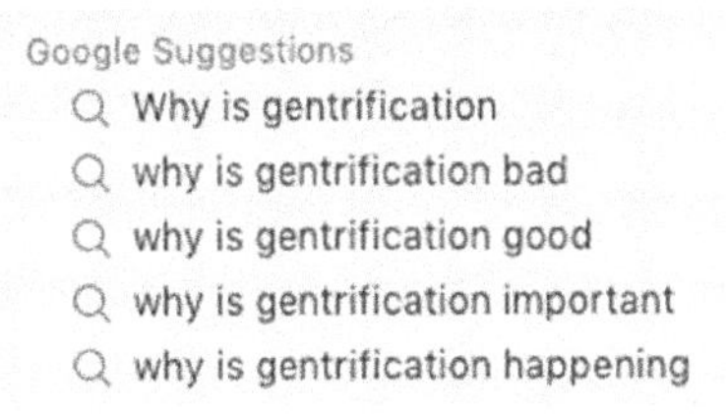

Google Suggestions
Q Why is gentrification
Q why is gentrification bad
Q why is gentrification good
Q why is gentrification important
Q why is gentrification happening

Figure 2.7 Why is gentrification ...

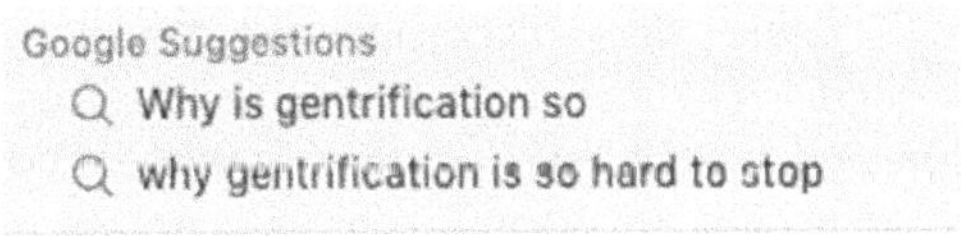

Google Suggestions
Q Why is gentrification so
Q why gentrification is so hard to stop

Figure 2.8 Why is gentrification so ...

to what *gentrification* is, or what it does, I just wanted to see how people talk about gentrification. Here's what came up (See Figure 2.7).

According to the Google algorithm, it seems that, in agreement with the Twitter responses, gentrification is a word that people associate with being "bad" – but also "good," "important," and "happening."

When I added the word "so," only one google search response came up (See Figure 2.8).

Why is gentrification so hard to stop? A lot of people must be asking this question – in turn illustrating that, indeed, gentrification (and talk about it) is hard to stop. Like linguistic gentrification, neighborhood gentrification seems to take on a life of its own. No matter how much we say about it – whether it is good, bad, important, or controversial, it is happening. And, like language change, it is hard to stop. We live in a world of others' words, others' intentions, and we navigate it. As citizens, and as citizen sociolinguists, through talking about language, we explore the range of perspectives on it – and we do it together. In the chapter that follows, we will detail the medium and methods for such exploration.

3 Doing Citizen Sociolinguistics
The Medium Is the Method

In the exploration of citizen sociolinguistics, our object of investigation is *How we talk about language*. Wherever those discussions about language happen, that is where our work begins. The medium may be everyday conversation, letters to the editor, comment threads on a city data forum, definitions and counter-definitions on urbandictionary.com, YouTube Accent Challenge videos and the feedback they receive, text messages, a Snapchat feed, or any other media yet to emerge. As we investigate the way people talk about language we follow where the media take us. The medium of the conversation creates the methods for our investigation. Slightly altering Marshall McLuhan's famous phrase about new media for our own citizen sociolinguistic purposes, *the medium is the method*.

In contrast to traditional sociolinguistics, in which media like an internet survey, a structured interview, or a dyadic conversation in the lab are designed to elicit data that will directly feed into a researcher's analytic plan, in citizen sociolinguistic inquiry, any medium can become a serendipitous tool for exploring how we talk about language. This means anything that happens within any context of language discussion – even much of what traditional sociolinguists might discard as non-objective data or noise – opens a new pathway to further investigation and inquiry. In this chapter I illustrate how this medium-as-method works, exploring how citizen sociolinguists pose everyday questions about language, how they gather and analyze that data around those questions, and how their findings are disseminated. Along the way, it will become clear that when we investigate everyday talk about language, not only is the medium the method, the process of inquiry – a cycle of endless question asking, answering, sharing our findings, reformulating, and asking new questions – is often itself the product.

This chapter will detail how data are gathered, analyzed, and debated in a way which distinguishes citizen sociolinguistics from typical social science methodology, exemplifying and discussing several distinctions: The tools used to gather data are often *mis*uses of other data tools like dialect surveys, language quizzes, or Google Translate; Objective "accuracy" of any data gathered, is less important than "likes" or popularity; Sharing data is commonplace and necessary, given the importance of popularity for validity: Transcripts are not kept in a locked drawer, but openly circulated; Transcription of talk (often in the form of phonetic spelling, emoji, or creative punctuation) is not presented as "accurate" or "inaccurate" but is a form of interpretation in itself; Making friends with research participants is not considered creepy overstepping, but the essence of citizen sociolinguistic inquiry and a serendipitous way that findings are disseminated. This chapter illustrates how citizen sociolinguists find answers to their questions by building a community that cares about the same questions, building a discussion and popular consensus, and then disseminating those findings through more discussion via social media. Validity then, is built through participation in this community, rather than appeal to another knowledge base (like published academic research). As a way of pushing readers into their own acts of citizen sociolinguistics, this chapter concludes with a short guide for fostering and exploring everyday conversations about language, whether fomented by curiosity and wonderment, or critique and arrest.

Asking Questions: Where Do They Come From?

Pick up any book or manual on "how to write a research paper" and you will find instructions that research questions must address a "gap" in the previous research literature. Whether these guides are discussing quantitative or qualitative, scientific or social scientific studies, the standard protocol calls for questions that emerge from a research gap. A generically worded gap statement might read like this:

While studies have shown that young people do this when they encounter X, and old people do this when they encounter X, there is no research addressing what middle-aged people do. This is problematic, because research has shown that middle-aged people are those most frequently seen with X. The proposed research addresses this gap in the literature by asking the following question: What occurs when middle-aged people encounter X?

This gap-motivated research builds from a specific context of expertise – in the hypothetical case above, the researcher presumably has a broad sense of the field and the research on X. In contrast, citizen sociolinguistic questions typically do not emerge from any known gap in the research literature (though, they may address that literature unintentionally, unearthing unexpected gaps). Instead, citizen sociolinguistic questions arise from everyday ruptures in their experience of language – arrest and wonderment in the face of language difference and distinction.

When everyday people happen upon research tools that real linguists have actually used to investigate language and plug holes in the previous research, they just might start using those tools themselves. But in the hands of citizen sociolinguists, these research tools take them down a completely different path of inquiry, fomenting language wonderment, and promoting more talk about language. This do-it-yourself (DIY) citizen sociolinguistic method is a way of repurposing and making the most of old linguistic research tools.

Repurposing Old Linguistic Tools

Google "old tools, new uses" and you will find a host of innovative ideas for how to recycle old rakes, hammers, screwdrivers, clamps, and even the toolboxes that once held some of those things you no longer use (e.g., www .bobvila.com/diy-hooks/46399-think-outside-the-toolbox-9-new-uses-for-old-tools/slideshows#!3). These sites offer new life for our favorite old (but now unused) implements by giving them updated roles in our updated lives. I don't need this old (though charming) rake, but I do need someplace to hang my scarves and necklaces. Voilà! Problem solved. I don't need these extra hammers, but they could do a great job holding up my iPad.

Just like old rakes, hammers, and pitchforks, old linguistic tools have been repurposed by citizen sociolinguists and their new uses have multiplied on the web. For example, a dialect survey created in the 1930s by the linguist Hans Kurath has become widely known via internet-mediated social circles. This survey includes two parts: a list of words to read aloud to illustrate how you say them (including *water*, *crayon*, *caramel*, *syrup*, *pecan*, and *New Orleans*), and a list of prompts to elicit what locals call certain items (for example, "How do you address a group of people?"). The original purpose of this survey was to gather data that could be used to construct Regional Linguistic Atlases, and Kurath created several of these, in multiple volumes, using his survey and careful statistical mapping to characterize local dialects of the United States. You may recognize these prompts as they were repurposed in Kelly's Konglish Accent Challenge, discussed in Chapter 2, and when they appeared briefly in the discussion of crowdsourcing in the Introduction.

Kurath's survey has reappeared in many different modified and internet-ready forms, including the popular "dialect quiz" in the *New York Times*, "How Y'all, Youse, and You Guys Talk," mentioned in the Introduction (Katz and Andrews, 2013). Rather than using this quiz to create regional dialect maps, the *New York Times* quiz offered to predict "where you're from." Many people I know took the quiz at least one time and declared astonishment as to its accuracy. But others also took it several more times, "playing the part" of certain places they had lived at some point in their life. Others laughed at its extreme inaccuracy – like an Australian friend who was pinpointed as being from "Yonkers." People were using the tool and relishing it, but instead of using the old survey tool to pinpoint regional variety, the new use seemed to foment talk about mobility. Discussions like, "When I lived in Atlanta ..., but in Chicago ..."

Another re-tooled version of Kurath's dialect survey surfaced before the *New York Times* "Dialect Quiz" and circulated through Tumblr and YouTube as the "Accent Challenge" or "Accent Tag." There are now thousands of Accent Challenge videos (like Kelly's from Chapter 2) posted on YouTube and voluminous comments about them. These performances illuminate features of English in today's world that could never have been predicted by Kurath as he and his research assistants traversed the United States with their trusty notebooks and gigantic recording devices. As the wonderment in language difference grew, varieties of accent challenge videos multiplied across the Internet. As discussed in Chapter 2, Kelly, the makeup tutorial YouTuber, illuminated her Konglish/English duality by recording a version of the accent challenge in which she reads through the word list and prompts twice: once, as she would say things when she is with her Korean friends, and again as she would talk with her American friends.

Other accent challenge videos go far beyond Kurath's boundaries of the United States, including Jamaica, Australia, New Zealand, and dozens of finely divided regions of Ireland, Scotland, and England. Some accent challengers have even used the survey as a way to compare the different varieties of foreign-accented English – and comparisons of the differences between Swiss, German, and Italian accents in English. Almost all accent challengers take their time with the survey, prefacing the reading of the list with long stories of how they grew up speaking certain ways and with whom, and interrupting their survey with asides that add to their story. All of these accent challengers (and there are many more varieties) display an awareness of their own speech, and that of others, that Kurath could never have fathomed, and would not have welcomed as he set out to document the *unmonitored*, regional speech of rural folk.

Ultimately the accent challenge has become an ever-morphing medium/ method for gathering different kinds of language samples and stories. I've also worked with high school language arts classes as they've developed their own New and Improved Accent Challenge, to explore language close to home, near Philadelphia. They've devised new word lists and prompts that depart from the standardized goals of Hans Kurath to ask peers, parents, and locals about more contemporary local distinctions in language. Instead of asking "What do you call a small bug that rolls into a ball when touched?" for example, they'll ask "What do you call the dairy dessert that comes from a machine?" and the frozen custard/soft-serve ice cream language debate has emerged as a robust medium/method of inquiry!

Most old tools probably did their job well. Rustically beautiful rakes and hammers remind us of simpler times, while lending a hand in our modern homes. The new role of linguistic tools can also bring to mind a simpler communicative time, and simultaneously illuminate some features of our updated communicative world. Repurposed and in the hands of citizen sociolinguistics, Kurath's old survey does not lead to several more pounds worth of bound volumes of linguistic detail; instead, it builds awareness and sparks dialogue about complex forms of linguistic diversity. The conversations brought on by these repurposed linguistic tools go beyond *roly-poly* or *custard* and *soft-serve*, building awareness of linguistic difference and how it separates us, but also how linguistic difference exists *within* us and can draw us together.

Today, the language quiz medium itself has become an online clickbait industry (See Figure 3.1). Each of these quizzes provides the sparks that foment conversation about language, often in other media, like YouTube and Facebook. This spark of wonderment and the follow-up inquiry creates a buzz about language and builds awareness in a way that goes beyond any objective "results" these quizzes offer on completion. In some cases, language researchers, like those at Boston College who created the "Which English?" quiz discussed above, still use these quizzes, surveys, and maps to build a database they use for cognitive science or dialect research. But most of

---

The three quizzes listed here give a sense of the more widely circulated language quizzes that have emerged following Katz & Andrews' (2013) *NYTimes* Dialect Quiz. Take them, enjoy them, share them, change them, and make new ones to take, enjoy, share, change, etc!

Which British Accent is Closest to Yours?
This UK version is designed to illuminate the different regional varieties and then pinpoints celebrities who characterize each. Not surprisingly, given the sparks of wonderment these quizzes create, the quiz and associated news story was featured as BBC Future's "Best of 2018" collection:
http://www.bbc.com/future/story/20180205-which-british-accent-is-closest-to-your-own

Are You *On Fleek*?
This language quiz was another New York Times contribution to language wonderment:
http://www.nytimes.com/interactive/2015/02/22/upshot/internet-language-quiz.html?smid=tw-upshotnyt&_r=0&abt=0002&abg=0

Which of the World's Englishes Do You Speak?
Stepping out of the UK and USA English-speaking circle, this quiz simultaneously addresses your language variety, and spreads awaress of world Englishes. http://archive.gameswithwords.org/WhichEnglish/.

Figure 3.1 Examples of online language quizzes

these quizzes – and by far the more popular ones – are now built on a cycle of curiosity and conversation, and savvy publishers have probably realized that readers like these things, so they continue to proliferate. In contemporary parlance, one might even call these new uses of old tools citizen sociolinguistic "hacks." Linguists, citizen sociolinguists, and publishers alike are hacking into the vaults of linguistic research to reprogram tools for modern-day purposes. Moving on now from the language quiz industry, technological hacking probably best applies to how citizen sociolinguists have devised new ways to use another online language tool, Google Translate.

Google Translate Hacks

Many people, across contexts, use Google Translate, the online translation robot, to translate talk and text. But like all robots, Google Translate makes mistakes. And so, ingenious humans figure out nuanced ways of using it in not exactly the way it was intended: Google Translate hacks.

Hack #1: The Stereotype Detector In an essay on language translation robots, the blogger Loving Language asked "Is Google Translate sexist?" and then suggested that, indeed, it is (Loving Language, 2014). He showed this by running tests in German, in which, for example, the word "teacher," when used in the phrase "cooking teacher" translates as "Lehrerin" (feminine) while in "math teacher" it translates as "Lehrer" (masculine). A few years ago I tested this myself with Spanish: Sure enough, a "cooking teacher" was a "profesora" (feminine), while a "math teacher" was a "profesor" (masculine).

This does not necessarily mean Google Translate is sexist. Robots need to be programmed to be sexist. Google Translate does not have a mind, and as usual, people are behind the choices it makes. The Loving Language blogger also points out that, while Google relies on algorithms to build its translation robot, people (not robots) create those algorithmic models. People also create the corpus of language that feeds into the Google Translate algorithm. If more people in the corpus are referring to math teachers as men and to cooking teachers as women, Google Translate will reflect that. The robot then, becomes a voice box for a sexist society. But here's where the "hack" comes in. Citizen sociolinguists' recognition of the process behind Google's "sexism" makes it possible for them to repurpose Google Translate as not just a translation tool, but also a potential stereotype detector. Some words collect in gendered ways. We recognize these stereotypes – in concert with Google Translate – and have the citizen sociolinguistic potential to expose them.

And since that blog post in 2014, Google Translate has changed. This Google Translate hack showed that it could not only be a stereotype detector, but a stereotype fixer. I first performed the Loving Languages hack in 2014.

Retesting in 2019, it appears Google has changed the algorithm. Every possible type of teacher under the sun now appears as "Lehrer." Okay, everyone is masculine, which raises another sort of gender problem. Maybe if we discuss this at length online, in citizen sociolinguistic forums, next time I check, they may all be Lehrerinen!

Hack #2: The Bilingual Expertise Detector and Multilingual Wonderment Provocateur Multilingual families, immigrants, teachers, and schools also rely on Google Translate. Often this can be painfully problematic, as Google Translate's literal bent and lack of communication skills can often lead to more confusion than simple old-fashioned, face-to-face negotiation of meaning. But sometimes, the inadequacy of the Google Translate robot also functions to highlight the importance of real, human bilingual expertise, pinpointing those moments when literalness just doesn't function. Consider this family's use of Google Translate, for example. In the transcript below, from Meredith McConnochie's dissertation research on bilingual family literacy, a bilingual mother is helping with homework, and explaining to her two boys (aged five and six) the translation of the English idiom, *school of fish*:

MOTHER: ¡Porque aquí dice *school of fish* y abajo dice banco de pescado (.) pero si fuera eh si como dice arriba *school of fish* sería escuela de pescado!

Because here it says *school of fish* and down there it says *bank of fish*, but if we were to go as it says above *school of fish* it would be *fish school*.

Bilingual parents, like this mom, have special knowledge. This mother is drawing attention to the nuance of language and translation. The boys will not be able to simply use a dictionary or Google Translate for an idiom, because *school of fish* does not translate literally. While they may be more computer savvy and know more English than their mother does, she knows Spanish better than they do – and better than Google Translate, which translates *school of fish* word for word as *escuela de pescados*.

If we look up *banco de pescados*, Google Translate doltishly supplies *fish bank*. Google Translate doesn't get it. But this mistake reveals how Google Translate can work well, if not as a fail-safe translation tool, as a citizen sociolinguistic tool. In its dumb errors (or "sexist" oversteps) Google Translate can reveal the nuanced knowledge of human beings, like this bilingual mom. It also provides a new language exploration game: Try querying Google Translate with a few of your favorite idioms in your language of choice and enjoy the amusing literal translations supplied by the Google robot.

Hack #3: The Bilingual Collective Expertise Leverager Flash forward 10 years in the life of a multilingual family. Often, multilingualism is distributed across a family, parents having expertise in one set of languages, children in another. Robert LeBlanc's (2019) research on teens and literacy at a massively multilingual Catholic Church (services offered in English, Spanish, Vietnamese, and Tagalog) revealed this hack.

Teens who attend this church regularly use Google Translate as just one of several translation steps to read scripture in Church. One teen, who doesn't speak much Vietnamese, or write it at all, manages to expertly recite scripture aloud in Vietnamese in church. These are his basic steps:
(1) Type bible passage into Google Translate.
(2) Print out Vietnamese text from Google Translate.
(3) Ask mother (who speaks and writes in Vietnamese, but not English) to edit, smoothing over the inevitable Google Translate errors.
(4) Record mother reading the passage aloud, using smartphone.
(5) Listen to audio from smartphone during spare moments and repeat it until committed to memory.
(6) Recite memorized Vietnamese bible passage in church.

With this hack, Google Translate, impersonal and error-prone, combines with a syncretic blend of family tech expertise, multilingualism, and ingenuity to function as an intimate medium/method for language learning, forcing at least one teen to engage deeply on a multilingual task with his mother.

Hack #4 Give Up! The Language Educator Teachable Moment After talking about Google Translate hacks with my friends and colleagues, a couple of language teachers mentioned how, with every new semester, they have a discussion with their students about the problematic use of Google Translate as a homework aide. One of these expert instructors had found the perfect entertainment to drive this point home with her students: a Disney YouTube video put through the wringer of Google Translate.

In the video the artist has used Google Translate to convert the lyrics from Disney's *Frozen* hit song, "Let It Go" into a hilarious mess (www.youtube.com/watch?v=2bVAoVlFYf0). By translating to at least a dozen languages, and then back to English, she arrives at an entirely new and nonsensical lyric. At its peak, Elsa, the Disney character who has, at long last, unleashed her uniquely expressive gifts, belts out the song's inspirational chorus, *Let it go!* which has, via Google Translate contortions, been converted to this:

> Give up!
> Give up!
> You can not do it back in.
> Give up!
> Give up!
> Tune in and slam the door.

The distinction between *give up* and *let it go* comes through crystal clear for any English speaker watching this video. Rather than the call to self-actualization implied in the original *let it go!* lyric, *give up!* suggests Elsa might be ready to just stop trying. The instructor whom I spoke with used this entertaining hack to convince her students not to rely on Google Translate as their only source when working on their homework assignments or term papers. In addition to this highly practical pedagogical message, engaging with Google Translate in language classes can illustrate to language learners how subtle and contextually sensitive language is – how learning a new language is much more than translating words.

Because Google Translate is imperfect, much is lost in translation. But when we use Google Translate as citizen sociolinguists, in concert with multilingual acquaintances, friends, or family members, much more can be found. The medium itself, in all its creative permutations, becomes the method.

Language Pies

Repurposing old linguistic tools like dialect surveys, and newer tools like Google Translate, generates wonderment, that wonderment sparks more questions about language and, in turn, more discussions, and more questions, blossoming into cycles of citizen sociolinguistic inquiry. Creating personal "language pies" is another medium/method and language-question generator, used by one high school language arts teacher, Mr. Z, when faced with the question, "Who speaks the most perfect English?" Rather than attempting to answer this question, Mr. Z had his students produce "language pies." He's found the language pie tool generates critical discussions about language and can get students out in the world talking to others about their own language use.

When Mr. Z's 11th graders were first prompted to make their own language pie charts, in just a few minutes many had divided their pie up into seven or more sections, including different language for the following slices of social life:
- Friends
- Close friends
- Adults
- Parents
- Parents' friends
- Home
- Texting
- Babysitting
- With siblings
- With brothers
- With animals

- At work
- At school
- With teachers
- With sports coaches
- Just Dad
- Just Mom
- Nice friends
- Vulgar friends
- Girlfriend
- Professional situation
- Writing papers for school
- Writing sentimental texts
- When complaining
- When angry or snarky
- When giddy or happy
- When tired or depressed

Most students specified slices for "friends," "adults," "home," and "school," adding varying degrees of nuance. "With animals" was a pie slice only one student came up with at first – but after being reminded of special animal pet voices, many classmates agreed they would add this slice to their pie, too. Momentary moods were crucial to a few students – clearly different ways of speaking come out when tired or depressed, angry or giddy.

Nobody spontaneously mentioned anything about languages other than English. But when I asked about multiple languages in their lives, several students had more slices to add to their Language Diversity Pie:

- Mandarin with Mom (not Dad)
- Danish with Mom (not Dad)
- "Asian"-accented English with Mom, or when ordering dim sum in Chinatown
- Persian with parents
- Mix of Persian and English in general when at home

A ten-minute discussion revealed a profusion of ways of speaking, languages, and "accents" that fit into any one individual's pie.

These teens easily recognize the distinctive relevance of all the slices of their pie at different moments, or with different people, or to convey different moods. Even these young 16- and 17-year-olds, in Honors English, most of whom have spent their entire lives in one suburban community, have wide-ranging ways of speaking, and can recognize the distinctive utility of each.

As these wise 11th graders illustrate through this type of inquiry, there is no one most perfect way of speaking, and our language goals should lean toward developing awareness of the language diversity needed to navigate all the sections of our pies. Today's teens will need to use different kinds of language to do many things: babysit, snuggle with their cat, comfort a friend, talk to grandma, write poetry, apply for college. These needs will continuously grow and change as they move away from home, meet new people, travel the world, work in the community, be President. One unitary language pie called "Perfect Language" could never do all that, and as the language pies medium/method illustrates, most teens already know this.

Once students make their own language pies, they also have a new research tool that they can use as a medium/method for asking others about the different ways they use language throughout the day. They can go home, ask their parents, cousins, or peers in different social networks. In the process of asking questions about language, they'll develop even more questions, and along the way, increase the language awareness of everyone involved in the conversation.

Getting "Accurate" Answers

Once we start asking questions about language – those generated from everyday experiences with language, fomented by the spark of wonderment or the sting of arrest, carried forward through repurposed tools like language quizzes and hacks, or with new inquiry tools, like language pies, we will also start accumulating answers from those we talk to. What counts as "good" or even "accurate" in everyday conversations about language differs from what more formal linguistic researchers consider good data. We don't necessarily care, as citizen sociolinguists, whether someone's language pie factually represents their language use, whether the percentages of time they say they've spent in each slice are accurate, and whether the vocabulary they cite in that slice is used only in that context. Most importantly, language pies illuminate *the way people talk about language*. Students have noted after talking with their parents about language pies, for example, that many fathers claim they only have two halves of their language pie – Work and Home – while their mothers have many thin slices in their pie. What does this mean? We don't discount these fathers as unreliable – they've given us some great insight into how they talk about language, and probably sparked many more follow-up questions.

Any talk about language that happens is important when exploring the world as a citizen sociolinguist. Nothing people say about language should end up in our mental trash bin – we shouldn't discount the response of the father who seems to have oversimplified his language pie, nor should we discount the classmate who seems to be overrepresenting their own flexible multilingualism and expansive friendship network. Instead, we should think more carefully about what these different representations tell us about who is doing the talking and their world. A metaphor that illuminates this source of insight is the "outtake" genre.

Outtakes

Sociolinguistic Outtakes: Footnotes, Epilogues, Anecdotes, and Asides   Have you ever indulged in the viewing of a movie *outtake*? The DVD ends and scenes flash next to the credits, featuring the very same movie actors you just watched – but now they are breaking character. They swear or burp or burst into belly laughs when they are supposed to be exuding wisdom or dying or committing a felony. One outtake from *The Fellowship of the Ring*, for example, features Ian McKellen, who plays the wise wizard Gandalf. In the outtake, he's shown tripping over his flowy and dignified wizard robes, apologizing for his mortal awkwardness, "I'm sorry – cannot get up these goddamned steps smoothly!"

This genre, the movie outtake, has become so popular that high school students have started including them at the end of school project videos – showing the actors of a *Hamlet* scene, for example, in costume but breaking character after the taping, goofing around, grabbing a soda, or munching on chips in a suburban family kitchen. And even animated movies have outtakes, though obviously fabricated intentionally. *Toy Story* outtakes, for example, proliferate on the Web – as if the anthropomorphized toys are so real that, like human movie actors, they sometimes break character and burp or giggle at the wrong times.

Outtakes were once simple teasers to make people keep watching during the credits after the movie ended. Now they are specially produced and sought out on the Web for their own unique merits (one *Toy Story* compilation on YouTube has over six million hits). Why? What makes outtakes interesting to people? Outtakes show that actors – even computer-generated Pixar characters – have lives beyond the artifice of the movie set piece. They react to situations and interact with each other in a huge variety of ways, some of which may be familiar to us, others that may be idiosyncratic and new. Also, they make us feel like Hollywood insiders, like moviemaking isn't as elite and exclusive a process as we may have thought. Outtakes reveal the process. They also suggest the joy in it. Maybe making the movie was even more fun than watching it.

Now, how does this citizen enjoyment of movie outtakes relate to citizen sociolinguistic inquiry and the question of accuracy? Think of the "research article" in place of the "movie." The article, conference address, or book, like a Hollywood production, emerges from careful editing, the squeezing of countless interviews, observations, field notes, recordings, videos, into the professional medium of a journal article. As with moviemaking, quite a bit ends up on the cutting room floor. Language researchers seem to delight in resurrecting those bits that didn't fit their professional storytelling venture (or research methodology). Just as movie producers (and viewers) delight in replaying Ian McKellen swearing about his robes in *The Fellowship of the*

Ring, language researchers (and readers) relish the unexpected stories that emerge inevitably when doing research with our fellow humans.

It seems that the more rigidly traditional the research parameters, the more delightful the cutting room scraps. William Labov (2006 [1979]), for example, in a write-up of a study that focused on five phonological features and their stylistic variation across five domains of use in New York City, honors his readers with dozens of asides and footnotes that call attention to the personal idiosyncrasies of the humans involved. One subject, Steve K, for example draws these anecdotal descriptions from the staunchly quantitative researcher:

> He studied philosophy for four years at Brooklyn College, but left without graduating; he had turned away from the academic point of view, and as an intense student of Wilhelm Reich, sought self-fulfillment in awareness of himself as a sexual person. (2006 [1979], p. 79)

While Labov includes many of these descriptions of his subjects (and this one continues in a footnote), he concludes that they play no part in the focus of his research on stylistic variation. Yet these sorts of Steve K descriptions remain a hallmark and entertaining highlight of all his research.

Linguistic anthropologists, like sociolinguists, also indulge in the anecdote and the aside, without more directly accounting for it in their research analysis. I still recall clearly the story one of my anthropology professors relayed about a white (Caucasian) anthropologist working in a remote South Pacific island community. In a discrete epilogue to his book-length ethnography, he revealed that, during his entire time living as a participant–observer, conducting interviews, participating in local rituals and routines, the community thought he was a ghost. Only those diligent readers who found the epilogue would be able to read the ethnography with the insider knowledge of that researcher's unique position in the community.

More often, these behind-the-scenes secrets don't even reach the written record. In the spontaneous moment of an introduction or over wine at the post-talk reception, a researcher will spill something about a key informant who was always drunk, a research assistant who never returned from the field, or, on even more confessional occasions, the connection of their work to their own life. I recently heard a senior sociolinguist introduce his research talk (a quantitative, fine-grained analysis of language variation) with a story about his own experience as a graduate student with a stigmatized North Philadelphia accent. Long after he had finished his Ph.D. and had begun to emerge as a leader in the field, his mentor/professor confessed: From the way you sounded in class, I never thought you would really make it through.

These research outtakes reveal the artifice of the research project and even the research training process, throwing extra details, messy details, but often the most interesting ones, into the public's view. As Paul Kroskrity (2016) has pointed out, while these research asides often center on the conscious ideologies of those under study, they don't account for them as relevant to the language being studied. And yet, what were thought to be marginalia may be what drive the language we see and hear: Steve K's anecdotes about his own class-consciousness no doubt play into the kind of phonological variants the researcher, Labov, recorded him producing; The linguistic anthropologist who pretended to be a ghost probably gathered very unique data because of that positioning; The now-famous sociolinguist who admitted as a senior scholar to have himself been the speaker of a stigmatized variety was no doubt influenced to design his research studies and interpret them differently because of this personal history. And yet all of these features of the language being studied are treated as marginal to the research results.

These days, these sociolinguistic outtakes need not drift into obscurity or footnotes, or insider information learned during the post-talk reception. The structure of social media, the networked arrangement of the Internet, digital media that hyperlink footnotes and other information, all make asides nearly as easily accessible as the main research article. And those who are the objects of research in that article may be reading or listening to those asides. What if they joined the conversation? What if we focused on the outtakes? We would be engaging in citizen sociolinguistic research. Now with social media and hyperlinks to even the most obscure trivia, the institutionally sanctioned research question can easily fall into the background, and the footnote can become focal.

As the Cowgirl from *Toy Story* says in a blooper when she accidentally pulls off part of Buzz Lightyear, "Should we put this in the movie now?" That's the crucial question for citizen sociolinguistics and our own fascinating outtakes. Maybe we should put more of those sociolinguistic outtakes into the official research. We should talk to our subjects and hear their concerns. But should vitriolic spewing of trolls (like those comments on citizenship videos in Chapter 1) be included? Should Labov have included Steve K's pursuit of self-awareness more centrally in his analysis of Brooklyn language variety? Or should we let the trolls' thoughtless insults or the identity quests of our participants fall to the status of outtake, or even remain on the cutting room floor? Probably the best option, whenever possible, is to keep those voices intact and in view, and let the conversation continue. The questions emerging will inevitably be relevant to understanding language diversity, humor, and creativity, and the role they play in social life.

Looking Up Words by Looking Up Context

Every once in a while, I annoyingly can't remember the name of someone in my field and I need to contact them. So, instead of looking up their name (which I can't remember) I just look up their context. I can usually remember the university and department they work in, or the professional organization they are associated with, or the last conference panel I saw them on. A quick google search for any of those contexts, and I can instantly find that colleague and "remember" their name. The same process works for words too. The other day I asked my students to write down a word, any word, that's baffled them lately – many quickly wrote something down. But others took to their phones to find the conversation, Twitter thread, or Instagram post in which that word occurred – they couldn't bring the exact word to mind, but they could find the context in which it was used. The citizen sociolinguistic process of "looking up a context" runs counter to the traditional "look it up" routine – rather than going from context to the decontextualized dictionary definition, we search for the context that gave that word meaning in our world. Paradoxically, contexts like text message conversations, or social media threads, can function like a dictionary, being the "reference tool" we use to find a word and even to pinpoint its meaning.

On a recent morning I spent at a local high school talking with teens about language, this exact predicament came up. As is typical, after only 10 minutes of talking they had taught me – and each other – a few new words and a few new ways of exploring language. Then one word came up that we could neither name nor define. We were all just back from winter break, having made many new language discoveries during our travels or while hosting holiday visitors. Most of us hadn't traveled much farther than various remote corners of Philadelphia. Jack, however, had ventured south to visit family in Virginia Beach, where he noticed another 16-year-old using a word, which for now we will call *pow*. Jack couldn't remember the actual word, but he was using *pow* as a placeholder. He could sort of remember what the word did (which seemed to be just about everything), but not what the actual word was. As Jack explained, someone who is really amazing can be *pow* or something really bad can be *pow*. You can say things like, "Those shoes, man. Pow." This could mean that your shoes are very cool. Or horrible.

By now, the other boys listening were getting very distracted by the stand-in word *pow*. One of them kept making a slow-motion punching gesture. Another kept saying "Pow?" quizzically. Jack insisted the word was *not pow*. He was just using *pow* until he could remember the actual word. Jack promised he would find it, and this is when he began to look up the word by finding its context. He began searching through his phone, and after a minute or less he came up with the word: *Weg*!

How did he do that? The others were quick to point out that *weg* sounds nothing like *pow*. How do you find a word you do not remember and that means both awesome and lame? How do you look that up? You can't look in a dictionary: What would you look up? *Pow*? You can't do a Google search, though I suppose you could try asking a question like: "What word would a teenager in Virginia Beach use to say something is either great or awful?" You can't ask the professor sitting there. She has no idea, since the above Google search did not work when she tried it. So, how did Jack find the word *weg*? He went back to the context, using one of the crucial tools of the citizen sociolinguist: Social media! He looked up his Virginia Beach friend's Instagram and scanned the comments. *Weg!*

In this instance, the most accurate way to find both a word's meaning and the word itself was to use Instagram as a reference source. For this everyday conversation about language, no dictionary could have solved our query and nothing could more accurately pinpoint the meaning of the word *weg* than the Instagram image Jack had pulled up on his phone – an image which, unfortunately, is still a mystery to me.

Urban Dictionary as Context Provider

In the case of *weg*, Instagram was the context that provided the definition and the word. In other cases, when one at least has a word to start with, urbandictionary.com may take on that role of context provider. Despite its name, Urban Dictionary functions more like a social media context provider than an actual reference dictionary. In this role, however, it has become increasingly used as a source for all questions about language and context. Often, the words in question may not even really be considered words by many people (including publishers of standard dictionaries). Thus, the social media context of Urban Dictionary is not only a good source, but the only place to go.

Is That a Word? Urban Dictionary as a Site for Citizen Sociolinguistics

Urban Dictionary also gives us a new way of thinking about what words mean – and even what counts as a word. From a citizen sociolinguistics perspective, the best way to find out about word meaning is not to ask "Is that a word?" (which might pointlessly lead one to a traditional dictionary, which might not even contain that word), but to figure out how people use the item in question and what impression it makes. Here's where Urban Dictionary can be a handy first stop. Despite the word "dictionary" in its name, it hardly conforms to a dictionary's role of providing standardized definitions. Instead, like Instagram in the *weg* example, it provides a social context in which that word works.

Let's think this through by puzzling over an often-maligned English word, *irregardless*. Most of us probably have a sense of the meaning of this word. But the way people use it, and why they use it at all, still baffles. When discussing the word in a high school classroom, one of the students, Bert, offered up a popular anti-*irregardless* argument, to an audience of nodding heads:

BERT : I feel like people say "irregardless" to sound like they know what they are talking about. Go on Facebook arguments and you'll see it: "Irregardless" [said with funny pompous voice]. People use it to try to sound smart. "Irregardless" [pompous voice again]. They are trying to sound smart.

I almost agree with Bert on this one (*almost agree* – another pompous posturing device?) But if saying *irregardless* is so obviously just pompous posturing, why do people use it? Again, is there any context in which one might use this word without being criticized? The very first and most popular entry on Urban Dictionary for *irregardless* gives us some insight:

Used by people who ignorantly mean to say regardless. According to Webster, it is a word, but since the prefix "ir" and the suffix "less" both mean "not or with" they cancel each other out, so what you end up with is regard. When you use this to try to say you don't care about something, you end up saying that you do. Of course everyone knows what you mean to say and only a pompous, rude asshole will correct you. (2,790 thumbs ups, 917 thumbs down)

When I first read this definition, I assumed it was making the same point as Bert: People who say *irregardless* are being pompous in an ignorant way. But this "definition" is making quite a different point – in which Bert would be the pompous one! As the author of this definition points out, technically, people who say "irregardless" probably mean "regardless." However, his criticism is not of those people but the people who would call them out for it: If you are someone who says *irregardless*, "only a pompous, rude asshole will correct you." So, whether it is a word or not, whether it is right or wrong, from this author's point of view, one should let it slide.

This "definition" first struck me as strange. When I realized it was defending the *irregardless* speaker by insulting those who correct him, I had a moment of wonderment. I entered a more enlightened and humble perspective in which we don't need to worry about people who say *irregardless*. But I also got the sense that the author of this entry may have been reacting to an experience he had, a citizen sociolinguistic arrest perhaps, following his own use of the word *irregardless*. His entry may have been his own passive-aggressive response to that occasion. The slightly horrifying dialogue he provides to exemplify his definition further underlines that interpretation:

WIFE: Irregardless is not a word, dummy
HUSBAND: Kiss my ass bitch! I'm still going to the strip club tonight!

This example illuminates how, like other social media, Urban Dictionary is less of a provider of "definitions" than a social context. This swatch of dialogue is not really about "irregardless" and when to say it, but about the kind of response the word might get. The dialogue begins with the "wife" *referring* to the word *irregardless*, but we never see the instance of its actual use. By reading this "top definition," and all the definitions of *irregardless* below it, I learned much more about the impression I (or Bert) might give by using or correcting someone's use of *irregardless* than anything about the word itself: People who use *irregardless* look ignorant; People who call them out look like "pompous rude assholes."

Whether some spoken item like *irregardless* officially counts as a word is only the tip of the citizen sociolinguistic iceberg. As these contrasting views on *irregardless* illustrate, questions about conversations in which that word is used seem more critical:

- What type of impression do I make when I use this word?
- How should I respond to someone else using this word?
- What impression might my response give?

While Urban Dictionary may provide an inscrutably wide-ranging set of answers of variable quality, it makes a good a first stop on the citizen sociolinguistic exploration of a word's social value. This is not a case for accuracy in any standardized sense, but a case for citizen sociolinguistic data sharing, discussed below.

Sharing "Data"

Since citizen sociolinguistic inquiry proceeds through conversation and collaboration, sharing language data and being transparent about our modes of understanding and interpreting that language data are crucial. When someone tells me something about my language, they usefully illuminate the world I'm participating in with my words by showing how others might perceive me. But I would also like the opportunity to provide my own perspective to add to the picture they are painting. This process of sharing language "data" and perspectives on it forms the foundation of citizen sociolinguistics. But this commonplace practice of sharing and being public with our own language (talking to each other) contrasts with much of the traditional research ethics of academic researchers.

Keeping Language in a Locked Drawer (Not!)

As all university researchers working with language know, if you record language, you must keep it in a locked filing cabinet, or a password-protected web location. Our Institutional Review Boards will insist on this, but even as researchers lock up the drawer or type up a passcode for a website, people continue to talk. The voices we record for our research do not stop once we turn off the recording device. Speech – our own and others' – is all around us. However, there may be unethical things being done with those locked up speech samples. How do we protect those people from being interpreted in irrelevant or inaccurate ways by the professional researchers analyzing how they speak? If our samples are locked away in a drawer somewhere, we don't.

Fortunately, in real life, we don't need to hack into some password-protected site to hear our own language, to use it with others – or to analyze it. We don't even need to be professionally or academically affiliated in any way. Many people out there listening to and commenting on the freely available language samples we all experience every day, are expert language analysts in their own right. Their expertise may differ from that of a Ph.D. linguist, applied linguist, sociologist, or linguistic anthropologist – but those everyday *citizen sociolinguists* are not necessarily any more or less responsible in their interpretation of other people's speech than a trained academic researcher. Nor are those everyday analysts necessarily more or less tuned into their sense of ethical obligation toward speakers. Nobody – university researchers or everyday citizen sociolinguists – holds the ethical high ground when it comes to making statements about people's language. Nobody has a premium on dumb or misguided interpretations – or on the most definitive explanation. However, when we officially gather up and lock away some bits of language, we also place limits on the expression of everyday language expertise, because we only let a few people interpret those words and publish the results. Locked-up language isn't even available to the people who spoke it. As a result, the ability to comment and, if necessary, defend ourselves, becomes locked up along with people's language.

For this reason, an open source approach to language is most consistent with citizen sociolinguistic inquiry. If you are recording some language, be open. Tell your participants this is now public data – it's not locked up. If you have some opinions about language you've heard, share it! And certainly share it with the people who spoke it. But also share your analysis. Let ordinary speakers share theirs. Just as open source software improves when more coders are involved, inquiry into language and society will inevitably become more useful and relevant when it includes more perspectives. Any time we speak with each other, we publicly share our language – and the right for others to interpret it. And, in general, we tailor our speech accordingly, attending to how other people engage with our words.

Transcription: Eye Dialect

Because we open ourselves to public interpretation when we are in a conversation, we have many subtle ways of trying to manage the interpretation of our words. We change our tone of voice, use gestures, or shift our eye gaze, all in an effort to influence how others interpret our message, using what John Gumperz (1982 [1976]) calls "contextualiztion cues." The management of these subtle cues becomes more difficult in a medium like text messaging, where we can't hear someone's tone of voice or see their eye gaze or gestures. For that reason, when we transcribe our own speech into a text message, we have developed some special ways to guide others' interpretations of what we are saying. In this way, we are shaping how they use our "language data" as we share it freely.

If you have ever had to transcribe oral speech you know it can be a tedious process – listening to a recording and then typing out utterances word for word. Word. For. Word. But transcription is not as easy – nor necessarily as boring – as it sounds. It involves translating spoken language into written words and, like any other translation project, this requires some interpretation and finesse. For example, when a speaker says what sounds like "I'm gonna leave now," should that be written as "I'm going to leave now"? or "I'm gonna leave now"? If an adult English teacher says this, would you be more likely to write "going to"? If a 16-year old in the class says it, would you be more likely to write "gonna"? How do age, race, gender, socioeconomic status, institutional role, and any other aspect of the situation figure into that interpretation?

The sociolinguist Mary Bucholtz, in her article "The Politics of Transcription," (2000) has pointed out that even established researchers often make transcription decisions in ways that indicate underlying biases. When someone uses a certain spelling for one demographic or social role and a different spelling for another, Bucholtz calls this "eye dialect." So, the tedious act of transcription becomes political, and the stakes can be high: A courtroom transcript, for example, that represents a defendant's speech in a stigmatized eye dialect could leave a record that unfairly influences a jury's perception of that individual. Bucholtz urges transcribers to be mindful of the choices they make when they transcribe – accounting for how their representations create identities for speakers.

When discussing "The Politics of Transcription" in my graduate class on classroom discourse analysis one day, one of the students pointed out that many individuals – especially teens these days – use something like "eye dialect" to purposefully add nuance to their text messages, Facebook and Instagram posts, Snapchat stories, or any social media that mimic face-to-face conversation. In these kinds of self-transcriptions, people usually call on eye dialect to deliberately construct identities for themselves. In this way, they are creating *citizen transcriptions* of themselves, calling on their own knowledge of local social value connected to transcribed forms of talk. Citizen self-transcribers crafting a text message, just like reflective researchers transcribing language "data," can be painstakingly mindful of the identity they present when they translate a speech-like message into a social media message. Here is an example of my own speaking-to-my-son self, self-transcribed in eye dialect:

> Okay. ☺ . See you later tonight! Text me if you are going to be late! Pleez!! ♡ 👵

Figure 3.2 *Pleez* as an example of eye dialect

This message, I hope, captures my kind yet concerned loving self. The spelling of "Pleez" conveys my sheepishly earnest need for my teenage son to keep me in the late-night loop.

Probably the best guard against bias among social scientists or courtroom transcribers is to treat all speaking the same way and be as uniform as possible. But when we everyday individuals transcribe our own voices into text messages, we participate in an unstandardized, yet high-stakes world of eye dialect. My own emoji smiley-face, heart, and old-lady face probably also convey some stereotype of middle-aged white lady dialect. But that's okay. That's who I am. And, I'm the one who transcribed it.

These comments on Sean Monahan's YouTube video about "Phillytawk" illustrate participants crafting a more exaggerated version of eye dialect for their own speech (my own standardized versions provided in square brackets):

LUVJOISEY [LOVEJERSEY]: Ahm frum Roxbro. You soun like yur frum over by da riber. Maybe Fishtun? In Philly evry naborhood's got their own dilect.

[I'm from Roxborough. You sound like you're from over by the river. Maybe Fishtown? In Philly every neighborhood's got their own dialect.]

JOSHUA GOODMAN: I'm from Sou' Jerzy an I like my spageddy cooked owl denny

[I'm from South Jersey and I like my spaghetti cooked al dente]

Those same features of transcription that can seem to unfairly bias social science research or stigmatize a defendant in the courtroom become powerful communicative resources for the citizen self-transcriber, and tools for humor and irony. The citizen self-transcriber might have a more sophisticated command of bias than your average social science researcher – because they know that there is not a "correct" way of doing it, only better and worse ways of communicating one's identity in each unique socially mediated context. And of course, the cases above may not be cases of "self-transcription" but the representation of stereotyped voices they have decided to perform in this context. Even so, representing voices in this form of eye dialect opens up the forum for debate over those voices.

While we needn't keep data in a locked drawer, we do need to learn how to interpret the messages people are making publicly, and to be mindful of how we interpret and present interpretations of public language data. By recognizing these forms of transcription as publicly available interpretations, rather than objective representations, we build important awareness of language and its contextual effects.

Dissemination across Social Borders

Questions of data-sharing overlap with concern for how and with whom we share findings and interpretations of that data. In the research community, every grant-funded research project requires a dissemination plan. Usually this refers to how any research findings will be communicated to the broader research community. And, since research subjects are not usually part of this research community, what happens in the research community usually stays in the research community. While publishing papers in peer-reviewed research journals is the gold standard for most research institutions, the readership of those journals is unlikely to include any of the research subjects. The research article or report remains a relatively restricted genre. Research is usually designed and conducted with the assumption that subjects will never read about the findings, and many researchers would like to keep it that way – the research should be disseminated, just not to the subjects of the study. Why? For many researchers, one of the lingering worries is that they might be confronted by their research subjects. If research subjects end up reading about themselves in published articles, for example, if those findings are also circulated in the popular press, there can be friction, shame, embarrassment, and even legal trouble. The veneer of research ethics might be chipped off when boundaries between the researcher and the researched are breached.

Citizen sociolinguistics potentially opens up these boundaries, because citizen sociolinguists, as they are talking about language and sharing their views, never remove themselves from the community being researched. They comprise that community. But even within a "community" we inhabit different contexts, participate in multiple situations with different participation expectations. Speaking flexibly across social boundaries, contexts, and situations is not only a problem between researchers and their subjects, but a perennial problem for human beings living among each other. Those boundaries reveal themselves more vividly now that we are communicating more and more via social media, and when we use those media both as methods of everyday inquiry as well as a medium to share our findings. One way knowledge about language can be communicated (and mis-communicated) across social boundaries is by "crossposting" any findings. Increasingly, even research centers have communication plans that focus on this type of cross-posting to different communities. But this practice also has its hazards.

Cross-Posting – Dumb or Delightful?

Cross-posting, literally, is the practice of posting the same message on two or more of your social media accounts. For a while, this was happening to me by accident. My Twitter account was linked to my Facebook account and it was dumb – and delightful at the same time. Dumb, because suddenly all my more geeky language tweets focused on an audience of students and colleagues were now posted to my family and friends from across the myriad phases of my life. But also delightful, because suddenly my friends from high school started tagging me on language-related posts on Facebook, sending me breaking news about the Word of the Year, or drawing on my presumed expertise ("What is dabbin'?").

Eventually, I figured out how to unlink the two, and unlinked them, probably saving the majority of my Facebook friends from a lot of annoying (to them) posts. But the value of cross-posting came through to me. Not only did I discover Facebook friends who cared about language like I did – I also became more careful about the kinds of language posts I was making on Twitter. Would my mother be offended by this? As long as I was cross-posting to Facebook and Twitter, that question always had to be in the back of my mind.

But cross-posting also raises important questions about the way we talk about language and social boundaries more generally. Cross-posting – and its ramifications – as a metaphor for the dissemination of language expertise seems worth considering. What happens when you "cross-post" to the various social groups you are part of? Being completely oblivious of the participants and audience in each of these groups seems socially naïve – at best. And, this seems to be what happened at Yale in October 2015, when the professor Erika Christakis notoriously posted, to a campus-wide email listserv, the comment that Halloween is a chance to be a little bit "obnoxious," countering the campus-wide email suggesting students be sensitive about Halloween costumes (and, for example, avoid blackface). Bringing up the value of obnoxious Halloween costumes might be a nice debate on one of Professor Christakis' more intimate social media platforms – say dinner with like-minded colleagues, or a small group-chat among friends – but, as it turns out, it may be a dumb thing to cross-post to the entire Yale student body.

These days, social media may be making a younger generation more aware than their elders about the ramifications of cross-posting in real life. People who use Facebook, Twitter, Instagram, Snapchat, etc., tend to mindfully tailor their messages to whomever they imagine is listening/reading/overhearing on one of those apps. High school students I work with, for example, know a lot about mindfully cross-posting. We have had them represent the various sectors of their lives as pie charts (discussed above) and talk about the language they use differently in each of those sections. Many students list a dozen or more sections in their pie, making fine-grained distinctions, for example, between language used with one's own parents, other adults, and one's girlfriend's parents. They include "slang" in some sections and not in others. Sometimes they include languages in certain sections, including separate spots for "Chinese," "Chinglish," and "English." They seem intuitively aware that certain ways of speaking work well in some slices of their daily language pie, but that it would be very dumb to speak that way in others.

This does not mean students don't engage in some forms of delightful "cross-posting." These same students have also mentioned that, sometimes, the most fun people are the ones who don't keep their language rigidly aligned with a certain slice of their language pie – mixing slang with formality, French with English, or purposely mispronouncing certain words. Still, students also admit, part of the joy of this language cross-posting is the inherent risk involved. The danger of overstepping remains – cross-posting might be dumb or delightful. Cross-posting might be offensive and even incite mass protest (as in the unfortunate case at Yale). In either case, cross-posting reveals the borders we cross repeatedly in our everyday lives. When we start crossing those borders, we are taking risks. But in many cases, it may be worth it, especially when the subject of our cross-posting is talk about language and communication, and the result is more communication and talk about how to use language creatively and productively together.

Laugh Tracks

Laugh tracks, like cross-posting, also illuminate the boundaries between groups who might react differently – but to supposed jokes or situational humor. Those recordings of canned laughter, which at one time predictably accompanied all TV comedies, are supposed to cue an audience response, anointing certain comments, actions, or dialogue as funny. The laugh track itself is a commentary on language. It says: It's good to laugh now.

Laugh tracks also suggest we are similar. We are all part of an audience that laughs at the exact same things. One reason laugh tracks were originally created was to provide that feeling of shared laughter – the pleasure you get in a movie theater or at a live performance, when the entire audience is laughing together. But usually in life we don't have laugh tracks to cue that laughter. And, increasingly, we don't have that shared background with those in the theater, or even in our living room. As audiences become more diverse, who laughs (at what and why) becomes more divided. Just as we need to think twice about sending an email message to a campus-wide list-serv, we need to be aware of how humor works differently for different people.

This division within audiences becomes especially apparent when comedy lampoons different ways of speaking. A lot of humor depends on stereotyped portraits of speech-types. These depictions can be hilarious at times, offensive at others – and often simultaneously so to different groups of people. So, creating one unified laugh track would be impossible. But why can't we all laugh together? Sometimes, we don't all get it. For example, during a graduate seminar recently, a student pulled up a YouTube video depiction of Asian-accented Englishes (including Japanese, Korean, Chinese, Cantonese, Thai, Filipino, and Indonesian). On watching this video with others in the class, half of us – those from China and Singapore – laughed heartily. The other half – those of us from the United States – just sat there, fascinated and puzzled. Not laughing. We weren't trying to be tasteful or polite, expressing our offense at the crass depictions of stereotypes across East and Southeast Asia. We didn't even know enough to make such judgments. We just didn't get it.

In other cases, everyone "gets it" but in a slightly different way. Then laughing together may be possible – but complicated. Many comics build their routines through self-mocking depictions of their own (or their parents' and grandparents') ways of speaking English. When humor depends on this kind of linguistic self-mockery, laughing "with" someone might border on laughing at them, or at an entire imagined group. Russell Peters, for example, has a popular routine that involves imitating his dad, who moved to Canada from India, through easily recognizable stereotypes of Indian English: (www.youtube.com/watch?v=4BWUFpzPYRc). And in her comic routines, Margaret Cho mocks her mother's Asian accent at length (www.youtube.com/watch?v=gevWOlEI5cc).

In each of these live performances, the audience laughs with gusto. They laugh heartily at Peters' imitation of the many different ways his father says "Come!" in stylized Indian intonation, his eyes growing wide, and his head bobbing from side to side. Similarly, Cho's audience enjoys her depictions of stereotyped guttural, r-less Asian speech. The YouTube comments immediately savor Cho's portrait of her mother's accent, attempting to replicate her accent in their direct quotes:

FOSSILMUSICTV : dis is da best mothas day. eva.
FERD617: ... Oh, dere was one mudder day dat was a little bit bettuh.

This savoring of stereotyped accent, gestures, and demeanor can also be troublesome. As the sociolinguist Elaine Chun (2004) points out, sometimes Margaret Cho's depictions of Asians are such stark caricatures it seems okay for Asians and Asian Americans to laugh along but disconcerting when white people join in. She writes of Cho's performance at a show in Austin, Texas, where more than half the audience appeared to be "non-Asians":

I had feelings of both pleasure and discomfort when hearing peals of laughter from non-Asians who seemed to profoundly enjoy her caricatures of Asians and Asian speech. (2004, p. 278 n. 17)

For Chun, Asians' enjoyment of Cho's stereotyped versions of Asian speech seemed more straightforward then "out-group" laughter. Cho's TV show *American Girl*, was canceled after one season, in 1995.

But Asian accents are increasingly surfacing as mainstream TV material. *Fresh Off the Boat,* a comedy about an Asian American family, premiered to mixed reviews. Many critiqued the stereotypes and, specifically, the stereotyped language used in the show. Angela Tom wrote in the *Huffington Post*:

Eddie's mother played by American actress Constance Wu must fake a Chinese accent throughout the show. It hurt my ears even more when I heard Wu speaking in her normal, unbroken, smooth-as-silk English during a TV interview. (Tom, 2014)

Other reviewers appreciate the negotiation between ways of speaking depicted in the show. Wu's accent is not necessarily "fake," but a performance. Like Tom, Shalini Shankar points out that the parents in the show perform stereotyped "Chinese" accents. But she also stresses the importance of getting these performances out there:

As we get to know these more well-rounded accented English speakers as people, hopefully it will make it harder to see them as one-dimension punch-lines. (Shankar, 2015)

And this critic's list of "8 Reasons to Catch *Fresh Off the Boat*" (www.8asians.com/2015/02/04/8-reasons-to-catch-the-fresh-off-the-boat-premiere-tonight/) includes this observation:

Fresh Off the Boat *is blessedly absent a laugh track.* (Dwyer, 2015)

Language variety and stereotypes of talk seem to be fodder for humor. But the humor may appeal in different ways to different audiences, in ways the universal presuppositions of a laugh track could never capture. At least leaving the laugh track absent from shows like *Fresh Off the Boat* means the audience can figure it out for themselves – and with each other. These depictions of language are giving different types of people an opportunity to listen to and think about language together – and to witness each other laughing at different moments, and to wonder about the reasons for those differences.

Validity as Participation

Ideally, citizen sociolinguistic inquiry – everyday conversations about language, about how we use it across social media platforms, about the perils of cross-posting or composing and interpreting a text message – expands our understanding of language and society, making it possible to communicate better with each other and to flexibly traverse the various slices of our language pie. Findings of our citizen sociolinguistic inquiry emerge from and feed directly back into our interactions with others – those we are already conversing with about language. The validity test for citizen sociolinguistic research happens the moment we try out our newly found language awareness by participating in another conversation about language. In this sense, for citizen sociolinguistics, validity is participation. Research participants and researchers are one and the same.

In traditional social science and sociolinguistic study, unlike citizen sociolinguistics, research participants and those conducting the study remain distinct from one another. When research subjects talk to a researcher about their language and their lives, and the researcher reports on those conversations, both usually proceed with the tacit assumption that the researcher with degrees and research assistants will be using their language data to inform an important, if inscrutable, mission for the greater good. But, that delicate veneer of expertise begins to crack when research relationships change. In some cases, for example, an "interviewee" and "research subject" may even begin to consider themselves as a "friend" or "research collaborator." The people we are working with are no longer objects of study, but participants in language inquiry. And we as researchers may then start to feel more engaged with those participants than with the research mission that sparked our initial interview. In traditional research, these changing relationships can call into question the meaning of an entire research program. A paradox emerges: On the one hand, this newfound closeness and trust with our subjects is crucial to developing new understandings. On the other, if our goal is to communicate these findings to the research community, to publish, to succeed in that community, we can be seen to be using our subject "friends" as career fodder. The project breaks down, ethically and existentially: Who are we, as researchers, to presume we have the exclusive expertise to speak for our subjects? For whom are we really speaking?

In 2014, Alice Goffman published an ethnography, *On the Run* (2014), chronicling the lives of African Americans in Philadelphia, and the controversy that followed its publication foregrounded precisely these questions. For years, she had lived with the subjects of her book. In many respects she was their friend. But they were also her "data." When her book began to receive mainstream attention – massive success! – many people took issue with the way she, as a white, upper-middle-class sociologist (daughter of the world-famous sociologist, Erving Goffman) chose to speak for African Americans in

Philadelphia. While her own mission with the book was to make real the struggles and injustice faced by African Americans in the city, another important, possibly more powerful story emerged from the dialogue that followed the book's publication and initial popularity: the story of the unexpected impact research can have when the wall between researcher and subjects breaks down, when the private lives of those subjects and their interactions with the researcher become public.

If *On the Run* had languished in academic obscurity like most research publications, Alice Goffman might be still flying under the radar, pursuing a happy career as a sociologist in Wisconsin. But the publicity around the book unleashed trouble for her both in the world of her participants and in the academic world into which she was launching a career. Her attempt to bridge these worlds ended up saddling her with the trials of both: Legal issues for Goffman ensued when she began to be associated with the crimes of her participants – those she described in detail in her book. Some suggested she had committed a felony by driving one of her participants around the city on a revenge manhunt. In the world outside of her participants, she instead referred to this event as a ritual of mourning. Among the academic community, different accusations accumulated about her entitled sense of privilege, her ability as a white woman to mine the lives of others for her own professional stature. In the years since the publication of this book, accusations have died down, but the complexity of representing the practices and language of another community as an *expert outsider* remains. A *New York Times Magazine* article on the controversy elegantly detailed this dilemma, framing it as a controversy over "who gets to speak for whom" (Lewis-Kraus, 2016).

The controversial relationship between Alice Goffman and her research subjects, between their community, the media, and academia, illustrates a tension endemic to social science research, and one that the citizen sociolinguistic medium/method attempts to transcend. It should be clear now, that when we consider *How we talk about language* as itself a form of inquiry, the paradoxical relationship between researcher and researched disappears. And, as the barriers between the world of academia and everywhere else become more permeable – as university lectures are posted on YouTube, as Twitter circulates posters about academic talks, as neighborhood Facebook groups contain both everyday sociolinguistic subjects and the graduate students and professors studying them – even traditional research will become more like citizen sociolinguistics. Researchers will begin to be participants in the community, as much as community members are participants in our research. Certainly, new controversies will arise (and we will see explicitly what such controversy looks like in Chapter 4), but the forms of expertise contributing to those controversies will inevitably be more varied and the discussion will be more inclusive.

A Guide for Getting Started

Readers are now stocked with wonderment about language, apprehension about arrest, and, I hope, many ideas for how to investigate those curiosities across communities of speakers. The guide below provides a set of steps to get started along a path of citizen sociolinguistic inquiry. Or, if you are a teacher, a loose set of guidelines that can guide you as you facilitate your students' growing language awareness.

A Guide for Exploring How We Talk about Language

1 **FORMULATE A QUESTION.** Write down one question about language that has piqued your curiosity (any language or consider an emoji or meme).
  (a) a word, phrase or even an emoji ("gas," "citizen," "feminism," "hygge," "sipping tea," ghost emoji, or other emoji)
  (b) a grammar point ("double negatives," "singular 'they,'" "graduate high-school")
  (c) pronunciation (*orange* versus *AREange, tooooer*-guide versus *tore*-guide, the pronunciation of *Wim Wenders*, the *Goethe Institute* or *Croissant*)
  (d) a way of speaking (speaking Chinese in the lounge, certain types of greetings or apologies, teacherese, stylized foreign languages, etc.)

2 **GATHER DATA.** Instead of looking for the ONE right answer, look for the huge range of answers out there. Talk to people, look online, in the media, listen, and ask questions. Inevitably, one of those answers will be from an institutional, standardizing authority – a dictionary, or a research paper, for example. But gather all the other perspectives too, even if they are sarcastic or irreverent. ***REMEMBER: We don't need standardizing authorities to think! They could even INHIBIT our thinking! They are but one perspective among many! Take in everything you hear and see!***
  (a) How have you experienced this language in context?
  (b) How have others? (Discuss it with a friend, professor, family member.)
  (c) Online dictionaries?
  (d) Urban Dictionary?
  (e) Blog posts?
  (f) Twitter?

: Cont

3. **ANALYZE/INTERPRET.** Think about all the views on language you've encountered and try to make sense of why they all exist and how they are related to each other.
   (a) What are the different views?
   (b) How are they distinct from each other?
   (c) How are they similar?
   (d) Why are there so many different answers?
   (e) What points of view do they represent?
   (f) What have you learned from this investigation that goes beyond the textbook, the dictionary definition, or the academic explanation?
4. **DISSEMINATE** and **FOSTER MORE DELIBERATION.** How would you like to present this new knowledge? *REMEMBER: We don't need standardizing authorities to tell us what is interesting or who our audience is! Talk about what is interesting to you and to those you want to have a conversation with!
   (a) Conversation
   (b) Web site
   (c) Social media: YouTube, Twitter, Facebook, Instagram, Weibo, etc.
   (d) Blog post or podcast

Gas and Gains Podcast

Here is example of this process in podcast form: https://podcasts.apple.com/us/podcast/gas-and-gains/id1470682949?i=1000444023454.

4   Fomenting Wonderment and Critique
Feedback Loops

Anyone who has ever been a teacher can probably recall a semester when a small number of students were always at the ready with a comment or response regarding anything under discussion. And, of course, as a teacher, it is nice to be able to count on those students who always seem to understand where our lesson is heading – and to push it there in exciting ways. In turn, these students may develop a sense that they are part of the "smart" group. The ones who know what's going on, who have, if not always the "right" answers, always the smartest questions. There may be plenty of other smart kids in the room, but these big talkers will be seen as the smartest ones. Their answers train the conversation to their interests, and as the teacher responds to the perspectives these students are voicing, these students have little trouble following the conversation because it's about them, and they respond again. Often, this can also be pretty exciting for those included – once the conversation gets rolling, as students and teacher get involved in their ideas, in expanding those ideas, they may stop noticing that nobody else is participating. Their "smarts" become real in that class through a positive self-reinforcing feedback loop.

In many ways, this is a wonderful feedback loop – probably one most readers of this book enjoy being part of. But this conversational feedback loop may also have negative consequences, driving other ideas underground, out of view. In classrooms, particularly democratic, Deweyan classrooms, in which, ideally, we probe underlying assumptions behind differences of opinion as discussed in Chapter 1, positive feedback loops that build only one line of argumentation can be problematic. As teachers, even as we are enjoying our back-and-forth with the vociferous minority in our classroom, we no doubt have a niggling sense that our obvious engagement with a minority of students may negatively affect more inclusive class participation for the rest of the discussion and possibly the entire semester. Even the most positive feedback loops can lead to the engagement of a minority, and the silencing of many others. The views of those "smart" kids will have become well-known to everyone in the class, while many other smart ideas may have gone unspoken.

The function of feedback loops is particularly pertinent to internet-circulated social media, where "comments are content" and language phenomena (or any ideas for that matter) can become important simply because they become widely circulated. What counts as smart or insightful or correct can be produced through those feedback loops. The "best answer" moves to the top of Yahoo Answers, the "top definition" is the first seen in Urban Dictionary, and the most-viewed hits for "proper pronunciation of succinct" move to the top of a google search. All the other answers drift further down your screen. As discussed in Chapter 3, people also create the corpus of language that feeds into the algorithms, like the one powering the Google Translate tool. If more people in the corpus are referring to math teachers as men and to cooking teachers as women, Google Translate will reflect that. And when the translate algorithm reflects that, more people might understand those professions as specifically gendered, and these stereotypes will feed into the Google Translate algorithm, which again reproduces those gendered norms. And so on.

To understand how we talk about language and the effects it can have, we need to understand how these feedback loops produce ideas about how language works in context, what makes certain ways of speaking valued, stigmatized, criticized, or coveted. This chapter illustrates what such investigation might look like by investigating both the positive and negative effects of feedback loops on how we talk about language and how we function as citizens. We'll look at how feedback loops have the potential to both create a reality through the sense of shared identity and positive affiliation they can create, and also put up barriers that keep people isolated from others' ideas. Then, we'll look closely at one case at Duke University in which citizen sociolinguists were able to disrupt entrenched social norms by breaking down those feedback loops and exposing different assumptions behind the way we use language.

Positive Effects of Feedback Loops: Fomenting Wonderment

When excited about their own language, citizen sociolinguists tend to fortify and elaborate one another's linguistic descriptions, creating cocoon-like happy places where people can use language with pride and creativity that draws on hyper-locality or internet-fostered affinity. The tendency to jump in and agree not only occurs online, but is a feature of everyday life and a staple of any interaction in classrooms.

Retweet! and Other I-Agree-with-You Signals

Teachers and their feedback are a defining feature of classroom interaction, but they are not the only providers of positive feedback. Students generally pay as much or more attention to the kinds of impressions they are making on their peers, and as any teacher knows, a response from peers can wildly change the direction of any classroom interaction. Recently, listening in on a heated high school discussion, I heard someone shout out "Retweet" from across the room. I wasn't sure what was going on. Was our conversation being tweeted about? Later, in another class, while gathering lists of words (using pencil and paper) for our semester-by-semester "slang" tracking, the word "retweet" appeared on someone's list. I had to ask, "Do people actually say that? Even when they're not on Twitter?" Sure. It means "I agree with you," or "I feel the same way," or "I TOTALLY AGREE!" Some teenagers say "retweet!" out loud – in the same place other people might say, "thumbs up!" "here-here!" "right on!" or "I concur."

Why so many expressions for "I agree"? And why do we keep coming up with new ones? We seem to have a species-wide love of agreement in whatever form it takes. Even as countless ways to talk about being "wasted/lit/turnt/smashed" etc. proliferate among teenagers, so do ways of expressing how much they agree (retweet!). Look around you and you will see all kinds of evidence that people like to agree. Many of these, just like many other new words, may seem boring and sheep-like (virtual thumbs ups, likes, exaggerated Instagram compliments, proliferations of exclamation points!!!) But others tip toward the profound, or at least show that how we agree may be a powerful glue holding us together.

Call and Response, for example, is one of the most enduring and primordial forms of "retweet!" Listen to all the buzzing agreement, for example, during Martin Luther King's *I Have a Dream* speech. Enthusiastic agreement happens when reading too. Look through a book that someone has read and appreciated. Underlining! Highlighting! Post-it notes! I happily notice when students show up with heavily annotated, bookmarked books in class. So many post-it notes point to serious engagement with a piece of writing – and a need to express it and share it. Inevitably, certain underlined post-it noted sections will find their way back into the class discussion, a term paper, or even a published article.

I often feel a need to underline not only scholarly books and articles, but also non-academic books, and sometimes even fiction and poetry – simply agreeing with what someone else has said and the precise way they worded it. Often those underlined gems end up in new feedback loops when they are included in an article or a book like this. Consider this one, for example, from Gloria Steinem's autobiography:

> ... ordinary people are smart, smart people are ordinary, decisions are best made by the people affected by them. (2015, p. 39)

Thanks for saying that, Gloria Steinem! It's an idea that forms the foundation of this volume.

But when there is a buzz of agreement in a class, it can also be difficult to intercede with a more nuanced opinion, or even an added angle on agreement. If not included from its inception, it may be hard to stay engaged in an all-out agreement-fest. To ensure that discussion remains inclusive, some teachers use silent hand signs, "talk moves," to signal agreement and understanding (Chapin, O'Connor, and Anderson, 2013). At a Teaching Channel website discussing "talk moves" (www.teachingchannel.org/video/student-participation-strategy), one teacher illustrates her strategy to include ordinarily quiet children by teaching her students "I agree" hand signs to use during group discussions. By holding up a closed hand, with only the thumb and pinky outstretched, even quiet kids can stay involved by signaling their agreement (or not) with whoever has the floor.

Comments on this video on the Teaching Channel also enthusiastically agreed that the "I agree" sign improves classroom discussions:
- Excellent, positive participation! (1 found this helpful)
- I like the positive quality of the interaction. It promotes positive thinking and gives permission to take risks (1 found this helpful)
- That's a smart way to give terms and body language to different ways that allow the kids to speak appropriately in groups! I give this an A+ (1 found this helpful)
- I have watched your Talk Moves video more than once. Each viewing has made me think more deeply about the whole group conversations in my own classroom. Your silent signal for "I am thinking like you" has such a positive impact on student engagement. I began doing it myself, just to try out the strategy. My students picked up on it and KABOOM! We had deeper dialogue, without necessarily having to speak out loud. Your encouragement for students, to rethink based on new information, is a mantra that I routinely recite. It, too, is powerful for positive classroom culture. Thank you. (2 found this helpful).

Piling on the positive feedback, readers of these comments that agree with them add on their own "I found this helpful" positive feedback. These comments in turn create an enthusiastic positive feedback loop, changing what teachers do in classrooms as a result. Many of the teacher comments responding to this video mention, "I'm going to implement this on Monday!"

As the "talk moves" teacher explains, finding ways to express agreement, even silently, is a way to "encourage discourse in the classroom." Agreement signals involvement. Humans thrive and grow through interaction, and teachers especially may even have a primordial urge to react to what other people are saying just to keep the talk going! Often, the easiest way to do so is to agree. But we also want to keep it real and display our unique identities. The "I agree" hand sign, obviously, can only take us so far. Finding ways to display affinity through agreement in more unique ways multiplies exponentially in everyday conversations about language on the Internet.

Language Wonderment Feedback Loops: Konglish, Welsh, Phillytawk

The "I agree" hand sign appeals to classroom teachers because it fosters student engagement with the teacher's curricular goals. Outside the classroom, we don't have regimented hand signals to register our thinking and positively align with views being expressed. But we do have different "I agree" signals that validate different forms of knowledge and expertise. The Internet provides its own version of this hand signal in the form of literal retweets, thumbs up, likes, and comments, and these provide a way to provide support to even the most marginal of views – and through positive feedback loops, to make those views more visible.

When it comes to talking about language, the Internet also provides a place to display one's more idiosyncratic self, or a persona that thrives outside the norm. Those citizen sociolinguist personalities mentioned in Chapter 2, for example, build visibility for ways of speaking by putting their language style on full display, opening themselves up for feedback – and for building, ideally, positive feedback loops validating their perspective on language. To illustrate, let's briefly walk through three of these prototypical citizen sociolinguistic postings and get a sense of the positivity that grows within the conversations around language sparked by each of those videos. Each of these videos varies in its popularity, and none of them come near the popularity of what Google identifies as the most famous viral YouTube video of all time, Charlie Bit My Finger, which has received over 869 million views and nearly 2 million thumbs up. However, all of them exceed Charlie Bit My Finger in the overall "thumbs up" ratio calculated by dividing likes by dislikes. And, most notably, each of these citizen sociolinguistic videos has an active comment section, whereas the comments for Charlie Bit My Finger have been disabled (see Table 4.1). Let's discuss the feedback loops for each in turn.

Kelly and Konglish As discussed in Chapter 2, Kelly introduces her Accent Challenge video with a series of hedges about her unique way of speaking – and yet she boldly performs the accent challenge in two different ways. As of this writing, her video has received 202,867 views, 1,400 likes, and 127 dislikes. Her like ratio of 10.2 far exceeds the baseline set by Charlie Bit My Finger (7.6). And, the quality of the comments illustrate the positive way that viewers are engaging with her English and Konglish Accent Tag. The first ten comments, those that rise to the top through positive feedback accumulation, are as follows:

Table 4.1 Feedback for language self-portraits (baseline: Charlie Bit My Finger)

Video	Views	Likes	Dislikes	Like ratio (likes/dislikes)	Comments	Involvement ratio (comments per view)
Accent Tag: English + Konglish (Korean + English) www.youtube.com/watch?v=GWOVL2bUKMI	202,867	1.4 K	137	10.2	527	.0026
The South Philly Accent Challenge www.youtube.com/watch?v=TXt1flZJHtk	8,378	43	5	8.6	27	.0032
Common Welsh Sayings www.youtube.com/watch?v=XcHMD0_DVe0	376,396	4 K	218	18.3	1,654	.0044
Baseline: most popular viral YouTube video of all time, Charlie Bit my Finger – Again! www.youtube.com/watch?time_continue=1&v=_OBlgSz8sSM	869,742,279	1.9 M	249 K	7.6	COMMENTS DISABLED	

- I've lived in Korea for the last 5 years, and find it very interesting that you can switch between English and Konglishee so effortlessly. I understand that you spent some time here in your formative years, but doesn't the Konglish bother you, especially since you know the correct English (spelling AND pronunciation)? Or, is it like how you talk one way with your parents and another way with your friends. I guess the reason I ask is that usually when I meet a Korean who speaks English very naturally, they usually don't resort to Konglish, but maybe that's just when they are speaking English to other English speakers . . . Really would be interested to hear your thoughts on this. (14 thumbs up)
- I have no idea what you are talking about your english to me sounds like normal english I dont think you say words funny or weird or different. And as for the Korean accent is concerned I dont think its an accent its just how native Korean and many native Asian non english speakers sound like when they try to speak english because lots of the english pronunciations are not the same in the Korean language. I just really dont understand the point of this video. And of course you being a native english speaker living in Korea I am quite sure they were intimidated/jealous that you can speak perfect English (6 thumbs up)
- That "Konglish" xD . . . it sounds very cute. (6 thumbs up)
- . . . Kourtney Kardashian?! (4 thumbs up)
- That's surely what Koreans pronounce English!! I guarante it. (3 thumbs up)
- I like accents in general! You should be proud of yours it's so pretty and unique! ;) (3 thumbs up)
- i dont think you from korea right ? konglish defo not like that, you dont looks like korea too (1 thumb up)
- Well, I came across this video because I'm just curious how a half english/half korean accent might sound (I'm writing a story with a character who is fluent in both and is a performer, so is in situations where he speaks both and more). So this turned out to be helpful~ thank you~~ BUT, I would also like to add, this video was also very interesting while being helpful for my personal needs. Thank you for the video, it was entertaining, interesting, and informative ^w^ (2 thumbs up)
- I can explain why Korean say like that*konglish. cuz in now days, so many vocabularys come in to being and come to korean from the world. and we can't change whole words to korean since those are totally new definition. so we just pronounce as korean way Korean is different from English in where such as pronunciation and how to say, even accent. so that's normal. some American who stay in korean for long time and learn korean say their english become so weird. that's normal. :) (4 thumbs up)
- Your accent sounds fine, stop worrying about it (1 thumb up)

Because comments rise to the top, based on readers' votes and not on their supportive or detracting content, these need not necessarily be in agreement with the points presented in the YouTube video. Instead, they represent views that other viewers have endorsed. Whatever point of view they articulate, however, gets top billing once they receive the most positive feedback from other viewers. Like the "smart kids" who speak on the first day of class and continue to be called on from that day forward, the "top comments" get amplified through positive feedback loops – even if they start out in first position with only one or two thumbs up, their location at the top of the list will likely draw disproportionate attention from that point forward, and disproportionate numbers of thumbs up, maintaining and even augmenting their top position through those positive feedback loops. In turn, the other comments, like the quiet kids in class, drift further down the page and out of view, even more unlikely to get seen and thumbed up.

Whatever content appears in the first top comment, then, becomes a point of view that more viewers engage with – so to get a sense of citizen sociolinguistic sentiment, and of the power of self-fulfilling citizen sociolinguistic feedback loops, we also now turn our attention to the content of those top comments. In response to Kelly's accent tag, the first two most popular comments here do not voice simple agreement, but instead engage with Kelly in more detail, illuminating a critical perspective on her English and Konglish. The first comment, while admiring the fluidity of Kelly's ability to switch between Konglish and English, shows muted interest in Kelly's Konglish accent, describing how Koreans they meet in Korea don't "resort to Konglish." This commenter goes on to speculate that, perhaps, the reason people they know don't "resort to Konglish" is the fact that that person is addressing English speakers. This raises the important issue of context and the need to accommodate to one's audience – one that Kelly discussed in her video. The 14 thumbs up in response to this comment suggest others have queries along this line. And the second most popular comment follows along this same Anglophilic line of thinking. This author wonders: Why would you ever speak Konglish when your English is so good? Both these comments suggest Kelly's Konglish is useless, not a valuable marker of identity in the way Kelly portrays it in her video. And, appearing as they do at the top of the comments list, this point of view gets amplified.

However, the third-place comment (with six thumbs up, the same as the second-place comment), registers unwavering appreciation of Kelly's Konglish: "That "Konglish" xD ... it sounds very cute." And most of the remaining seven of the 10 most popular comments represent a range of views, all (maybe with the exception of the Kourtney Kardashian comment) adding substantively to the deliberation around Kelly and Konglish. The presence of positive feedback loops, in this case, seems to sustain a diversity of voices in the top 10 comment area, potentially fostering a forum for more discussion about Konglish/English and its many forms and effects.

Thethugyone Thethugyone, from South Philadelphia, is another bold accent challenger. Compared to Kelly's transnational presentation and audience, his circulation is more minimal, his presentation of self much scruffier, and his appeal far more localized. Still the views (8,378), thumbs up (43), and affirmational comments (27) proliferate. With only five thumbs down, his thumbs up ratio (8.6), like Kelly's, comfortably exceeds the ratio for Charlie Bit My Finger. And since first posting this video in 2013, he has continued to respond to comments and add his own. This self-commenting may also have boosted his involvement ratio up to .0032 comments per view, the highest of the three citizen sociolinguistic videos being considered here.

Sampling the ten most popular responses, there is a clear qualitative difference form Kelly's comments:
- South Philly's accents are totally different from New York (3 thumbs up)
- Don't get cocky! SP represent! (2 thumbs up)
- The acAme is a Philly thing. I have a deep Philly accent. (2 thumbs up)
- I love the accent. A man I loved very much was from South Philly with a deep voice and odd irish accents. I miss him, thanks for talking online. (1 thumb up)
  - thethugyone responds: You're welcome and thanks for the compliments :)
- Yeah but you should really make more videos this one is highly entertaining and hilarious! (1 thumb up)
  - thethugyone responds: you got it!
- Dude I agree with you throughout the entire vid. I don't know why Californians think that it's New York. Idiots! (2 thumbs up)
- I don't think you have an accent. (1 thumb up)
- very good o yeah nice want some scrapple
- Wayne AVE
- Your right about the NY/PA accents. I'm from Buffalo and I don't sound anything like ya. Take it easy

With the possible exception of one of these comments ("I don't think you have an accent"), they are all affirming. While small in number, these comments suggest detailed engagement with the content of thethugyone's video. In contrast to Kelly's comments, some of whom don't seem to have taken in her comments about her life, the multiple places she has lived, and how this background goes in to choosing her "accent," thethugyone's comments all engage in the specifics of his accent tag – agreeing with his comparison of Philly to New York, savoring his South Philly pronunciation of the Acme Grocery Store chain ("Ac-a-me") and the South Philly phrase he performed ("Don't get cocky!"), offering up more Philadelphia area food items ("want some scrapple"), and joining thethugyone by sharing a specific location ("Wayne AVE seems to be a response to thethugyone's statement that he is from, specifically "12th and Reed to be particular about it.") While Kelly's top comments illuminate the contrasting views around Konglish, thethugyone's comments illuminate a more specific community of like-minded South Philly people, who recognize his idiosyncrasies and locale, all constructing together a sociolinguistic identity for thethugyone and themselves through positive feedback.

Common Welsh Sayings KatieMayoxx, in her YouTube video, Things Welsh People Say, departs from the "accent challenge" genre, but instead uses the category "Common Welsh Sayings" to provide a catalogue of her own local ways with words. Notably, of the three language self-portraits here, Katie's Welsh Sayings video not only has the most views (376,396), but also has the highest positive feedback ratio (18.3) and the highest level of involvement (.0044). Compared to the baseline video, Charlie Bit My Finger, which has an feedback ratio of 7.6 and no involvement at all, Katie hits it out of the park. People are engaged with this language, and, as the top responses illustrate, they are also engaged with each other. Each comment on the video receives generous thumbs up, and many follow-up replies. Here are the ten most popular responses:

- Anyone can hug but only the Welsh can cwtch [referring to one of the "common Welsh sayings," *cwtch*, translated as *hug*] (171 thumbs up, 12 replies)
- South Wales people where u at (84 thumbs up, 22 replies)
- The Welsh are cool people (90 thumbs up, 15 replies)
- im welsh and im from south wales, im from cwmbran and i say all these<3 welsh and proud! x'D (148 thumbs up, 56 replies)
- You forgot to mention "Thanks/Cheers Drive" when people leave the bus. (23 thumbs up, 2 replies)
- OH MY GOD WHEN YOU GOT TO THE I AM'S I DIED. OH LORD. My grandparents are Welsh and my grandma is always like, "it's cold it is" "you're hungry, you are?" "I'm hot I am" (45 thumbs up, 17 replies)
- "Scram" means "get the hell out and quickly!" in American English. You'd say it to a dog or a cat underfoot, or to a little brother getting on your nerves. Hahahaa (46 thumbs up, 2 replies)
- I'm African American but I'm 8% Welsh hello my fellow Welsh people ! ! ! ! (14 thumbs up, 3 replies)
- I say all of these, I also live in South wales!!!! WELSHIES!!!😊 x (14 thumbs up)
- I'm originally for Chepstow I am 😊 but I moved to North Carolina, USA. One thing I noticed that was very different is that little thing at the end of a pencil used to erase your mistakes. Yep you guessed it! but apparently

depending what part of the world you are in you called it something different. If you are from USA you most likely called it an eraser. But if your from back home (South Wales 😊)) you probably called it a rubber. Well here's the funny bit. A rubber in the USA is slang for a condom. So at my work in the USA I announced very loudly I needed a rubber. Of course I worked out fast that it wasn't exactly what I was asking for when a kind gentleman pulled a condom from his wallet and proudly said I have one! (86 thumbs up, 10 replies)

As indicated in the reply-comment numbers listed after each comment above, unlike either Kelly's Konglish video or thethugyone's South Philly video, Katies' Welsh Sayings video comments themselves receive voluminous comments. The reply-comments further foment that positivity. Here, for example are the first ten reply-comments under the top comment:

COMMENT: Anyone can hug but only the Welsh can cwtch (171 thumbs up, 12 replies)
REPLY 1: Agreed! :D (4 thumbs up)
REPLY 2: I have a sign that says that (3 thumbs up)
REPLY 3: I love a good cwtch :3 (4 thumbs up)
REPLY 4: Yep ! (2 thumbs up)
REPLY 5: i have that on a fridge magnet (2 thumbs up)
REPLY 6: My dude, do you like D&P?? I hardly find any other Welsh people who do :'))
REPLY 7: everyone know that's saying in wales 😊 I'm glad I'm welsh
REPLY 8: You didnt make this up. Its been a quote for years
REPLY 9: Truer words were never spoken ! It's actually the first welsh word I ever learnt. I've been learning three Celtic languages for the past couple of years gaidhlig (Scottish Gaelic) gaeilge (Irish Gaelic) and cymraeg (welsh) all are beautiful in their own ways. Fave welsh words of mine are cwtch, pili pala (butterfly 🦋) hiraeth and cynefin. Tolkien thought it beautiful himself and was such an afficianado of welsh that he actually based the elvish language of middle earth on it so that's something you can be proud of!
REPLY 10: Love it

As indicated, many of these replies in turn receive thumbs up, and the feedback loop grows. And as comments foster thumbs ups and replies and more thumbs up, "Welsh sayings" grow in popularity. An online affinity group grows up around them, a momentary support group for KatieMayoxx, for those interested in Welsh, or who think they might be.

Hearing the Quiet Majority

These three examples of positive feedback loops shine a light on the power of everyday talk about language to build communities of speakers who might otherwise not be heard. "Talk moves" in classrooms can pull new students into a discussion, building more inclusive classroom communities and discussions that engage different points of view. Similarly, the Internet has provided a way to expand our conversations about language. Anyone is free to post, and their voice can be magnified by those thumbs up, comments, replies to those comments, and subsequent thumbs up. Moreover, those participants, while they may never have considered creating a video of their own, learn that others out there might share their perspective and have created a forum for displaying that positive affiliation publicly. Ultimately, it is not the content producers, but these likers and thumbs-uppers, and the still-silent participants witnessing that affirmation, who are the majority of participants on the Internet – and in our society.

Unofficial and non-verbal channels of communication – from thumbs-upping to "talk moves" in a classroom to affiliative comments on YouTube videos like Things Welsh People Say – can change how people engage with school and society. These feedback loops have the potential to harness voices, creativity, and new perspectives that might otherwise go unrecognized. For example, what some people call "Black Twitter" represents a positive feedback loop that has given voice to perspectives previously limited from white racialized spaces, bringing new voices into academia, politics, and journalism, building affinity groups among those voices, allowing previously unheard perspectives to circulate more widely, and for those voicing those perspectives to receive affirmation and find their extended community of support – by creating it together.

This same process has also opened up how we talk about language. Unlike the answer to an arithmetic problem or the facts listed on someone's tax return, norms for communication are not true or false, right or wrong. Instead, the "right" way to speak involves joining a community of speakers and adapting to the norms of that group. YouTube threads, like those that unfurl under KatieMayoxx's video, have become sites of consensus building around language and identity. Through positive feedback loops of thumbs-upping, commentary, and sharing across the Internet, everyday people build representations of language, who speaks certain ways, and what counts as right and wrong, good and bad, building wonderment around shared language, fomenting more discussion.

These explanations can serve, if understood only in the isolation of those forums for conversation, as self-fulfilling prophecies. This is the horror of the Internet some people fear – we just talk to people who are like-minded, who reinforce what we already believe, stating opinions as if they were timeless truths. Fortunately, however, there is always a next turn, another site to visit, another point of view. Participants may go to other contexts to talk about language, and with each new context, participate in new norms and develop more nuanced understandings of language in context.

On Disabled Comments

Unfortunately, sometimes those forums for deliberation close down. Sometimes, we see the notice "comments disabled" under videos. We saw this when the word "citizenship" was under discussion (see Chapter 1). And now, again, with Charlie Bit My Finger. No doubt the decision to disable those comments was the result of someone protecting those two babies (now grown boys who likely also watch their share of YouTube videos) from the damage those comments could cause. Similarly, in face-to-face classroom conversation, sometimes we don't want to hear from some students because we fear what they might say. However, when it comes to conversations about language, we need to invite everyone to the table, and by taking steps into those conversations and following the sparks of wonderment we can enter into deliberative conversations about how language works. Each of the citizen sociolinguistic videos considered above include comments that critique the video creator's perspective: For Kelly, commenters question why she doesn't just speak English, why she bothers with Konglish; For thethugyone, some deny he has any accent at all; For KatieMayoxx, honestly, it's hard to find a criticism, but there are those who pile on with suggestions for additional Welsh sayings, phrases, and words, and alternative explanations for Welsh syntax. These videos invite dialogue and the dialogue promotes more views and more comments, which in turn invites more views, comments, and involvement with conversations about language. When it comes to talking about language, comments are not only crucial to conversations about language, they and the feedback loops they foster are the substance of citizen sociolinguistics.

Negative Effects of Feedback Loops: Producing Isolated Elites or Righteous Critics

Digital Enclaves and Ideological Echo Chambers

With all this discussion of happy feedback loops of positivity, readers may be worried about the power of the web to create ideological echo chambers, or digital enclaves where like-minded people gather to repeat the same tired truths – "truths" that may even directly contradict "alternative truths" being voiced on another social media platform. Of course, positive feedback loops can also have negative consequences. While affinity groups of like-minded people may start off as a simple matter of finding our friends, talking with those we feel comfortable with sharing our ideas, the massive scale of the Internet, and the ability to make money off these like-minded enclaves, has created an industry that perpetuates them, not always to positive ends. In her essay on "The Targeted Citizen," Cathy O'Neil illustrates how the science of "microtargeting" has been able to find these like-minded enclaves and reinforce them on a massive scale through algorithms that feed people's "like" profiles back into the system, attracting them to more products, and using their attraction to certain categories in their internet browsing to attract more people, more "likes." Today, political campaigns have entire teams of data scientists who mine the Internet to develop stereotypical portraits of types of people and the associated messages that appeal to them. They can funnel news stories accordingly: For those who like the Welsh language, there will be news stories that focus on certain incidents and not others, and sometimes new stories that have little basis in reality, that have long been discredited among other target groups. This process can threaten democracy. As Cathy O'Neil writes:

Successful microtargeting, in part, explains why in 2015 more than 43 percent of Republicans, according to a survey, still believed the lie that President Obama is a Muslim. And 20 percent of Americans believed he was born outside the United States and, consequently, an illegitimate president. (2016, p. 194)

As we become targeted as enclaves of like-minded people, or even individuals of a certain identifiable and targetable type, these metrics then reinforce the barriers between those of us who have different views. Deliberation stops and we receive information that simply reinforces our pre-existing beliefs. What does this have to do with conversations about language? One result of these isolated ideological enclaves is that they become places where we use language in ways that make sense only to members of those peer groups. Remember when we discussed the word "citizen"? In certain peer groups, the word *citizen* carries varying sets of impressions – idealism, cynicism, fear, propaganda. When feedback loops enforce the ideological enclaves around these views of citizenship, people develop ways of using the word that have not cultivated the sensibilities of the other groups. People begin to use the word "citizen" in ways we might call "tone-deaf."

A Condition of Isolated Feedback Loops: Being "Tone-Deaf"

Implementing something called a "citizenship grade" in a school district in which many of the families are of missed citizenship status, living with day-to-day fear of being deported or separated from one another, qualifies as being tone-deaf. When the school district considers this a "translation problem," this suggests they have not spent enough time among other types of people who have different experiences with the word. The mixed-status families in that community certainly understand the meaning of "citizenship." They just have very different experiences with that word than those school district administrators who created the "citizenship grade." For the families who saw that phrase on their report care, the word "citizenship" struck a very painful note.

Readers can probably all call to mind other instances of everyday tone-deaf uses of language. Examples I've encountered include

- a college student, charging meals and shopping sprees to their parents' credit card, complaining about how *poor* they are in front of peers who struggle to pay tuition on their own
- a museum docent welcoming a Korean American visitor from Santa Barbara with the Mandarin Chinese greeting *ni hao*
- a professor repeatedly referring to the women in his graduate seminar as *girls*.

Every day, people use language in ways like this, slightly out of tune with the immediate situation, ways we might describe as tone-deaf. Considered more literally, a tone-deaf musician cannot hear what their instrument sounds like relative to the pitch of others. A tone-deaf singer can sing loudly and clearly – while completely unaware of the cacophony their voice causes when surrounded by a chorus of voices singing in a different key. This can lead to some pretty painful listening. In conversations, metaphorical tone deafness can also lead to painful situations. Often and understandably, the person most directly affected by tone-deaf turns of phrase may not feel they can speak up. Or, that if they do, the tone-deaf person may become defensive and the conversation will go nowhere. Tone deafness is an unfortunate state, but one with a remedy: more talk about language, across communities, that is, citizen sociolinguistics.

Almost nobody purposefully intends to be communicatively tone-deaf. For this reason I prefer the formulation tone-deaf to the commonly used term *microaggression*, which might also describe the example scenarios above. But the term *microaggression* suggests these instances of tone-deaf language use originate from a malicious individual, intentionally using language aggressively to demean another person. In contrast, the term tone-deaf describes a societally induced state, one fostered by poor language education – even among our most privileged classes. Advice to combat microaggressions usually involves highlighting words or speech events to avoid: Don't use the n-word; Don't ask Asian Americans where they are from – things to NOT say. Unfortunately, this kind of advice can lead to accusations of "political correctness," or to people simply clamming up in the face of the unfamiliar. Instead of leading to further conversation about assumptions behind our language choices, conflicts around language across diverse groups continue to seethe beneath the surface.

Citizen sociolinguistic inquiry provides an alternative to these prescriptions for sensitive language use: more discussion about language and more consideration of different perspectives. We do not need a prefabricated list of words to use and not use, but an increased level of language awareness, and the skills to inquire about words and their uses and meanings across contexts. Situations of tone deafness arise every day, but they can be curtailed by improving language education, by specifically teaching our children how to tune in to the everyday workings of language in context.

While a tone-deaf person may have excellent language skills according to one context and set of criteria, skills that have been developed and praised through positive feedback loops over their entire life, they have an underdeveloped ability to assess the effects of their words in new contexts. A tone-deaf use of language, if unchecked and fostered through positive feedback loops of an isolated enclave of like-minded speakers, can have the opposite effect of citizen sociolinguistic discussion. Instead of fomenting conversations about language, it can silence less powerful voices. Unless someone speaks back – for example, by calling someone out on the type of language they use – that tone-deaf perspective becomes the only one people hear. Nobody learns from alternatives. People who are literally tone-deaf may be discouraged from ever pursuing music. They just won't be able to participate. The equivalent action for the conversationally tone-deaf would restrict those who are tone-deaf to their own neighborhood of language use, be it an Ivory Tower, fraternity or sorority, family or clique, or other any other walled-off language community that "understands" them.

Fortunately, however, being metaphorically "tone-deaf" is something we can work to avoid by having conversations about language and including language awareness and inquiry as part of any language arts education: Let's investigate who uses the word *girl* in different ways and why, explore uses of *ni hao* and all the ways Asian Americans experience that greeting, discuss how people relate to the word *poor* and the implications. Any tone-deaf encounter provides us impetus for a discussion about language and how it affects all of us. Each conversation about language can illuminate the ways we have all been socialized into different understandings of how certain words work.

Breaking Down Feedback Loops, Building Up New Ones: A Case Study

Acting to combat tone deafness – breaking those positive feedback loops that have negative consequences – may be the primary way that acts of citizen sociolinguistics can have powerful consequences. Case in point: In January 2019, a very tone-deaf email from a Duke University professor went viral. This professor was talking about language. Specifically, the language of Chinese students in her program. She was recommending that they not speak "Chinese" with each other when in the Duke Biostatistics Department. Ironically, this directive to not speak Chinese led to a huge amount of talk about speaking Chinese – and this talk about language now gives us a window into the power of acts of citizen sociolinguistics to disrupt damaging feedback loops and create new feedback loops that counter institutional norms.

In this incident, many of the mechanisms that fuel citizen sociolinguistic inquiry were involved:
(1) A status quo, isolated feedback loop, generating a tone-deaf demand: When in the presence of English speakers, speak English only.
(2) First citizen sociolinguistic arrest: Please do not speak Chinese in the building.
(3) Cross-posting on multiple Internet platforms, reaching multiple audiences, breaking the isolated feedback loop of the professorial email list.
(4) Citizen sociolinguistic counter-arrests:
   (a) Your English is not perfect, time to brush up!
   (b) You can't tell us what language to use with each other, during our break.
   (c) Don't assume we can't speak English, just because we are speaking Chinese with our Chinese-speaking peers.
(5) Each of these counter-arrests fomented embedded comment threads and *positive feedback loops*.
(6) Embedded dialogue fomented more conversation and deliberation about language, exposing other isolated feedback loops and tone deafness far beyond Duke.
(7) Consequences: Conditions of initial email rescinded. Public apology issued.

Let's explore the incident by looking at the conversations that followed it – from discussions online, to offline, and back.

First came the tone-deaf demand: When in the presence of English speakers, speak English only. Here is the complete text of the circulated email, subject line, "Something to think about":

Hi All,

I have two separate faculty members come to my office today and ask if I have pictures of the MB [Masters in Biostatistics] students. I shared with them the head shots of the first- and second-year cohorts taken during orientation. Both faculty members picked out a small group of first-year students who they observed speaking Chinese (in their words, VERY LOUDLY) in the student lunge/study areas. I asked why they were curious about the students' names. Both faculty members replied that they wanted to write down the names so they could remember them if the students ever interviewed for an internship or asked to work with them for a master's project. **They were disappointed that these students were not taking the opportunity to improve their English and were being so impolite as to have a conversation that not everyone on the floor could understand.**

To international students, PLEASE PLEASE PLEASE keep these unintended consequences in mind when you chose to speak in Chinese in the building. I have no idea how hard it has been and still is for you to come to the United States and have to learn in a non-native language. As such, I have the upmost [sic] respect for what you are doing. That being said, I encourage you to commit to using English 100% of the time when you are in Hock or any other professional setting.

Copying the second-year students as a reminder given they are currently applying for jobs.

Happy to discuss more. Just stop by my office.

This was not the first email sent by this professor. Another, sent nearly a year earlier, had not been circulated more widely at the time, but stayed within the department. The basic directive, Don't speak Chinese in the building, functions as a citizen sociolinguist's arrest, calling students out for speaking a certain way and even threatening them with "unintended consequences." Apparently, over the year, nothing suggested to the author of this email, or the professors who asked her to send it, that this might be offensive and overreaching. Within their faculty enclave, it went unquestioned. Before going on to the fervor created by the recirculation of this email, it's worth noting the characteristic features of this citizen sociolinguist's arrest. It drips with moral censure (these professors were "disappointed" with students speaking Chinese, because they were not taking the "opportunity to improve their English"), it assumes that simply because the students were speaking Chinese, they don't speak English well – and thus need to constantly work to "improve their English," and it accuses them of being rude by speaking their own language ("being so impolite as to have a conversation that not everyone on the floor could understand"). The email also includes a threat: Continue to speak Chinese in the building and there will be "unintended consequences" regarding internship opportunities or master's projects. Were this email to have stayed within the Biostatistics group to which it was addressed, it might easily have contributed to the common pedagogical feedback loops readers might recognize in their own academic settings: Multilingualism is treated as lack of English, so international students have fewer opportunities to interact with native English speakers and stay among themselves, which creates a climate of isolated language enclaves. This in turn creates a culture of mistrust and minimal understanding, in which people feel threatened by languages other than English. Since the English speakers hold the power and the internships, Chinese speakers who read this email would most likely keep their Chinese to themselves from this point forward, and the isolation and mistrust between international students and their monolingual professors would grow. This is a feedback loop with negative consequences. And it appears that it had been going on, without pushback, for at least a year, given that there had been a similar email from the same professor in February 2018.

The second time around, however, an act of citizen sociolinguistics broke down the barrier that kept that faculty enclave isolated, because the 2019 email, reproduced above, led to a citizen sociolinguist's counter-arrest: Someone took a screenshot of the problematic email and recirculated it to an entirely new audience. First it went viral on Weibo, the Chinese micro-blogging platform. The subsequent English discussion on Twitter (https://twitter.com/siruihua/status/1089219853725122561)included the text, "one professor from Duke University sent out an email asking Chinese students not to speak Chinese in school building," and the entire screenshot of the email.

Citizen sociolinguistic cross-posting then generated a battery of citizen sociolinguistic counter-arrests! In contrast to the 2018 email, which stayed within the Biostatistics community, when this email, originally also meant only for the Chinese biostatistics students, was sent out on Twitter, the conversation exploded. The day after it was sent (January 26, 2019), it had received 13,970 retweets and 28,541 likes. It had been retweeted over 14,000 times. Even a cursory review of this single Twitter thread reveals multiple concerns, among them the hypocrisy of this language policing, the threat that these students may be jeopardizing their future job opportunities within the department and beyond, and the assumption that, because they are speaking Chinese, their English is not good.

The more innocuous of these citizen sociolinguistic arrests draw attention to the Duke professor's use of the phrase "upmost respect" instead of the standard, "utmost respect":

TWEET : This professor also wrote Upmost so she probably needs an English language brush-up as well. (1.5 K likes, 27 retweets, 21 comments)

The tweets become more pointed about discrimination when discussing the email's threat to these students' future opportunities – that if they do not refrain from speaking languages other than English while in the building, they may have difficulty finding internships in the department. This, the email warns, may be the "unintended consequences" of speaking Chinese. In response:

TWEET : Reread this, even angrier now. The language is incredibly menacing: "unintended consequences" for simply speaking Chinese during free time indicates there's no end to the Othering of international students to make them feel inadequate and unwelcome. (2.8 K likes, 184 retweets, 14 comments)

This tweet's emphasis on the email's ominous threat of "unintended consequences," and its broad "Othering" of international students receives 2,800 likes and 184 retweets, fomenting more tweets on this theme. Repeatedly, more tweets like this one point out that denying students opportunities because they have been overheard speaking Chinese amounts to unfair bias – because this denial is not based on relevant skills, or even English ability, but simply the fact that these students speak Chinese in public.

Another thread more specifically points out the false assumption that those speaking Chinese need more English practice. As the response to Tweeter A's initial tweet below illustrates, "Speaking Chinese" does not necessarily mean students cannot speak English well:

TWEETER A: Speaking from personal experience a lot of Chinese students backed in my high school didn't speak English unless they had to, and their English skills remained just about the same four years later, I don't know the actual situation here but she's atleast very respectful (133 likes, 48 comments)
TWEETER B: I scored top 1% on the GRE, 119 on TOEFL, and hold a B.S. in philosophy with distinction from @UBC [University of British Columbia], do I get to sepak Chinese with my friends on my own time when I'm on a university campus w/o my professional dev opportunities getting stripped away? (2.3 K likes, 34 retweets, 14 comments)
TWEETER A: That is super impressive! You're right, I need to think more about this situation. (381 likes, 1 retweet, 15 comments)

Tweeter B's response to A illustrates that students at English-medium universities who speak Chinese to each other may also be highly proficient English speakers. To his credit, Tweeter A rethinks his previous tweet.

These observations and deliberation represent a level of citizen sociolinguistic language awareness that would never have been aired, had this email (and it had been preceded by others like it) been left to contribute to its isolated and tone-deaf feedback loop. This is one small drop of the outpouring of internet dialogue generated by the Duke email, after it was cross-posted – and the sheer quantity of this outpouring led to more coverage in the print and TV media. Swiftly, the professor who wrote the email issued an apology and stepped down from her post as Graduate Director. The Dean announced they would be embarking on an investigation into the program's cultural climate.

Then came the backlash – a history professor (Zimmerman, 2019) argued in the *New York Daily News* that readers should not "rush to judgment" of the Duke professor. He discussed his own experiences with an NYU student from China and how he helped her realize that "her speech patterns" outside the classroom might be "deeply limiting her professional opportunities." This description echoes the "unintended consequences" mentioned in the Duke email – the threat that students would be judged poorly when applying for internships simply because they had been overheard speaking Chinese. It also suggests the tone deafness evident in the Duke professor's email extends to academic contexts beyond Duke University.

The controversy continued to burn, sparking more email and face-to-face discussions, including many among my colleagues and our students. Suddenly issues of Chinese language and its role in our increasingly internationalizing campuses became something many people were talking about. And now we were discussing these forms of language policing more broadly – not simply as something that happened at Duke, but something we recognize in many contexts, including in our own communities.

Disrupting Status Quo Feedback Loops, Creating New Ones

Despite being cloaked in the passive, agentless phrase "unintended consequences," the Duke email actively produces discrimination. Warnings to students were not simply pointing out a harsh reality to which students must accommodate lest they face "unintended consequences." These emails were producing that reality and those consequences. Discrimination against Chinese students, or any other ethnic group, is not a matter of "unintended consequences," nor even solely the result of intentional choices by people in power. Rhetoric about students' best interests in the face of "unintended consequences" reproduces this discrimination each time it's used, creating a self-fulfilling feedback loop, where to "get ahead," people must conform to an English-only context – a context produced repeatedly in the rhetoric of these warnings.

How can one disrupt that rhetoric and the context of discrimination it creates? Here's where we may have been witnessing social change: These Weibo, Twitter, and otherwise mass-mediated discussions created a rupture in a feedback loop that has been reinforcing a status quo policy of "English-for-their-own-good" for centuries in this country – centuries that have led many "well-meaning" people to reproduce ethnocentric and racist norms. Colleagues of mine pointed out in our discussion of the Duke email that forcing people to speak English, and specific types of English, is nothing new in the United States – a nation built on language eradication. Hundreds of distinct languages were spoken in North America when Columbus arrived centuries ago. Far fewer than half are still spoken today, and most of those are endangered. Only decades ago, our school systems erupted in controversy when it was suggested that we recognize and respect speakers of African American English in K-12 classrooms rather than relegate them to remedial classes; and, until recently, most children of immigrants in this country were instructed to speak only English both in school and at home, even with their family members who knew almost no English. Not surprisingly, most children of immigrants to this country lose their mother tongue and become monolingual English speakers.

Much of this centuries-old pattern of language eradication, including the forced education of indigenous people in English-only boarding schools, was done to individuals ostensibly to save them from the "unintended consequences" of limited opportunity. These policies and actions, like those of the Duke professors, were not simply pointing out a monolingual reality to which multilinguals were advised to accommodate, they were creating that monolingual culture by talking about different languages as if they are inherently detrimental to an individual's success.

When we tell people to change their "speech patterns," presumably for their own benefit, we continue the eradication of difference, even while publicly most academics now recognize such eradication as ethnocentric and racist. In the feedback loops made visible in the Duke controversy, we've witnessed a rupture in the "unintended consequences" rhetoric. Instead of discussing how students can change their speech patterns, we're thinking about how institutions might change the way we treat linguistic diversity. Instead of reproducing monolingual achievement norms, we're questioning the institutional discourse that upholds those norms.

When students used the Internet to circulate that email outside its usual institutional range, they made a collective citizens' counter-arrest, and brought new voices into the conversation. They questioned the *tone-deaf* "unintended consequences" rhetoric that has built monolingual institutional power for centuries in this country and in institutions of higher education worldwide. While we can lament the idiocy of Twitter and other social media, these platforms function as a valuable tool for cross-posting, breaking down isolated enclaves of feedback, and fomenting new cycles of retweets and likes. Via these multiple platforms, an email message meant to be seen by only a chosen few was able to circulate more widely, attracting a huge diversity of everyday opinions about language – including those opinions we've heard before and those that are new to us, those we agree with and those we don't. In the Duke controversy, someone's ordinary institutional email became a springboard for discussions about language policing. Online, via viral tweeting, we began to see a rupture in the usual feedback loop that reinforces the old monolingual status quo – and to see what social change looks like.

This response from the students was sparked by a citizen sociolinguistic arrest, spread via cross-posting, and subsequently picked up by mainstream media. The massive dialogue about language that followed the posting illustrates that citizen sociolinguists also have the potential to foment social change by breaking down self-affirming feedback loops and creating large-scale counter-feedback loops, bringing huge numbers of new voices into the conversation.

I suspect (I hope!) professors who have followed this controversy will now think twice before policing the languages students use with one another. Online and offline, we will soon be able to see what new forms the feedback loop takes – and we are all free to play a role in those conversations, voicing our own opinions in whatever language we choose.

5   Citizen Sociolinguistics and Narrative

> ... there is a democracy implied in narration, the lowest rank in that activity is not very low by society's standards – the right and obligation to listen to a story from a person to whom we need not be in a position to tell one.
>
> Erving Goffman, *Forms of Talk* (1981, p. 152 n. 11)

Most students and professors, parents and children, leaders and subjects probably recognize the "democracy implied in narration" that Goffman describes in the quotation above. When an instructor pauses their lecture to provide an illustrative story, the feeling of the room can palpably shift. Students may suddenly perk up, sensing they might be privy now to something more than the facts and concepts enumerated in the syllabus – instead bearing witness, as story-listeners, to the instructor's human connection to that material. Children listening to parents attempting to teach them an important "lesson" might be unconvinced by a reasoned didacticism but drawn in by a story about the parents' own distant adolescence and their common struggles. Even powerful and iconic personages can be humanized in the eyes of their subjects through storytelling: Introducing the comment above about the democratic nature of narrative, Goffman describes how the Queen of England, as subject of a BBC documentary, was followed around by the film crew through every moment of the day. While she seemed to maintain a studied decorum through even the most mundane activities, on those moments when she broke into a story, the regal curtain seemed to be pulled aside. As Goffman writes, these stories were no doubt carefully selected, but the act of telling them changed how the queen and the documentary crew (and, ultimately, the documentary viewers) were related to each other in that conversational moment: "The royal personages could not but momentarily slip into the unregal stance of storyteller, allowing the hearers the momentary (relative) intimacy of story-listeners. What could be perceived of as 'humanity' is thus practically inescapable" (1981, p. 152 n. 11).

Up to this point, we have not explicitly addressed the role of narrative in citizen sociolinguistics, but many of the examples of citizen sociolinguistic commentary we've discussed have included storytelling. It seems that citizen sociolinguists inevitably tell stories that contextualize their own language use. Given the apparent democratic quality of narrative, it follows that citizen sociolinguists would draw on stories to talk about language and convey how language works in their lives, and that an audience from varied backgrounds would be drawn in. This chapter focuses more explicitly on the affordances of the narrative genre for citizen sociolinguistics, exploring the kinds of stories people tell about their language use, and how narrative logic informs the conclusions of those storytellers as well as the responses from their audience. I focus on the narratives that most YouTube "accent challenge" videos include as introductory material as well as the response narratives that appear in the comments underneath those videos. These data illustrate how narrative builds affinity spaces for highly localized communicative practices, and in the process constructs an emergent sociolinguistic validity to the language claims being expounded.

In the context of internet-circulated social media, narrative ways of knowing feature prominently. To illustrate the potential power of internet-circulated social media to facilitate narrative logic, this chapter compares the information-storing and -sharing functions of Web 1.0 and Web 2.0, making an analogy between these two conceptualizations of the Internet and Jerome Bruner's (1986) two different modes of knowing: logico-scientific and narrative. Just as discussions of Web 2.0 (like the sorts this book has been engaging in for the last four chapters) highlight collaborative construction, dissemination, and uptake of information, analysis of narrative illuminates the accrual of socio-cultural meaning in collaboratively constructed stories. So, in this chapter we are going to look more closely at narrative and dialogue in the Web 2.0 context to investigate the social value that citizen sociolinguists put on "accent" in Philadelphia Accent Challenge YouTube videos (and the associated comment sections).

Whereas in Chapter 4 we focused on how feedback loops and accumulating thumbs up generate value for social valuations of language, in this chapter we will see how social value accrues via the snowballing of "small stories" (Bamberg and Georgakopoulou, 2008) about these accent performances. Just as the Internet amplifies the effects of feedback loops discussed in Chapter 4, it also affords the proliferation of smaller-scale, narrative ways of recirculating certain emblematic features of accent. This perspective on analyzing YouTube video-based accent data illuminates the value of YouTube accent performances as a medium/method for narrative modes of knowing, as narrative accounts circulate language ideological discourse via internet-based participatory culture.

Web 1.0 and 2.0

While more of a continuum of functions than a stark dichotomy, *Web 1.0* commonly refers to the use of the Internet as an information stockpile (or simply a digital version of what used to be books and libraries), and *Web 2.0*

Table 5.1 *Web 1.0 phenomena and their Web 2.0 analogues*

Web 1.0	Web 2.0
Personal websites	Blogging
Publishing	Participation
Britannica Online	Wikipedia
Content management systems	Wikis
Stickiness (of a single post or website)	Syndication (cross-posting and feedback loops)
Directories (taxonomies)	*Tagging (folksonomies)*

Source: O'Reilly 2005 in Herring 2013

refers to the use of the Internet as a generative network of connections through which information about social value accrues. Herring (2013) and others attribute this distinction to Tom O'Reilly, who coined the term *Web 2.0* in 2004. Table 5.1 illustrates the types of distinctions O'Reilly was trying to capture through this description.

For anyone who wonders about the social implications of certain ways of speaking, Web 2.0 provides new types of social information and expertise not available within a strictly 1.0 paradigm. A 1.0 linguist may describe phonemic distinctions like "vowel length," "nasalization," "voice onset time," or "[h] dropping," measure them with precision via Praat or other computer software packages, and compile them in databases or *directories* (as noted in Table 5.1). While students of Linguistics will engage with these findings, and perhaps seek to reproduce or refute them, the uptake and recirculation of these findings outside of the Linguistics community will likely be slim. The broader social value of these data (according to *non*-disciplinary linguistics) emerges through reports circulated online by people who embed descriptions of speech in narratives including remarks like "That sounds ignorant," "He talks white," or "If I actually talked like that I'd pull a gun on myself" (Moore, 2011). These *folksonomic* descriptions (see O'Reilly, 2005) may correlate to vowel length, voice onset time, or nasalization, but disciplinary labels for those linguistic distinctions, backed by their precise measurements, are far removed (practically and epistemologically) from the networked participatory culture that builds social meaning around certain emblematic distinctions, through Web 2.0 networks (see Table 5.2).

Web 2.0 networks expand the reach of sociolinguistic understandings beyond contained "directories" of linguistic information. Traditional repositories of sociolinguistic knowledge reside in a 1.0 world and rely on "stickiness" of those repositories to attract consumers of that information. If a Linguistics undergraduate needs to understand what "vowel length" is, she might go to one of these 1.0 repositories to get that information. In contrast,

Table 5.2 *Metalanguage for 1.0 taxonomy of acoustic features vs. 2.0 folksonomy of social value*

Linguistic information (1.0)	Socially networked value (2.0)
"Vowel length" (Jacewicz, Fox, and Salmons, 2007)	"That sounds ignorant"
"Voice onset time" (Flege, 1980)	"He has a strong foreign accent"
"Nasalization" (Moore, 2011)	"If I actually talked like that I'd pull a gun on myself"

Web 2.0 networks, offer a means to spread sociolinguistic understandings beyond those sticky repositories of specialized information. For information in these networks to go beyond a single website or journal article, it must be "spreadable" (Jenkins, Ford, and Green, 2014) – that is, it must offer something that appeals widely, that entices people to repost, to cross-post, to share with friends, and to recontextualize in newly meaningful ways. As illustrated in Table 5.2, in sticky 1.0 media, decontextualized metalanguage like "voice onset time" develops in a way that appeals to a group of insider linguistic researchers. In 2.0 networks, information becomes spreadable when the language used to express linguistic phenomena appeals to a wider audience – inevitably, the more widely that information is spread, the more diverse the manner in which it will be expressed (cf., the *diversity principle*, Rymes, 2014). Accordingly, conversations about language that spread in this way take on wildly varying forms according to the new contexts in which they occur.

As the examples in Table 5.2 suggest, everyday accounting for "accent" involves at least two types of knowledge. People must know enough about language to recognize differences in ways of speaking (though they may lack the linguistic metalanguage in the first column), but people must also know how their peers ascribe value to those differences in order for them to count as socially meaningful "accents" (as described in the second column). This second type of knowledge accounts not only for the sounds of language but also for additional aspects of an individual's communicative repertoire, including ways of dressing, contexts of talking, and the types of situations in which certain accents become relevant (Rymes, 2014).

Narrative 2.0

This nuanced talk about language relies heavily on the narrative genre to render more arcane sociolinguistic knowledge *spreadable*. Stories about accent emerge from human interaction and serve to build shared expectations for social types of speech in the same way that stories about death, marriage, immigration, child-bearing, career choices, divorce, or dating build normative expectations for those activities. YouTubers and commenters' stories, by depicting the travails of recognizable social types and their ways of speaking (and speaking about speaking), give a sense of the relative social indexical value of accent and a richer sense of the communicative repertoire within which discrete sound distinctions play a part (Blommaert and Backus, 2012; Rymes, 2014). Is a speaker of that speech token smart, annoying, pushy, sheltered, hip, slutty? Narratives provide an approachable medium to illustrate how these personality types may align with linguistic features.

Simultaneously, narratives can serve as a democratizing invitation to an audience to participate in these normative depictions of social types and the language forms associated with them. In the last 50 years, researchers in psychology, sociolinguistics, linguistic anthropology, and educational linguistics have been developing methods of narrative analysis as a tool for understanding both how individuals build a sense of their own identity, and how that identity is collaboratively constructed in conversation with others (Bamberg, 2012; Labov, 2013; Mishler, 1999; Ochs and Capps, 2001; Stein and Policastro, 1984; Wortham, 2001, 2005). As individuals communicate their personal experiences to others, narrative frequently becomes the genre through which they do it. To recount experiences in a narrative form, interlocutors typically orient to a generic set of expectations: They set the scene, build drama, reach a turning point or change in the course of events, include protagonists and antagonists and associated evaluative language, resolve the action, and conclude with an explicit or implicit message. Labov and Waletzky's (1967) classic structural description of oral narrative names these elements the *abstract, orientation, complicating action, evaluation, resolution,* and *coda* and Labov remarks that these comprise the necessary components of a "fully developed narrative" (2013, p. 5). While not all conversational narratives include all these components, they demarcate common expectations for narrative: listeners may expect a story to follow this general structure, and will interact with it accordingly.

More recent thinking about conversational narrative places additional emphasis on the interaction between the teller and those listening to (or reading) the story. This is most obviously the case in conversational narrative, where tellers must somehow secure the engagement of the audience so they can hold the conversational floor for an extended turn – suspending the usual back-and-forth of conversation (Bamberg, 2012; Bruner, 2003; DeFina and Georgakopoulou, 2012; Mishler, 1999; Ochs and Capps, 2001; Sacks, 1974; Wortham, 2001). From this interactional perspective, Ochs and Capps have offered the concept of narrative "dimensions" of "*tellership, tellability, embeddedness, linearity* and *moral stance*" (2001, p. 20) to which listeners orient, rather than the more decontextualized components of narrative

Table 5.3 *What narratives do*

Narratives...
• set a scene
• build drama
• tell of protagonists and antagonists
• engage an audience
• seize the floor
• have a message/coda

described by Labov and Waletzky (1967). Building on this understanding of narratives as often more loosely organized productions unfolding through conversation, some narrative researchers have further departed from Labov's (2013) ideal of the "fully developed narrative," emphasizing the importance of "small stories," or barely recognizable, nascent narratives, woven into the fabric of a conversation (Bamberg and Georgakopoulou, 2008). Combining these perspectives on narrative, Table 5.3 illustrates a generic composite of story and "small story" components, arguably of concern to most conversational storytellers.

Ochs and Capps (2001) emphasize how the shared expectations for generic features of narrative illuminate the role stories play in navigating an important human communicative paradox: the infinite complexity of individual experience and the need to put that complexity into a form that communicates to others. Through narrative, tellers collaboratively reach socially normative ways of formulating unresolved life events. As such, *stories* about language, unlike even the most precise *descriptions* of linguistic detail and variation, provide an ideal means for researchers of language and communication to trace how social value accrues around ways of speaking.

Dialect Surveys on YouTube: From Logico-Scientific Descriptions to Narrative Ways of Knowing

Over the last decade, the Internet has become a medium for both *descriptions* of ways of speaking and personal *stories* around those descriptions. Stories about accent and language almost always accompany descriptions, cross multiple internet platforms (Tumblr, YouTube, Facebook), and even where there aren't stories told as one cohesive and instantly recognizable genre, the ingredients are there (e.g., a protagonist, their motivation, an audience). These nascent accent narratives, circulated via multiple forms of Web 2.0 social media, exemplify what Jenkins (2006) has called "convergence culture," and a form of interaction that Herring (2013) has named "convergent media computer mediated communication," or CMCMC.

A preliminary illustration of CMCMC comes from the *New York Times* (Katz and Andrews, 2013), in the form of the web-based "dialect quiz" discussed in the Introduction, and once again in Chapter 3, as an example of a repurposed linguistic research tool. Even though the dialect survey on which that article was based was intended to identify regional language differences, its repurposing as a language quiz, circulated in the Web 2.0 context, has turned it into a highly spreadable foundation for narrative sense-making. As soon as the *New York Times* quiz was posted, people began to post their results on Facebook and share stories about their regionalisms or the geographic or social trajectory of their lives. Narrative accounts of taking the survey also began to circulate, and even generic versions of dialect survey stories began to emerge, setting the scene and embedding various survey responses (e.g., coke/pop/soda) in these stories as key features, generating small stories like these rough transcriptions of stories I heard from friends:

- During my first weeks at college, every time I'd say *pop*, I'd receive a barrage of insults, so I had to start saying *soda* ...
- I used to say *sow bug*, now I say *roly poly*, unless I'm with *my grandma*, then I say *pill bug* ...
- After a few years in the South, an "all y'all" would pop out of my mouth every once in a while, but I wouldn't be caught dead saying that here ... except, I guess I just did!

While the *New York Times* survey became a medium for sharing life stories surrounding dialect, the survey tool itself has very different origins. Unlike the usual quizzes one sees on Facebook or Buzzfeed, the *New York Times* survey was designed originally as a research tool by linguist and dialectologist, Bert Vaux, implemented as the Harvard Dialect Survey (Vaux and Golder, 2003). When Vaux originally conducted his survey, he was likely concerned with being able to measure and plot results on a map, and less so in the stories, thoughts, biographies or hedges of the survey-takers. For instance, the instructions ask participants to take the survey *without thinking*:

The Dialect Survey uses a series of questions, including rhyming word pairs and vocabulary words, to explore words and sounds in the English language. There are no right or wrong answers; by answering each question with *what you really say* and not what you think is "right," you can help contribute to an accurate picture of how English is used in your community. (Vaux 2003, emphasis in the original)

Rather than concerning himself with the biographies of people, their potentially multiple places of origin, or the way they strategically use different ways of speaking, Vaux intended to use this survey to objectively pinpoint "how English is used in your community." The *New York Times* version of the dialect survey drew on Vaux's, but because the results were so easy to share, and the survey so easy to repost on various forms of social media, it was talked about much more extensively. This survey and its rapidly accumulating findings became *spreadable*. The *New York Times'* circulation of the survey and its subsequent recirculation via social media illustrates not only that many individuals are interested in descriptions of how they speak, but also that they reflect on the contextualized social meaning of accent, and possibly that this influences the way they speak. When circulating their dialect survey results on social media, people embed this information in narrative accounts of when, where, and why they speak certain ways.

Jerome Bruner's (1986) distinction between "logico-scientific" and "narrative" modes of knowing provides a useful analogy to the contrast between survey results and the narrative embedding of those results (see Table 5.4).

Bruner (1986), pushing developmental psychologists to address the social and interactional aspects of human development, describes these two modes as two different ways for making sense of human experience. When operating in logico-scientific mode – typically prioritized in traditional experimental psychology – researchers necessarily focus on quantifiable data, often gained through surveys of individuals. Researchers analyze these data for statistical regularities, with the goal of obtaining objective, replicable results. Bruner contrasts this mode with the equally rigorous and important narrative mode of knowing, which he suggests might be more relevant to studying the psychological development of individuals. Individuals generally make sense of their own experience by recounting life events in narrative, and the measure of that narrative logic is not based on its objectivity or verifiability, but on its *verisimilitude*. Telling a coherent story that makes sense to one's audience and accounts for one's experiences can be more important and more psychologically relevant (and revealing to a researcher) than comparing one's experiences to statistical regularities or logical proofs or even the strictly causal connection of events in one's story. While statistical regularities and survey research can provide useful generalizations, Bruner argues that to conduct valid psychological research one must

Table 5.4 *Key features of logico-scientific vs. narrative modes*

Logico-scientific (formal)	Narrative (social)
scientific proofs	gripping drama
statistical regularities	audience involvement
survey research	ethnographic research
objective, replicable findings	verisimilitude

also analyze the kinds of meanings that individuals build up collaboratively with other people, through narrative.

Research on how individuals *create a story about* their experiences around dialect can provide an important trail of data indicating how social value accrues to certain ways of speaking. Such stories can illuminate how "dialects" and "accents" get recognized and named in the first place, and how they come to be associate with certain situations, local contexts, types of people, or walks of life.

The Role of Web 2.0 in Storytelling

The *New York Times* dialect survey article and its instant popularity (the most read *NYT* article of that year) exemplifies how the Internet has become an effective medium not only for telling and recirculating stories, but also for accumulating reactions and additions to those stories. Rather than being a repository of information like a linguistic atlas (for example, Labov, Ash, and Boberg's [2006] *Atlas of North American English*), social media's participatory momentum provides a medium for continued accrual of social information, and it fosters webs of connection between users and ideas.

While the socially generated value of accent is nothing new, convergence culture and Web 2.0 discourse analysis afford new ways to investigate this process. While Web 1.0 facilitates information generation and stockpiling in the logico-scientific mode, Web 2.0 facilitates collaborative sharing of ideas and the testing out of multiple perspectives, providing unique affordances for what Bruner describes as "narrative modes" of knowing (see Table 5.5). In their theoretical extremes, Bruner's epistemic modes of "logico-scientific" and "narrative" correspond analogously to the internet modes of Web 1.0 and Web 2.0.

Table 5.5 *Modes of knowing as analogues to Web 1.0 and Web 2.0*

Epistemic modes	Internet modes
Logico-scientific	**Web 1.0**
Knowledge as decontextualized, standardized	Internet as information stockpile; information valued and categorized via top-down sorting methods (taxonomically)
Narrative	**Web 2.0**
Knowing as culturally situated, achieved through storytelling	Internet as social web through which forms of information gain value; what counts as important emerges through collaboration and participation (folksonomically)

Convergence culture, specifically, "the flow of content across multiple media platforms" (Jenkins, 2006, p. 2) and Web 2.0 provide a context for collaborative narrative about accent and accounting for the different social value of distinct ways of speaking.

The YouTube Accent Challenge: Web 2.0 Pathways to Understanding the Social Value of Distinct Ways of Speaking

The field of sociolinguistics has as one of its primary concerns the "social value" that speakers place on certain acoustic features, or "accent." Originally, dialectologists made maps that made statistical correlations between phonetic features, lexicon, and specified geographical regions or social categories. However, as the field has developed, methods for understanding how dialect correlates with place have departed from traditional statistical field methods of dialectologists. Johnstone (2004), for example, looking at features of "Texan" and "Pittsburghese," emphasizes that it is people and their practices rather than geographers and their measurement tools that make "localness" come to life. For example, "Pittsburghese," she writes, "is a set of linguistic features that overlaps with but is not the same as the set a sociolinguist might choose on the basis of observation" (2004, p. 78). Recognizable features of a local dialect, like the word "yinz" for you-plural in "Pittsburghese" or "y'all" in "Texan," do not necessarily mark a person as living in Pittsburgh or Texas proper, but as identifying with a complex array of social identifiers related to being a speaker of "Pittsburghese" or "Texan."

Echoing Johnstone, Eckert emphasizes that speech "localness" is "never an association with a generic locale but with a particular construction of that locale as distinct from some other" (2008, p. 462). Speakers negotiate performance of identity by stylistically choosing to use certain socially recognizable dialect features, like "negative concord" or "/t/ release." Eckert has conceptualized the dynamic nature of these social identifiers as the "indexical field" – the "field of potential meanings" – of certain variable speech features. Just like features of "Pittsburghese" or "Texan," these features do not map statistically onto static identities. Rather, they suggest stances, which in different contexts may have different meanings. The indexical field of maximal /t/ release, for example, includes the stances like "formal," "clear," "polite," or "exasperated," which may or may not index social types of "British Person" and "School Teacher" but also "Gay Diva" and "Nerd Girl." How stances accumulate to point to these social types becomes a matter of highly localized negotiation. As such, these social types are not objective labels, based on decontextualizable variables, but dynamically and collaboratively produced identities, contingent on interaction.

Given the globalizing nature of interaction in both face-to-face and internet spaces, such indexical fields become more layered and complicated.

Individuals who gather, say, in an airport bar, or a YouTube comments section, bring multiple indexical fields into contact. Blommaert and Backus (2012) describe the contemporary complexity of each individual's "indexical biography," noting that in today's context of mobility and globalization, individuals may know bits and pieces of many languages and varieties of speaking, and the meaning of each of those portions of one's repertoire may have highly variable identity value depending on the context. In online spaces like YouTube, such indexical emblems may come together in increasingly common mash-up form and include elaborated comment threads, or what Androutsopoulos (2013) calls a "participatory spectacle." Looking specifically at German dialect tagged videos and responses to them Androutsopoulos analyzes the complexity of dialect discourse in the comment sections. Commentary illustrates that speakers are attuned to the 1.0 descriptions of dialect, but also to the 2.0 understandings of what those dialect features index. Even when German dialect performers include all features of local dialects officially recognized and documented by linguists, "this does not make their dialect performances authentic in the eyes of some commenters, who assess authenticity based on the entire performance rather than isolated dialect features" (2013, p. 61). Androutsopoulos here points to the necessarily contextualized nature of the social value people place on distinct ways of speaking.

To understand the social value of "Pittsburghese," (Johnstone, 2004) or the properties of an "indexical field" (Eckert, 2008), one's "indexical biography" (Blommaert and Backus, 2012) or an online "participatory spectacle" (Androutsopoulos, 2013), we need a medium/method that allows us to trace the accumulation of social value. The best medium/method available is those conversations (online or face-to-face) in which we can observe and participate in talking *about* language use (Rymes 2014). As Johnstone writes, to understand the local social value of categories like "Texan" or "Pittsburghese," researchers need to spend time "listening to and looking at local representations of local speech as they are created and drawn upon in various genres of *metalinguistic* talk" (2004, p. 78, emphasis mine). Narrative accounts in YouTube accent challenge videos exemplify one such "genre of metalinguistic talk," and are an ideal medium/method for investigating such local representations of speech types. The Accent Challenge videos also illustrate a path from 1.0, logico-scientific context (as exemplified by the original dialect survey and statistical methods for compiling linguistic atlases) into 2.0 narrative context, as hundreds of thousands of people have voluntarily posted videos of themselves reading a version of a dialect survey, collaboratively and *thinkingly* turning the survey into a narrative performance.

Table 5.6 illustrates the list typically used for the Accent Challenge. Unlike the ideal scientific subjects envisioned by the original researchers, YouTube performers never read the list through without interruption. Instead, they

Table 5.6 *Sample word list and lexical prompts for the Accent Challenge*

Sample word list
Wash, Oil, Theater, Sure, Data, Ruin, Crayon, Toilet, Spitting Image, Syrup, Aunt, Roof, Route, Theater, Iron, Salmon, Caramel, Fire, Water, New Orleans, Pecan, Both, Again, Probably, Alabama, Lawyer, Coupon, Mayonnaise, Pajamas, Caught, Naturally, Aluminum, Envelope

Sample questions
- What is it called when you throw toilet paper on a house?
- What is the bug that when you touch it, it curls into a ball?
- What is a bubbly carbonated drink called?
- What do you call gym shoes?
- What do you call your grandparents?
- What do you call the kind of spider (or spider-like creature) that has an oval-shaped body and extremely long legs?
- What do you call the wheeled contraption in which you carry groceries at the supermarket?
- What is the thing you change the TV channel with?
- What do you call it when rain falls while the sun is shining?
- What do you say to address a group of people?

---

alternate between performing the word list and elicitations and offering side-commentary to their viewers. The YouTubers behind the Accent Challenge videos choose to emphasize or dismiss whatever they wish, and usually tell stories, give examples, and talk at length about the nuanced uses and pronunciations of any given word or phrase, thus providing stories about their accent and eliciting series of second stories from viewers.

Accent Challenge Narratives

Let's now look more closely at two performers, thethugyone (also a star of Chapter 4) and LifeTracking, both illustrative of the Philadelphia Accent Challenge. Each of their performances includes lengthy asides and stories about their own experience of accent and their decision to perform the Accent Challenge on YouTube. Characteristic of most YouTube accent challenge videos, both thethugyone and LifeTracking's videos include long introductory narratives. Thethugyone, for example, narrates at length before starting to read the word list and lexical prompts:

THETHUGYONE: All right so yeah, um, for the past twelve days, or whatever, I've been sick with the flu. And then on top of the flu, I got pneumonia, and, um, sinusitis on top of it. So, today's like actually the first day I'm feeling better in a long time. In a looooong time. So, um, being sick I've been on YouTube watching videos, like, incessantly, just for entertainment, you know. And I came across like different Accent Challenge videos so I figure, I'm from South Philly, I can do a accent, too. I mean, just the way I talk, or whatever. So, um . . . yeah. I figured I would do it, and, maybe you guys can relate to it? I don't know if there's anyone from South Philly or from Philly in general who knows this accent. Um, people who aren't from like the East Coast hear the accent and they think it's New York. But trust me, I'm from here, I'm from Philly, and when I hear a New York accent, it's not the same. So you're all craaazy. Anyway, so the Accent Challenge here it goes ...

Thethugyone's (2015) introduction includes many standard components we think of as "narrative"-like (see Table 5.7). It sets a scene by talking about how he came across Accent Challenge videos while he was at home sick and watching YouTube "incessantly." He builds drama around his own pending performance by introducing a common misconception about Philadelphia accents ("they think it's New York"), and provides some foreshadowing, suggesting his own accent will be not be anything like a New York accent. He sets himself up as a protagonist ("trust me I know") and those other "craaazy" people as antagonists. And he engages his audience of viewers by appealing to them directly to empathize with his performance ("maybe you guys can relate to it?"). Finally, he concludes with a generalizing message ("trust me, I'm from here, I'm from Philly, and when I hear a New York accent, it's not the same") based on the expertise he is presumably about to display when he reads the word lists.

While most Accent Challenge introductions include these components, the message around the various accent performances varies considerably, even when individuals are performing, ostensibly, the "same" accent. LifeTracking, for example, narratively introduces her performance of the "Philly" accent, but her story conveys a very different message:

LIFETRACKING: A friend of mine suggested that I make a Acc–or do like an Accent Challenge? Make like a video about my "Philly accent" because I "talk funny" . . . I really don't think I have [an accent], but researching "Philly accents" and like, what the hell is a Philly accent, and like, a Accent Challenge? And last night,

Table 5.7 *Narrative components of thethugyone's introduction*

Narratives generally ...	Thethugyone says ...
set a scene	"been sick for 12 days, watching videos incessantly"
build drama	"some people think the Philly accent is New York!"
tell of protagonists and antagonists	"some people" vs. "trust me, I know"
engage an audience	"maybe you guys can relate to it?"
seize the floor for an extended time	holds the floor with a promise of reading the list
have a message/coda	"I'm from Philly, and when I hear a New York accent, it's not the same. So you're all craaazy."

I came across Tumblr's Accent Challenge, which is about a year old but I didn't really know about it, I don't really use Tumblr ... so basically I'm gonna read off a bunch of words and answer a couple of questions ... and I think the vowels in the words, they choose these words because the vowels kinda show off your accent, like, if you have one, wherever your accent might come from, um and the answers to the questions I guess show, what kind of words or slang you use from where you're from or what you call certain things ... So I guess today it's all about the Accent Challenge, and I accept it! And I'm gonna do it, [puts on baseball cap backwards] Philly style.

Like thethugyone's introduction, LifeTracking's (2012) narrative includes typical narrative elements. She sets the scene, saying friends encouraged her to record her accent and describing how she came across the word list on Tumblr. She builds drama by emphasizing the "challenge" aspect of the activity ("Today it's all about the Accent Challenge – and I accept it!"). In this way she also positions herself as a protagonist in this story, and those who say she talks "funny" as antagonists. She also makes an effort to engage the viewing audience, providing a little information about why she thinks these words have been chosen for the list she's about to read ("the vowels kind of show off your accent – if you have one"), and like thethugyone, she holds the conversational floor (or the YouTube listener captive) with the promise of going through the word list. However, her coda or message differs substantially from thethugyone. Rather than concluding that anyone who makes pronouncements about the Philly accent is "craaaazy," she accepts these critiques as real challenges. She also has some Philly pride, like thethugyone, but she explicitly "accepts" the fact that people might be challenging her and, further, that they may indeed be correct by saying her accent is funny, even though she doesn't think she has any accent at all.

Table 5.8 *Narrative components of LifeTracking's introduction*

Narratives generally ...	LifeTracking says ...
set a scene	"A friend of mine suggested that I make a Acc–or do like an Accent Challenge?"
build drama	"A friend of mine suggested ... I 'talk funny' ... what the hell is a Philly accent, and like, a Accent Challenge?"
tell of protagonists and antagonists	"A friend of mine suggested ... I 'talk funny'" ... versus "I really don't think I have [an accent]"
engage an audience	("the vowels kind of show off your accent – if you have one")
seize the floor for an extended time	holds the floor with a promise of reading the list
have a message/coda	"it's all about the Accent Challenge, and I accept it! And I'm gonna do it, ((*puts on baseball cap backwards*)) Philly style."

Collaborative Narration of the Accent Challenge

While it is possible to understand these YouTuber's narratives as individual productions, their relevance beyond the individual emerges in the way their viewers comment, contributing to the story or message presented in the original narrative, building a collective narrative – and piling on distinctly contextual social value – around certain ways of speaking. While the performances by thethugyone and LifeTracking are both based on the identical language prompts, the narrative quality of the comments around their sociolinguistic portraits are unexpectedly distinctive.

Thethugyone: Comments about Place

References to place dominate thethugyone's comment feed. As of early November 2015, there were comments posted by 12 different viewers and nine of them made remarks about place:

COMMENT A: I love the accent. A man I loved very much was from South Philly with a deep voice and odd irish accents. I miss him, thanks for talking online.
COMMENT B: South Philly's accents are totally different from new York
COMMENT C: Don't get cocky! SP represent!
COMMENT D: Hahaha! Numonyeh! I hate the Philly accent. I live in California now, and always get mistaken for a New Yorker.
COMMENT E: Wayne AVE
COMMENT F: 10th and reed here, this is legit, all of these other philly accents on youtube are so crazy I thought I was losing my shit but this has grounded me
COMMENT G: Hey I talk da same way..huh Maybe cause I'm From south Philly
COMMENT H: Dude I agree with you throughout the entire vid. I don't know why Californians think that it's New York. Idiots!
COMMENT I: Your right about the Ny/PA accents. I'm from Buffalo and I don't sound anything like ya. Take it easy.

These viewers' comments contribute to the crafting of thethugyone's story and message – in the process of talking about accent and enacting its social value. For example, Comment E, "Wayne AVE," and Comment F, "10th and reed here," accentuate thethugyone's mention of his own South Philly location at "Tenth and Wharton." Through these local shout-outs, the comments highlight the drama of the controversy over accent in South Philadelphia and their own very real place in it. Other comments build up the theme of Philadelphia as distinct from New York. Comment H supports thethugyone, against the "idiots" who think "it's New York." Even Comment I, from Buffalo, joins the thethugyone's side, "your right about the ny/PA accents," despite taking an outsider's perspective, "I'm from Buffalo and I don't sound anything like ya." Each of these voices contributes to thethugyone's initial claim: "I'm from South Philly I can do a accent too."

These comments and the threaded interaction they cultivate also bring out the strong emotions associated with place and accent, from love to hate: One commenter brings out the "love" side of the story, "I love the accent. A man I loved very much was from South Philly ... thanks for talking on line," and thethugyone responds with his own comment, "You're welcome and thanks for the compliments :)". Even the one person (Commenter D, above) who says he "hates the Philadelphia accent" precedes it with a "hahaha" and seems to savor thethugyone's pronunciation of pneumonia as "numonyeh." Thethugyone himself responds to this comment in good humor, "I hate it too! lol." Ten months later, another YouTuber registers her "hate" of the Philadelphia accent – in contrast with her "love" for New York:

COMMENTER J: Ahh I hate my Philly accent too lol. But love the New York accent.

This remark, though it mentions "hate" for the Philly accent, has nuance. It echoes the jokey delivery of Commenter D's "hate" for the Philadelphia accent and thethugyone's response to it and has a tone of underdog-like self-deprecation that Philadelphia is arguably infamous for. Over several months, these YouTube comment threads include proclamations of love and hate accompanied with degrees of hedging (lol) or irony – all contributing to the ongoing accrual of camaraderie around South Philadelphia ways of speaking.

LifeTracking: Comments about "Water"

While comments for thethugyone are dominated by place, some very specific, they include zero mentions of the word most frequently discussed in other South Philadelphia accent challenge video comments: "water" (also referred to in the comments sections of these videos as *wooder, wud-ur, wooter,* and *wutta*). Comments for LifeTracking, in contrast, focalize the word "water." LifeTracking's commenters mention places, but primarily to highlight the non-local. This provides a sharp contrast to thethugyone's commenters, who highlight place names as a source of local pride and connection. LifeTracking's commenters bring up geographically large, faraway places like Florida and Las Vegas, where people have a hard time understanding their "funny" accent, as exemplified in stories about "water":

COMMENT A: I can remember being about 6–7 years old and bein in florida on vaca n askin the waitress for water n she had no idea wat i was sayin cause we pronounce it wuter
COMMENT B: i've lived in florida since I was 11 ... I still can't order a "wooder wida lemon" without people saying "huh?"
COMMENT C: I am from Levittown and when I say "water, clicker, or burogh (you know a piece of furniture you put your underwear in!) I get so much crap from my new friends here in Las Vegas!! Another word for you to add to your list is ... WATER ICE

Just as thethugyone's comments construct an emergent message out of his narrative ("You're from South Philly, you have an accent, it is super-local, and you out there are the crazy ones if you think it's the same as New York"), comments on LifeTracking's Accent Challenge construct an emergent account of the social value of "wooder." Through statements like, "she had no idea wat i was sayin cause we pronounce it wuter," "I still can't order a 'wooder wida lemon' without people saying 'huh?'," and "when I say *water* . . . I get so much crap from my new friends here in Las Vegas!!" commenters support *and help to construct* LifeTracking's message: This accent definitely *is* funny and it has given me a lot of grief!

Internet-circulated YouTube accent narratives illustrate one way that linguistic tokens of "accent" get their social value through storytelling and, more specifically, storytelling sparked by the opportunity to talk about language. In YouTube Accent Challenge videos, a performer initially constructs a narrative text and broadcasts it. In the process, this performer also elicits further talk about language, often in the form of more stories. Through these comments, certain parts of the text – words like "water" or "Acme" or phrases like "Tenth and Reed, here!" – accrue social value or local prestige. Stories about using "wooder" may accumulate in the comments section, while stories about "pecans" (another word on the dialect survey) may never show up.

This narrative approach to YouTube videos about language goes beyond a simple count of views, thumbs ups, and comments to provide a sense of the process that builds the social value of a word, or a phrase, or a way of speaking. Messages emerge in the accent performance, but continue to be formed through comments and dialogue around those comments. For LifeTracking, a message emerges that might be paraphrased as "I guess I do talk 'funny'." For thethugyone, the emergent message might be, "My accent is super-local and I like that!" (with the added nuance of the layered and affectionate "I hate it too! Lol" comment). Both of these messages may continue to be constructed as valid or be debunked by further commentary.

The divergent narratives of thethugyone and LifeTracking continue, to this moment, to illustrate the contingent character of narratives about accent and their potential to accrue social value. As of this writing, LifeTracking has disappeared from YouTube, while thethugyone and his Accent Challenge video, first posted in 2013, continues to garner viewers, comments, and compliments. The thethugyone continues to interact with his following and, in the process, continues to build a YouTube self-portrait around his own South Philly way of talking and being.

The Dark Side of Web 2.0, "Stories," and Spreadability

Stories

Stories, and small stories, like those told by these YouTubers and in the replies to their videos, can propel ongoing engagement, a more detailed accounting of the role of language and "accent" in individuals' lives. These citizen sociolinguists have harnessed the affordances of Web 2.0 networking, the intimacy of small-storytelling, and the spreadability of narrative to share details about the ways they speak and how people react. However, not only citizen sociolinguists are using these media. Currently, marketers have harnessed the power of spreadability, and the intuitive draw of the word "story" to encourage users to share constantly online. A feature called "Stories" on apps like Snapchat, Instagram, and now Facebook, encourages users to incrementally post bits and pieces of "stories" as they unfold in their lives. Now, instead of using words, however, people on these apps largely tell their stories in pictures, the narrative of, say a surprise party unfolding in pictures of the set-up, the surprise, and the aftermath. While these pictures may mimic the arc of narrative, their production and "sharing" is so orchestrated by the technology to serve ulterior motives: to collect as much data as possible about the users – data that can be packaged and sold to marketing firms and drive advertising placement. The intimate moments of sharing we see on comment threads about accent are very different from the thousands (millions!) of likes generated by the stories of "influencers" on Instagram and similar apps. Is this the direction Web 2.0 and spreadability is taking us?

Technological Determinism versus Technological Affordances

To suggest that the Internet is doing this to humanity smacks of what has been called "technological determinism" – the notion that the technology itself is forcing humans to be a certain way. In the case of "stories" on apps, it can seem that the technology is turning us into self-absorbed people who are constantly snapping pictures of ourselves and trying to tell stories about the incredible amounts of fun we are all having (though we might be crying on the inside).

However, despite the specter of these apps, and the way they seem to take over our lives, technological innovations like iPhones and apps do not have the power to make us do things. They are made by people and used by people. Some may even argue that technology doesn't determine our actions or psychological states, it exposes who we are and the motivations we already have.

To account for the role people play when they interact with technology of any kind, it may be more useful to draw on the concept of technological affordance. James J. Gibson originally offered up the theory of "affordance" as a learning theory. As humans develop in any environment, they learn how to make use of its affordances. If we are going on a hike for example and start to get tired, we may see an old tree stump and recognize its affordance as a place to sit down. As we go on more hikes, we learn more about the environment we are walking through and its affordances. Not only is a stump good for sitting, but some stumps are better than others. Those surrounded by poison ivy might not be so good! Similarly, within the internet environment, early participants on the YouTube side began to interact with it as a social media site (2.0 style), even though its creators initially conceptualized it as a repository for video (1.0 style). As I've shown here, in the interaction with YouTube, users find new affordances: the possibility to share accent videos and to spin stories about the value of those accents in their lives. Technology doesn't determine how people use the site, instead new affordances develop as individuals interact with the platform.

Now tech creators have recognized the affordances of 2.0 networking, and the spreadability of stories and added another twist to our social media environment: the "stories app." Users have swarmed to Instagram to post their stories. And they have begun to use it to gather "likes," to become "famous," and to become influencers and brand ambassadors. It can seem like the technology is controlling them. But the technology was made by humans, those with motives to line their pockets. They have used the affordances of the 2.0 technology, of "stories" and "sharing" to build their databases of consumer information. In the process, even the words like "stories" and "sharing" seem to have been coopted. However, innovation need not always tilt in the direction of the bottom line.

As Rushkoff has pointed out, the networking affordances of social media also provide us with the tools to "find our people." These can be people who buy the same brands we do (what marketing companies are looking for) or they can be people who speak like we do, like the Welsh language, or think the Philadelphia accent is beautiful. They could also be people who want us to join a terrorist group. These networks are powerful. But they do not determine our actions. We now must be aware of our social media environment and its potential affordances. We need to be aware of how we are using these networks and the kinds of conversations we are having with them and about them. They do not determine our actions, but they do have affordances – for the better and the worse – that we understand minimally or that are yet to emerge. We need to talk about these apps, these technologies, these words like "stories" and "sharing" in ways that recognize their affordances – and how we interact with them can affect their uses in our world.

Rituals of Self-Exposure and Trust

Accent Challenge performances are one type of story – one way that people talk about language together – building a simple listing of linguistic tokens into a narrative. These performances in turn generate commentary – also often in the form of small stories. This process constructs the emergent social value of accent. These empirical points have some methodological implications – modeled in the medium we have used for our inquiry: Self-conscious linguistic performances, as opposed to "unthinking" responses to sociolinguistic surveys, count as data. Moreover, we can assess their validity by following social media-generated metacommentary.

These strangely intimate identity displays are also Goffmanian rituals (1981) of self-exposure and trust. Accent challengers spin out long biographical narratives that contextualize their relationship with language, offering an invitation to viewers to engage in their self-narrative: "I speak like this, maybe you can relate to that." Accent challenge performances provide a framework for narrating the "self," in concert with viewers, as performers and commenters co-construct emergent social value for certain ways of speaking. These YouTubers don't need to ask linguists "Who am I?" or even "Where am I from?" Their performances are narrative acts that allow speakers to explore those questions themselves and with any interested collaborators, as citizen sociolinguists.

6 Acts of Citizen Sociolinguistics

> How do we investigate acts through which subjects transform themselves into citizens?
> Engin F. Isin, *Acts of Citizenship* (2008, p. 18)

While Chapter 1 directly addressed the meaning of the word "citizen" and its meaning in different situations, this chapter focuses on the "act" itself of being a citizen sociolinguist. More specifically, we develop an account of citizen sociolinguistic "acts," as distinct from systemic social movements or organized social *action*. Citizen sociolinguistic acts are momentary ruptures that reveal tacit assumptions behind our everyday use of language. As such they may lead to change, but they might not. But in any case, these acts of talking about language transform subjects into citizen sociolinguists. As Isin (2008) puts it above, through such acts, "subjects transform themselves into citizens." Acts, as idiosyncratic and situationally specific, have existential qualities that remain outside typical top-down social theoretical explanations like Marxism's theory of capital, a Foucauldian system of discipline, a Bourdieusian habitus, or the enregisterment of language norms across a speech chain. Consider, for example, these commonly recognized discrete acts and what might exemplify them:

Act of kindness
Act of forgiveness
Act of faith
Act of courage, generosity, violence

Each of these brings to mind *instances* or *encounters* with another being, not necessarily a systemic set of forces that we might associate more with the term "social action." Similarly, acts of citizen sociolinguistics, like those we've been discussing throughout this volume, consist of encounters with another:

Act of sociolinguistic arrest
Act of sociolinguistic wonderment

These acts of citizen sociolinguistics do not, on their own, reconfigure systemic relations, ethics, or spoken language, any more than an "act of kindness" or an "act of violence" might. They are not large-scale curricular reforms or policy changes. However, they raise our awareness of our humanity and relatedness – our Bakhtinian "answerability" – and the role of language in it, in ways that can provoke further talk and have a societal impact. After discussing and exemplifying each of these types of acts, I'll contrast them with what Deborah Cameron has called "language policing." We'll see how the concept of "language policing" and related concepts like "undoing appropriateness" describe a more systematic imposition of a perceived order on everyday language, and the need for resistance to that order. This portrayal of language debates is existentially distinct from acts of citizen sociolinguistics – either whimsical acts of wonderment, or the more jarring acts of arrest. Acts of wonderment or arrest provoke new perspectives on language and society, and as such, are acts of citizen sociolinguistics that constitute their own chaotic moments outside of top-down systems of control.

Acts of Arrest and Wonderment

To review, let's consider an abbreviated docket of citizen sociolinguistic arrests that have appeared throughout this volume:
- *Greenwich Street* in Philadelphia is not pronounced like *Greenwich Village* in New York. It's *Green witch* street.
- Passyunk Ave is originally a Native American word and it's pronounced "Pashunk."
- What do you mean by "citizen" or "citizenship"? Have you considered using a different word?
- "Jawn in the fun" is a horrible use of the word *jawn*.
- Why bother with Konglish when your English is so good?
- "Everyone can hug but only the Welsh can cytch" is not an original statement.
- Don't speak Chinese in this building, or you will face unintended consequences.

We've also encountered instances of wonderment. Let's consider their range:
- *Greenwich Street* in Philadelphia is not pronounced like *Greenwich Village* in New York. It's *Green witch* street!
- "Hoagie" is a unique Philadelphia word! So is "water ice"!
- Teens in Virginia Beach use the word "weg" to mean almost anything
- People in Philadelphia really say "jawn"? It means "thing"?
- Konglish is so cute!
- People respond to online conversations about language with enthusiasm and engagement.
- Most language videos have a higher like ratio than the all-time viral hit, "Charlie Bit My Finger."

Readers may have noticed some overlap in these lists. A word or phrase or way of speaking that one person finds problematic may strike another person with wonderment. Some people find Konglish cute and wonder at it, others see it as a frivolous affectation, to be corrected in a citizen's arrest. This contrast in itself may spark a wonderment in readers, because it opens a window into the social historical layers that invisibly contribute to all our conversations.

Even the most unintentional act of wonderment or arrest – from savoring someone's pronunciation of the word "wooder" to arresting them over a ban on the Chinese language – is an act of citizen sociolinguistics. In some scenarios, these acts will spark conversation about controversial language issues, promoting social change. In others, that act of citizen sociolinguistics will simply get people talking. In either case, those small moments of savoring language or critiquing it, these acts of citizen sociolinguistics, have the potential to build conversations about language across groups of people, across situations, and across media platforms. Let's now consider how these small acts of citizen sociolinguistics differ from more programmatic approaches to critical language awareness.

Language Policing and Undoing Appropriateness

Frequently, issues about how to talk or what one can say become much more controversial than the whimsical pronunciations of Philadelphia street names. Most citizens are reluctant to make a real "citizen's arrest." Even in the face of an obvious crime, the risks – physical and legal – are also obvious. Even if I see someone pulling a gun on another human, I admit, I'm more likely to call 911 than step in and make a citizen's arrest. But what Deborah Cameron calls "language policing" happens constantly. This happens when people "police" the language of women, or African Americans, or multilingual people, or anyone noticeably outside the norm.

In her blog post, "Just Don't Do It," for example, Deborah Cameron specifically critiques the reams of advice to women about how they should speak to be successful (Stop apologizing! Lose the high pitch, use less body language, avoid uptalk). Cameron's insights about language advice for women have parallels in recent discussions about advice given to other non-mainstream-white-male groups in the United States. Just as women should mind their use of "women's language," African Americans should avoid their use of African American English, and bilinguals should be mindful of how they use their "home language." To be successful, just as women should not apologize so much, avoid the word "just," and stop ending sentences with "uptalk," African Americans should avoid "African American English" in "formal" spaces like classrooms or job interviews, and they should code-switch to "standard" English; and bilinguals should be proud of their multilingual resources but keep their "home language" at home.

Each of these pieces of advice smacks of double standard and stereotype. Underlining the double standard, Cameron points out that we never read articles that provide such advice for white men. She cites an ironically imagined article offering advice to men about not punctuating their sentences with words like "actually, obviously, seriously, and frankly" because "this verbal tic makes them sound like pompous bullshitters, so that people switch off and stop listening to what they're saying. If they want to be successful, this is something men need to address." While this (imaginary!) description is framed as friendly advice for success, it functions as both an articulation of a stereotype about men and a criticism of men's language. While this imagined article – stereotyping men and then providing advice about how they should speak to be successful – sounds preposterous, it succinctly pinpoints a specific act of language policing: Women are constantly being stereotyped inaccurately, then advised to adjust that stereotyped speech if they want to be taken seriously: Don't use the word "just" ... stop apologizing, avoid uptalk, no vocal fry, the list goes on. Cameron also points out that these descriptions of the speech are inaccurate, based on biased assumptions: Women don't necessarily apologize more than men. Instead, this is a stereotype about women that affects our everyday perceptions.

Nelson Flores and Jonathan Rosa have illustrated how stereotypes similarly affect how we perceive the speech of minorities as more "informal" or bilingual children as "long-term English language learners." They have also shown how a double standard exists for what counts as "appropriate" English in US classrooms. The label of "appropriate" is used far more flexibly for white students, who inevitably and freely range across levels of formality, than it is for African American students, whose language is far more rigorously policed. In the same way men "get away with" apologizing, hedging, and using uptalk, while women get called out for it, white people use "informal" language as much if not more than African Americans do – even in so-called "formal" spaces.

Similar advice about multilingualism exists and has been critiqued. Often, multilingualism is coveted and admired – unless the speaker is from a certain ethnic background. Rosa and Flores have coined the term "raciolinguistics" to describe the way a speaker's race influences perceptions of their language – as well as the type of "well-meaning" advice a multilingual individual might receive. Flores also points out the double standard: While white males are praised for even the most stumbling attempts to speak Spanish in a public space in the United States, Latinos are condemned for not speaking perfectly unaccented English. While a white man receives praise for even minimal Spanish proficiency, multilingual brown-skinned children are labeled "long-term English learners," despite their wide-ranging communicative abilities in both English and Spanish.

Reconsidering "appropriateness" and resisting the relentless quality of patriarchal advice to women, illuminating the self-deceiving "facts" that uphold arguments that keep women and minorities hustling to act in more normative ways, while discrimination against them marches on – these applications of sociolinguistic knowledge are different from bare acts of arrest and wonderment. They are instances of systemic social action, not individual acts. They are contributing to an established literature and debate, and they are put forward by those who presume already to be speaking for the citizenry. As such, instances of language policing, or recognition of such policing, differ from more quirky and situational acts of citizen sociolinguistics.

Acts of citizen sociolinguistics are performed every day by those substantial clumps of people who neither conform to nor directly react to norms of appropriateness or patriarchy, but who nevertheless reveal themselves and their concerns through everyday talk about language, talk that transforms them into citizen sociolinguists. These acts reveal how smart and savvy and subversive they are, sometimes intentionally, but more often just as a matter of everyday life. This happens in an act of arrest, for example, when someone posts a sign that says "Jawn in on the fun" as an instance of linguistic gentrification, calling out white gentrifiers for appropriating Philly's black language and character. Or, through an act of wonderment, when people spend 30 minutes discussing the word "gas" as it is used by one unique peer group. It's as if people surprise themselves with their own concern, insight, and interest. Citizen sociolinguistic "hacks" like cross-posting, or ingenious uses of Google Translate, reveal the even more nuanced, momentary, non-regimented forms these acts of citizen sociolinguistics can take.

Hacks like these, the repurposing of old linguistic tools, acts of wonderment and arrest, posting an accent challenge video, or commenting on one – all of these ways of talking about language collectively build an alternative ethic for thinking about language and how it accrues social value. Until we account for the knowledge circulating in these everyday conversations about language – unless we consider the expertise of individual acts of citizen sociolinguistics – so-called expert descriptions and prescriptions will have little relevance or impact beyond our own specialized world of language professionals (or non-professionals). Sociolinguistics, to be relevant, to have an impact, needs to account for all acts of citizen sociolinguistics. In this way, acts of citizen sociolinguistics differ in a subtle way from language policing.

Social media potentially provide us with the medium and the method needed to link up the roles of everyday citizen sociolinguist, academic blogger, and professional sociolinguistic researcher, creating what Henry Jenkins (2007) has called "convergence culture" – a collision between old media (e.g., scholarly publications) and new media (e.g., YouTube-circulated opinions about language). In the citizen sociolinguist/scholar convergence, the Internet does not simply provide "data" for professional linguists, nor do language scholars simply provide "expertise" for citizens. Instead, social media provide a mechanism for combined scholarly and citizen-centered pursuits. Ideally, as questions and concerns of citizens become more visible and salient to a scholarly community, the scholarly community addresses questions more relevant to the finely tuned communicative details of local social and political contexts.

Bureaucratic Control of Knowledge: Built-In Self-Preservation Mechanisms

As the Duke email illustrates, not only academics themselves but academic institutions can have slow, creaky bureaucratic ways of functioning and *built-in self-preservation mechanisms*. Academic expertise, for example, is ostensibly built on the shoulders of giants, or brilliant forefathers – and we do much to preserve the legacy of those giants, lest we all collapse. Similarly, institutions – of higher education and otherwise – maintain their legitimacy, not by airing dirty laundry, but by discussing any hints of scandal or controversy behind closed doors. Statements are issued, adjustments are made. Often cloaked in the passive voice, appearances are maintained. But this passive voice also hides the people who create those scandalous conditions. Unfair or inhumane conditions appear to be harsh, but pre-existent – a reality we must come to terms with, but that none of us created. A natural disaster or a genetic inheritance. The "conditions" are presented as "unintended consequences," as if nobody created them.

What these institutional tacks have in common is their attempt to control the discussion about language and indeed language itself. Institutions would like to avoid situations like Duke faced with their "no-Chinese" email scandal. From the perspective of the institution, life would have been much more convenient if someone had just quietly reported that email to the proper assistant dean – then millions of people around the world would never have participated in a debate about the place of multilingualism in the halls of elite universities.

In the hands of everyday people, however, outside the definitions and discretion of institutional protocol, discussions about language can go every which way. And they can become painfully – but often productively – public. In this way, everyday conversations about language are simultaneously acts of citizenship. When talking about language and what to do with it, individuals are contributing to civic dialogue about what can and can't, should and shouldn't be said. They are not subjecting themselves to a test of citizenship or producing the appropriate documents required to be in this or that nation state.

Everyday conversations about language, feature little control or predictability of the type bureaucracies or academics like to wield. Instead of conceptualizing citizens as mindless followers – which most of us in democratic societies do not – we have represented citizen sociolinguists here as any people engaging in everyday conversations about language. They are not docilely taking citizenship tests, or blindly following language rules. Instead, they are actively producing themselves as part of a sociolinguistic citizenry through discussions of language. While many may be ventriloquizing views about language that come from more entrenched institutional definitions, or stereotyped sociolinguistic shibboleths, inevitably, by being released from the control of institutional discourse around those rules and expectations and into the more chaotic interplay of difference and alternative perspectives, any view is subject to questioning. Truths about language will be called out as "myths"; bilingualism will be dismissed and praised; definitions of words like "harassment," "bias," "discrimination," or "freedom of speech" will be tested and rewritten; "proper" pronunciations will be posited and rejected and infused with new value. New stories will be told about how language helped, hindered, confused, or connected people – and schooled them about the world.

Journeying through endlessly recursive discussions of language on the Internet has the potential to create a broader culture of critical thinking around language – and a more democratic approach to language research, learning, policy, and practice. There will inevitably be roadblocks on this journey, but at least two of them, discussed below, are self-imposed, and as such can be overcome.

Roadblocks to Acts of Citizen Sociolinguistics: Self-Censorship and Gated Language Communities

As we've seen throughout this volume, comments on YouTube videos about language are for the most part positive – and often over-the-top enthusiastic! If someone is sharing some thoughts about Philadelphia Street Names, Things Welsh People Say, or the Konglish Accent Challenge, for example, most comment threads will unfurl with agreement, praise of the language portrayal, or provision of a few more examples or personal anecdotes to support the points being made. Most viewers give "thumbs up" to the videos and to any positive comments. "Thumbs down" are rare. Probably because of this field of positive engagement, there are quite a lot of very amateur citizen sociolinguists out there posting about their language videos and fielding comments from anyone who cares to watch and write. But when internet trolls roll into town, everyone's ability to comment can be cut off, and most of us want to hide. We present our views only to each other, not strangers invited to comment, and we take refuge in our gated communities of like-minded language users, the potential for either arrest or wonderment lost. Let's take a brief journey down this dark path now.

Self-Censorship: Comments on Gender-Neutral Pronouns

At least one set of language-related posts has emerged as a glaring exception to the general positivity surrounding posts about language: posts discussing gender pronouns. One of the more widely viewed YouTube tutorials on this topic, Gender Pronouns: Get Them Right, illuminates the negativity that can swarm to this more controversial topic. (www.youtube.com/watch?v=gXLFdYNEl_I)

Despite what seems to me to be a relatively even-handed discussion of gender pronouns (including "singular they"), this video's thumbs up, thumbs down ratio of *negative* 8.8 (283 thumbs up to over 2,500 thumbs down) stands as a stark contrast to the positive 18.3 ratio for KatieMayoxx's Common Welsh Sayings. And the comment thread is equally dark. The first and most thumbed-up comment (at 210) reads: "How to generate dislikes."

Paradoxically, it seems this YouTube video has turned into a site for affiliation – but not around respectful use of gender pronouns. Instead, there is a different group building agreement together here: those who feel strongly opposed to any non-binary framing of gender, those who consider Jake a representative of the "snowflake" generation, and those who see no reason why their personal "freedom of speech" should be restricted to attend to the needs of a "small minority" of people who want to be referred to with gender-neutral pronouns.

How did this happen? Why aren't there more voices here chiming in on Jake's side? Sure, there are a few comments that try to counter the thumbs-downers, but they are a small minority. Whatever your feelings about this issue, doesn't it seem odd that the dis-likers are out in such force? Maybe Jake foregrounds the gender issue too much and too abstractly and this takes the discussion away from issues of language and from his own personal experiences, usually big draws for positivity on language videos.

This led me to a search for other sites where affiliation around gender-neutral pronouns might, I imagined, come more freely, sites where members of the LGBTQ community told their own stories or anecdotes about pronoun use and how it made them feel. I found a few of these, but, almost universally, such sites have their *comments disabled*. No doubt they feared the same treatment as Jake Edwards. Are there no outlets for non-institutionally produced, positively affiliative public voices commenting on this issue? Thirsty for some more refreshing citizen sociolinguistic dialogue on gender-neutral pronouns, I pressed on.

Maybe, I thought, there would be more even-handed dialogue around the use of gender-neutral pronouns if I found a YouTuber who addressed this even more explicitly as a language issue and downplayed the gender-identity aspect. Along those lines, here is Tom Scott's video, episode 7 in *Tom's Language Files*, "Gender Neutral Pronouns: They're Here, Get Used to Them." (www.youtube.com/watch?v=46ehrFk-gLk). Despite having a title strikingly similar to Jake's, the focus on what he calls "grammatical gender," its role as part of his "language files" series, Tom's much more mainstream look, and his "proper" British pronunciation suggest a more neutral approach to gender neutrality.

This video is very popular – over one million views – and the thumbs up and down ratio is more balanced, though still very low at 1.8 (31,000 thumbs up to

17,000 thumbs down). And, scanning down the comments, I found some very appreciative and personal remarks, receiving many thumbs up, like this one:

COMMENT : As an agendered person, this video makes me so happy (^-^) ! Thank you! (392 thumbs up)

Then, Tom's own pinned comment caught my eye. It explained the more positive ratio – and the age (posted two or more years ago) of the positive comments I had noticed:

TOM: this comment section was reasonable a few years ago when I put this video up, but now it seems like there's a lot more kneejerk-reaction boors who comment without watching the video. Everything's already been said and I'm sick of banning jerks, so I'm closing these comments. (4.2 K thumbs up)

To his credit, 4,200 people like Tom's comment here. But to me, looking for real dialogue and personal engagement around this issue, the kind I've grown used to around other citizen sociolinguistic videos, this seemed sad. What happened to fuel such a dramatic change in the content of comments that he felt forced to disable them?

A glance to the "recommended videos" on the right margin of my computer screen provided the answer. Or rather, the name: Jordan Peterson. He is a Canadian psychology professor who made news when he posted a YouTube video (a PowerPoint lecture with voice-over) criticizing a bill in Canada that would include gender identity and expression as subject to human rights protections. Being legally forced to call people by gender-neutral pronouns, Peterson asserted, was a violation of his freedom of speech.

He has since blanketed the Internet with his views. His followers have also mastered the art and science of trolling, attacking anyone who dares speak out about their own experiences as a non-gender-conforming individual. For Jordan Peterson gender-neutral pronouns are no longer an issue about language and linguistics. Instead, language here is a proxy for other prejudices – and "freedom" not to use gender-neutral pronouns has become a means for suppression of difference. Peterson's quest for his own version of free speech, as an individual – a white, male, psychology professor from Canada – has, de facto, resulted in lack of free speech for those who hold views different from his own. Dialogue and deliberation has ceased. It seems that Jordan Peterson's internet empire and the way it has emboldened those expressing hate and fear of difference has led to comments sections being disabled on most of those sites where individuals try to speak for themselves about gender pronouns in their own lives.

When comments are disabled, the community-building and knowledge-sharing fostered by citizen sociolinguists stops. The positive feedback loops built by wonderment, the conversations and narratives, the supportive comments and encouragement have no home. These everyday acts of citizen sociolinguistics are blocked.

The potential power of citizen sociolinguistics lies in its ability to air points of view that otherwise might not be heard, to foreground local forms of expertise, and to build common ground. Often these forms of expertise might be held by a small minority of people. That is certainly the case with the group of citizen sociolinguists who would like to talk about gender-neutral pronouns. We need to hear from them and about their experience. They are the experts. And they need each other! We do not need Jordan Peterson speaking about these issues with which he has no experience or expertise, obfuscating in the guise of philosophizing, silencing civic dialogue in the name of freedom of speech.

The old ways of dictating language via standardizing institutions and documents may be losing their hold on how we think about language – and hurray for citizen sociolinguists who are sharing their nuanced and local expertise, building community and affiliation through conversations about words and ways of speaking. But what happens when trolls and negative attention-seekers lead us to "disable comments"? When this happens – as it seems to have in the case of gender-neutral pronouns – the control over how we use language and discuss it may have become more insidious than even the most prescriptive grammarian or authorizing institution. What alternatives are there to disabling comments? Is it possible to counter the negative-affiliative power of huge troll movements? We need to find creative alternatives to simply blocking comments.

When faced with the specter of negativity, however, many of us want instead to retreat into our own enclaves of like-mindedness. At worst, we start to view everything different from us as a potential threat, and we not only disable comments, we lock ourselves away too.

Gated Language Communities

Recently I had an encounter with a visitor to Philadelphia (a prospective Penn father, college touring with his son) who said, "I didn't realize the University of Pennsylvania was located in a *rough neighborhood*." When pressed, he elaborated. "I mean, West Philly – there are some nice houses, but mostly row houses. And some are really run-down."

Since I have a house in that neighborhood (I call it a "twin," not a "row house"), his comments forced me to reflect. I would never describe West Philly (especially the part within walking distance of Penn) as a "rough" neighborhood. Yes, some people do not have money to repair their homes. And the homes are old. And West Philadelphia, like the city as a whole, is not majority white. I don't equate low-income or non-white majority with "rough."

But this visitor also found it difficult to interact in this area. As he put it, "We were not threatened in any way, but neighbors were often out and just stared at us as we parked and walked to and from the car." Despite his denial ("we were not threatened in any way, but . . ."), his description of the neighbors as "just staring" suggests he felt uncomfortable and, well, threatened. But I would never equate neighbors being "often out" with his "rough neighborhood" description.

One of my favorite things about West Philly is that people are "often out." They do not have huge private back yards or indoor leisure spaces. But they do have front porches with tables and chairs for family and friends. Isn't it okay for them to be out? If a visitor is parking in their neighborhood, why should they not watch him? In addition to economic diversity there is a huge amount of ethnic and racial diversity here. And many residents of West Philadelphia speak different languages. This makes the neighborhood feel good – to me. I am happy when people are out after work, and if they "stare" at me, I stop and say hello. But for visitors like this one, from an exclusive gated community in Florida, interacting with a diversity of neighbors might feel slightly uncomfortable.

How is any of this relevant to citizen sociolinguistics? To how we talk about language? Citizen sociolinguistics thrives in spaces where people talk about language and communication, and where people feel free to share stories and personal experiences that illuminate how certain ways of speaking contribute to who they are. These kinds of discussions often happen online – they include voices across socioeconomic statuses, language backgrounds, and gender, racial, and generational differences. These conversations may be unique, even weird, sometimes misguided, or challenging, but like my neighborhood, they are not "rough." And like the richness I see in my neighborhood, citizen sociolinguistic richness depends on being open to encounters with others. Citizen sociolinguistic forums – discussions about "Spanglish" or "common Welsh phrases" or "gender-neutral pronouns," for example – are like West Philly front porches. But citizen sociolinguistic dialogue and community formation, like my neighborhood, can be damaged by visitors who don't engage in the discussion because they see that front-porch presence as a threat.

Even online, there are visitors who shut down points of view being voiced within the "rough neighborhoods" of citizen sociolinguists. Rather than engaging with the conversation, they react impulsively to an impression made by a certain word or phrase. Forums and videos on "gender-neutral pronouns," for example, have drawn many citizen sociolinguists to post about their own experiences with language, and are potentially a center for understanding the way pronouns are changing in the way they function in our society. But this very phrase – "gender-neutral pronouns" – can also draw in outsiders who don't engage in the community but react to what they view as a threat to their own identity. These are commonly called "internet trolls." They shut down dialogue. Trolling can lead to entire comment forums being disabled or expunged. The trolling comments turn previously amicable and open spaces for engaging with language into platforms for an alternative xenophobic or otherwise bilious message. All dialogue ends.

Trolls in the neighborhood of citizen sociolinguistics send everyone inside off their porch. Citizen sociolinguistic conversations are not gated communities. They are more like the front-porch society of West Philly. But trolls treat certain citizen sociolinguistic conversations as if they are rough neighborhoods, where the simple act of discussing certain ways of speaking are aimed at them – treating discussions of "gender-neutral pronouns" for example, like threatening "stares" of neighbors. The troll does not stop to say hello – but scares everyone inside, silencing them. The out-of-town visitor to a diverse neighborhood, like the outsider troll visiting a language discussion, creates a threat by imagining one. In doing so, walls go up around neighborhoods, barriers divide communities of speakers.

In his book about the city of Los Angeles, *City of Quartz*, Mike Davis identifies precisely this dynamic. He laments the "fortress" neighborhoods people build up around themselves in the LA area. Invoking a phrase from William Whyte, eternal sage of city life, he writes, "'Fear proves itself.' The social perception of threat becomes a function of security mobilization itself, not crime rates" (1990, p. 224). And, gradually, this leads to the destruction of public space. City planners' strategies designed to keep homeless people away – unsittable benches, randomly timed outdoor sprinklers, elaborately caged trash areas, non-existent public restrooms – end up driving not just the homeless but everyone away. Or almost everyone. Outside public spaces become the realm of drug addicts and dealers – precisely those targeted by the tactics of the city planners. Fear proves itself.

Conversations about language can also become places where "fear proves itself" in this way – where trolling drives away discussion of the language issues that most need diverse input and forms of expertise. Some see trolling as the playful practice of free speech online, some see moving to gated communities as exercising the freedom to safely raise our children. But both may also be viewed as self-fulfilling feedback loops of disengagement and isolation that come from fear – and end up generating more.

What can we learn from this? And how do we circumvent a feedback loop of fear that drives people into gated communities and shuts down language discussion? For urban planning, Mike Davis suggests we can drive away fear of crime and homelessness by creating a "dense, compact, multifunctional core" for the city (1990, p. 231). When people are nudged to gather in public spaces, the inevitable sociability builds community and motivates humane solutions for social issues. I'd like to think there are analogous solutions for conversations about language. It would be a mistake to isolate language discussions to their own gated community, with "comments disabled," away from the trolls. Instead, somehow, discussions will have to be more densely and diversely occupied, to ensure that trolling can't derail them and that engaged citizen sociolinguists continue to illuminate our understanding of language and each other.

The best way through roadblocks to citizen sociolinguistic productivity is through more citizen sociolinguistic activity, not self-censorship, and certainly not by hiding away in your own gated community of language. Citizen sociolinguists (not professional linguists) may be best situated, for example, to offer examples that counter perceptions of monolingualism, that maneuver around language bullies and trolls, or provide counterarguments to accent bias. Similarly, citizen sociolinguists are best situated to recognize commodification like linguistic gentrification and produce counterculture. This citizen sociolinguistic work leads to a re-examination of the "citizen" in citizen sociolinguistics and the potential for *acts of citizen sociolinguistics* to have an impact on social conditions in the real world.

Answerability versus Responsibility

Imagine you are grading papers, or editing the paper of a friend, and you see a sentence that pushes all your "language police" buttons. The word "utilize," for example, drives some professors nuts! The word "use" is simpler. "Utilize" can seem overblown and unnecessary. So, consider this hypothetical sentence in a persuasive essay about laptop use:

> A majority of those in attendance *utilized* laptops to take notes, indicating that computers can be an important tool for student engagement in classroom lectures.

How might one address this issue as a teacher and editor? Some options:
- Ignore it.
- Cross it out and write "use" above it.
- Cross it out, write "use" above it, and add a note: Too wordy!
- Circle it and write a more extensive comment: "Pro writing tip! Try to use the most simple word and let your ideas be the complex part of your sentence. In this case, 'use' is more effective and draws no attention to itself."
- Ignore it in this paper, but later have a discussion with the entire class about wordiness, building on their own "pet peeves" about language. In the context of that discussion, raise the issue of the word "utilize."

I list these options to illustrate the important distinction Isin (2008) makes in his discussion of "acts of citizenship": Drawing on Bakhtin

(1919), Isin draws on the distinction between "responsibility" and "answerability" in his discussion of every acts of citizenship. Extending this discussion to conversations about language, or acts of citizen sociolinguistics, responsibility and answerability provide useful ways of thinking about our options for engagement. When addressing a stylistic issue like "utilize," there are obvious codes that a teacher or editor adheres to in order to do their job, but also a sense of relationship and ethics that goes beyond the generalizable responsibilities of our position, to which we are answerable in that specific moment. As teachers, we have a responsibility to work with our students to improve their writing, extend their knowledge base, and fine-tune their ability to think critically. For that reason, it would be irresponsible to simply ignore what we saw as a stylistic problem in a student's writing. We would not be doing our job.

Exactly how we act within each moment of interaction within our job is also "answerable" to both the nuance of a momentary relationship, the interaction with that student, and to a more intangible ethic that provides us a sense of "the right thing to do." Each teacher may be answerable in different ways. Each of the options for action listed above observes differing degrees of "answerability" and "responsibility." In each option (with the exception of doing nothing), the teacher is acting responsibly with respect to the requirements of their job as teacher. But some of the options attend more to the nuance of the relationship and illustrate answerability to an ethic that goes beyond simply fulfilling one's duties. Bakhtin discusses answerability as our sense of ethical engagement with our inevitably incomplete knowledge of "the other." Each choice above attends in slightly different ways to "the other" (the student) and the relationship between that student and the commenting teacher. Each choice involves subtle understandings of the background that student brings to that moment of interaction. The student may work in an office where "utilize" is commonly bandied about and may have come to rely on it as a signal of sophistication. How to account for unknown histories like this in each editing encounter? By simply crossing out "utilize" and writing "use," one might be "responsible" to one's role as teacher – but not entirely answerable to the other, which involves attending to more subtle individual nuances of their unknown social history and habits of self-expression.

Were we to simply act as responsible citizens, responsible sociolinguists, life would be rule-bound, ordered, and unchanging. We would always know the right thing to do and we would all agree on it. In being answerable to the other in each act of human engagement, we have the potential to go beyond simple fulfillment of responsibility to a more finely tuned engagement with the situation and the relationships within it. Acts of citizen sociolinguistics, answerable to specifics of a situation, attuned to the unknowability of the other – whether in wonderment and awe or critique – have this same potential to push beyond the bounds of speaking about language "responsibly" to speaking about language in ways that are answerable. The answerability of each act of citizen sociolinguistics provides the most important rationale for continuing to explore it. We cannot engage with the other by simply creating rules for how to use language, what to say, and what not to say. We need to have the tools to be answerable to the nuances of ethical engagement involved in any interaction. This is why, as I'll discuss in the Conclusion, we must continue to talk about language.

Conclusion
Why We Must Talk about Language

> Education, even if it cannot by itself knock down the barriers by which human beings are divided, should at any rate not add to them.
> Isaiah Berlin, *The Power of Ideas* (1969, p. 214)

This volume has been about *how we talk about language*. In writing it, my goal has been to equip readers to think about language expertise in a new way: as locally generated. To illuminate this local expertise and investigate its power, I've also provided some strategies for carefully considering how we talk about language, noticing how those around us do so, and making the most of those conversations. We've discussed the seemingly frivolous (as when people discuss the pronunciation of "Greenwich Street" or the exaggerated "French" pronunciation of the word "croissant" by Americans) and the demoralizing, dark, and challenging (the copresence of cynical and idealistic meanings of the word *citizen*, the attempts of University faculty to control everyday lunchtime multilingual conversation among graduate students, or a trove of hate speech surrounding gender-neutral pronouns). We've seen how everyday feedback loops can reinforce and build pride in certain forms of language use, and can also build barriers between people, creating enclaves of narrow-minded assumptions about language in which people are socialized into ways of using language that can be hurtful outside of their closed circles. We've also seen how acts of citizen sociolinguistic engagement can disrupt those negative feedback loops, push people outside their linguistic comfort zones, and even push positive social change.

This act of pushing people outside their comfort zones, developing empathy for other perspectives, is both a crucial aspect of human development and one that has been overlooked in our schools. We have been so caught up in standardized forms of education and achievement that we have neglected to more broadly educate our citizenry. Nowhere is this more apparent than in today's increasingly diversifying schools, where verbal bullying has become endemic and divisive, drawing lines of difference and distinction, and harming those who do not match an imagined norm. In "high-achieving" suburban schools, where we might expect the best education to be happening, where a comparatively privileged cross section of the student population are schooled, these acts of verbal bullying – of language ignorance – are most prevalent (Ed Week 2018). In the words of Isaiah Berlin above, rather than functioning to "knock down barriers by which human beings are divided" our educational institutions can function to build up those barriers. While teaching language, and teaching other subjects *through* language, our schools have failed to become environments where students and teachers are able to talk *about* language. As a result, language has become weaponized in many school contexts, and teachers, students, administrators, and community members don't know how to have critical conversations.

This has become increasingly clear in the United States, where the public expression of hate speech has proliferated over the last five years. In March of 2018, *Education Week*, the United States' primary news source for all matters related to pre-K-12 education, published an extended story investigating three years (2015–2017) of "hate and bias in K-12 school settings" in the United States. Of 472 confirmed incidents of hate and bias, the reporters found that most

involved hate *speech, spoken and written* ... The most common words were: "the n-word," various versions of "build the wall" and "go back to [insert foreign country name here, usually Mexico]. (emphasis mine) (Education Week, 2018)

Since this book was researched, lawsuits around language bullying have proliferated in US schools. A nationwide study of bullying by the National Education Association found that teachers and staff perceive verbal bullying as their biggest concern (far above physical or cyberbullying). According to the NEA study, 90 percent of teachers also feel it is their responsibility to intervene, but most feel unequipped to do so, especially when abuse is around sexuality and gender (NEA, 2010). And, increasingly, due to nationwide anti-bullying legislation, school districts are facing lawsuits for failing to adequately address the issue (Kimmel, 2017). Schools are also struggling with how to account for and learn from the growing multilingualism in their communities. While the US values multilingualism, we have a poor track record for making the most of it in our education system (Marian, 2018). It's clear there is a need to equip teachers, staff, and students with strategies to be more mindful of the language in their schools and to engage in conversations *about* language and its ramifying effects. But how?

A simple solution would be to consult a language expert who could inform a school community how to use language properly in every context, to avoid fights and bullying, and to do well in school. Unfortunately, as we've discussed throughout this volume, no such expert exists. No one person can possibly understand all perspectives involved in the use of a words like "fag" or the "n-word," a mysterious acronym like "THOT," or the role of multilingual conversation in the halls, lunchroom, or class discussion. No expert can fully address the rapidity and specificity of language change. No linguistics professor will have a ready explanation for how, for example, "THOT" pops up and recedes over the course of months, in a single classroom, and how it affects people in that classroom. Instead of looking to some imagined expert for definitive diagnoses of language issues, this book has emphasized the need to develop heightened forms of language awareness in ourselves, in our students, in our children, colleagues, and friends. When we are befuddled by language use, we can begin down a path of inquiry: We must talk to people who use that word and ask them about what it means to them and why they used it; Look around, listen, and observe how people talk about language, and talk to as many people as you can *about their language*; Then share and compare the answers you get. Engage in *citizen sociolinguistics*.

Citizen Sociolinguistics: Everyday Conversations about Language

As I emphasized in the Preface to this volume, language is no trivial matter. Language is a human's primary way of communicating our experiences. As reports on hate speech and bullying in schools illustrate, language may also be our primary means for building barriers between each other and fomenting discord. For this reason, we must learn how to have conversations *about* language. While we can use language as a shield from others, a way to build boundaries between all our tiny demographic comfort zones, talk *about* that language opens up a way to engage meaningfully with other viewpoints and in the process develop shared understandings. Powerful learning can result from these discussions.

Discussions about language potentially start every moment someone notices and comments on something distinctive about their own or another's speech. In this book, we've considered two very different entry points into those conversations about language, *sociolinguistic wonderment* and *citizen sociolinguist's arrest*. Both these reactions to language difference, *wonderment* and *arrest*, can function as invitations to construct meaning together in new ways. The sting of arrest or a spark of wonderment can bring on conversations that take down barriers between groups of speakers by raising awareness about how language builds meaning differently in different contexts.

Language Wonderment: Shit!

Consider a three-year-old spontaneously belting out "oh shit!" over breakfast. The mind of any adult at the table will be launched on a lightening-paced journey through their associations with that word, their understandings of who uses it and how, and possibly an inventory of the last time they used it and whether it was in front of their three-year-old. Most likely they will not be offended, but amused. Everyone at the table (even the three-year-old) might enjoy a fantastic chuckle together – sharing their joint experience of the surprising might of a single word. Often it takes the unlikely remark of a child like this to jolt us into wonderment about the power of language. *Citizen sociolinguistic wonderment* (a blend of admiration and awe, sometimes touched with silliness, fear, or skepticism, regarding ways of speaking) best describes those conversations – which can also launch us into inquiry mode. Once language becomes a more habitual object of discussion, we may also start experiencing language wonderment more often and recognizing it as an opening for conversation and learning:

- Why do you say *lightening bug* instead of *firefly*? What does your grandmother say? Where did you grow up?
- Why *cinema* studies or *film* school versus watching a *movie*? Who uses these different words and why?
- Would British people really use the word *fag* for a cigarette? Is it offensive in that context?

These conversations start in the realm of the trivial, the non-threatening, but as such, they can be inviting and inclusive pathways into discussions about difference and distinction in our classrooms and society. Through discussions about language, we develop the habitual language awareness needed to respect the language of others in the future.

Citizen Sociolinguist's Arrest: Why Did You Say That?

On a recent afternoon I was having coffee with a friend, waiting for my cousin who was about to arrive with his new girlfriend and his three daughters, aged between 4 and 13. My friend asked, with a twinkle in her eye, "So will your cousin be bringing along his *harem*?" Ugh! The word *harem* disappointed me at that moment. To me it seemed like a disappointingly sexist and unanswerably crass way to talk about my cousin and the women and girls in his life. But I said nothing. No citizen sociolinguist's arrest followed. But I considered the possible forms it might take:

- Why do you call them a *harem*?
- Don't you consider yourself a feminist? Why would you use that word?
- Do people really use *harem* to talk about women these days?
- Would you be so uncaring as to use that word in front of my cousin and his daughters?

I asked none of these questions. I just seethed a little and then changed the subject. But the experience makes one point clear: As I've discussed, the sting of arrest can lead to important conversations about language, but it's still a sting. And it can be hard to "arrest" people we care about. We tend to avoid shaming those who are close to us. It's much easier to start from the shared experience of wonderment and awe. Later I looked up the word *harem* and confirmed my sense that it was an unfortunate choice of word: "the wives or concubines of a polygamous man." What my friend thought was funny struck me, again, as icky.

While I never addressed the issue directly with my friend, I noticed the situation. And I retroactively considered this word and my own reaction to it. And, next time I may have the wherewithal to make a *gentle* citizen sociolinguist's arrest and start a discussion about language. I might frame my questions as points of real inquiry. How could a friend of mine, history PhD, scholar of *women's* history, use the word *harem* this way? Am I becoming old and humorless? Has my friend lost any critical sensibility? We could *talk about it.*

I mention this opportunity missed because it exemplifies opportunities that we all pass up each day to have conversations about language. Those missed opportunities have losses associated with them. Unless we talk about this language, we continue to seethe, and we continue to use language in ways that can be hurtful, offensive, or blinding, and that build boundaries between social groups. Not having conversations about language is not sustainable – it leads to tone deafness.

On Being Tone-Deaf

If we can't talk about language, like the word *citizen* or *harem*, social issues, like the division between immigrants and other US citizens, or between women and men, can seethe beneath the surface: Opposing parties never confront one another as humans, nobody learns about the effects their words have. As a result, every day, people use language in ways we might describe as *tone-deaf*. As discussed in Chapter 4, in conversations, being metaphorically tone-deaf can be hurtful and damaging. It involves, for example, ordering people to not speak their own language, or using words like *fag*, *mental*, the *n-word*, or *harem*, in ways that are out of tune with the diversity of people with whom they are speaking, or using any turn of phrase in a way that is inattentive to the kinds of effects those words might have on others.

A tone-deaf use of language, if unchecked, can have the opposite effect of either wonderment or arrest. Instead of fomenting conversations about language, it can silence less powerful voices. Unless someone speaks back – for example, with a reposting of an email, as in the Duke case – that tone-deaf perspective becomes the only one people hear. Nobody learns from alternatives. Sadly, being tone-deaf, speaking without regard for the other perspectives in a community, can be the result of a privileged and overly standardized language education, in which expertise is seen only to be lodged in the voice of the teacher or the text of a grammar book. As the Duke "don't speak Chinese" email and the "harem" remark from my friend illustrate, even professors with PhDs, working at prestigious universities, can be tone-deaf until less powerful individuals have the courage to call them out. While a tone-deaf individual may have excellent language skills according to one context and set of criteria, they may have never learned to adequately consider the context in which they are speaking, and the way others might receive their words. An education that enables such tone deafness to develop is undereducation, because it never builds the expertise necessary to engage in the cycle of dynamic language awareness.

The Role of Internet-Circulated Social Media

Any consideration of conversations about language cannot exclude one of the places where most kids and many adults these days are most actively using language – internet-circulated social media. Discussion about language must include the way language is used in these contexts as well. Throughout this book, we have been exploring how everyday conversations about language can both inform us and pull us out of our more entrenched assumptions – and entrenchment of assumptions is infamously common on social media. Talking *about* that media, how it functions and how language works there, may be even more necessary. Banning certain apps or platforms, censoring access, will never develop in students the skill they need to manage that information flow on their own. Instead, we need to learn how to use social media as a medium through which we access multiple points of view, a treasure box of opinion we can dip into to explore what motivates different views of language and the perspectives attached to them.

As dana boyd (2014) has written, social media may not resolve our social divisions and it certainly has the power to exacerbate them, but it also provides us with an important view into what form those social divisions take:

The internet will not inherently make the world more equal, nor will it automatically usher today's youth into a tolerant world. Instead it lays bare existing and entrenched social divisions. (2014, p. 175)

If the Internet lays those social divisions bare, we probably should take a look at it. And, as has been illustrated throughout this book, the Internet has become a trove of conversation about language. In those conversations we see how people begin to build up communities of pride and shared identity around language, and as platforms for deliberation about how language functions across contexts and communities. As such, the Internet has emerged as a primary medium for engaging in citizen sociolinguistics.

Building the Cycle of Dynamic Language Awareness

When we talk about language, when we explore the language of others and compare different perspectives people have about language, whether face-to-face, in real time, or through messages on social media across stretches of time and space, we develop awareness of other conversations about language occurring around us and far afield. This is a form of expertise all humans need to develop – the ability to listen to others, to engage with different perspectives. The more we talk *about* language, the more deeply we understand how and why some language may be hurtful, and how some can be powerful; how words like "hoagie" or "hero," "firefly" or "lightning bug" come from different walks of life, but describe similar worlds, that "THOT" may be an offensive expression (I leave it to readers to Google that one), or how an individual speaking Chinese may also be highly accomplished as an English speaker.

How do we build this expertise in our population? In our classrooms and communities? We don't simply invite an outside expert in to tell us how language works. Though this might be one of many perspectives to engage, we also have to develop the tools to engage in inquiry as citizen sociolinguists, to follow the spark of wonderment or the sting of arrest to learn more about how language has an impact on people in different ways, in different contexts, and how language is always changing. Precisely because language is always changing, we need to stay attuned to it – there are no fixed rules that tell us what is right and wrong, who can and can't say this or that, where and when. This does not mean there are not better and worse ways to use language. There are terrible ways to use language! But we can only know how language works if we are aware of how people other than just us, other than just the teacher, other than so-called language experts, use it and understand it. But we need to listen, investigate, learn, and then share what we have learned to spark more conversations about language.

Any student, from pre-school through graduate school, and any human, of any age, can embark on this type of citizen sociolinguistic inquiry. Listen to your students, your colleagues, your children, your peers: What word, turn of phrase, or way of speaking has led to wonderment and sparked conversation? Hoagie? Lightening bug? Creaky voice? Eyebrows on fleek? Chinese? What sorts of "citizen sociolinguistic arrests" have you (or people you know) experienced? These experiences – good and bad – can be springboards to important citizen sociolinguistic inquiry. Over the years, I've developed the ideas in this book as a loose guide to push high-school, college, and graduate students and myself to explore language questions – whether sparked by wonderment, arrest, or something else, and to dwell with multiple possible answers to any of them (see also, more specifically, the Guide for Getting Started in Chapter 3). Readers, I hope you will use whatever insights and ideas this book has sparked to explore the different perspectives surrounding your own language curiosities, to build flexible and thoughtful habits with language in your lives, as citizen sociolinguists, and to share your discoveries through more acts of citizen sociolinguistics.

References

Androutsopoulos, J. (2013) Participatory culture and metalinguistic discourse: Performing and negotiating German dialects on YouTube. In D. Tannen and A. M. Trester (eds.), *Discourse 2.0: Language and New Media*, 47–71. Washington, DC: Georgetown University Press.

Bakhtin, M. M. (1919 [1990]) Art and answerability. In *Art and Answerability: Early Philosophical Essays of M. M. Bakhtin*, ed. by M. Holoquist and V. Liapunov. Austin, TX: University of Texas Press.

  (1981) *The Dialogic imagination: Four Essays*. Austin, TX: University of Texas Press.

Bamberg, M. (2012) Narrative analysis. In H. Cooper (ed.), *APA Handbook of Research Methods in Psychology (Vol. 3)*. American Psychological Association.

Bamberg, M. and A. Georgakopoulou (2008) Small stories as a new perspective in narrative and identity analysis. *Text and Talk*, 28(3), 377–396.

Bell, A. (2017) Giving voice: A personal essay on the shape of sociolinguistics. *Journal of Sociolinguistics*, 21(5), 587–602.

Berlin, I. (1969 [2000]) *The Power of Ideas*. Princeton, NJ: Princeton University Press.

Blommaert, J. and A. Backus. (2012) Superdiverse repertoires and the individual. *Tilburg Papers in Cultural Studies*, 24.

Blum, S. D. (ed.) (2017) *Making Sense of Language: Readings in Culture and Communication (3rd Edition)*. New York, NY and Oxford: Oxford University Press.

boyd, dana (2014) *It's Complicated: The Social Lives of Networked Teens*. New Haven, CT: Yale University Press.

Bruner, J. (1986) *Actual Minds, Possible Worlds*. Cambridge, MA: Harvard University Press.

  (2003) *Making Stories: Law, Literature, Life*. Cambridge, MA and London: Harvard University Press.

Bucholtz, M. (2000) The politics of transcription. *Journal of Pragmatics*, 32, 1439–1465.

Burgess, J. and J. Green (2009) *YouTube: Online Video and Participatory Culture*. New York, NY: Polity Press.

Cameron, D. (2012) *Verbal Hygiene* (2nd edn.) London and New York, NY: Routledge.

Chapin, S. H., O'Connor, C., and Anderson, N. C. (2013) *Talk Moves: A Teacher's Guide for Using Classroom Discussions in Math, Grades K-6*. Sausalito, CA: Math Solutions.

Chun, E. W. (2004) Ideologies of legitimate mockery: Margaret Cho's revoicings of mock Asian. *Pragmatics*, 14(2/3), 263–289.

Coupland, N. (2016) Five Ms for sociolinguistic change. In N. Coupland (ed.), *Sociolinguistics: Theoretical Debates*, pp. 433–454. Cambridge: Cambridge University Press.

Daily Moth (2018) Nyle DiMarco's *Black Panther* controversy. *Daily Moth*, February 19. Retrieved May 7, 2020 from www.dailymoth.com/single-post/2018/02/19/The-Daily-Moth-2-19-18.

Daniels, C. B. and Roetman, P. E. J. (2009) *The Possum-Tail Tree: Understanding Possums through Citizen Science*. Adelaide: Barbara Hardy Centre University of South Australia.

Davis, M. (1990) *City of Quartz*. New York, NY: Vintage.

DeFina, A. and A. Georgakopoulou. (2012) *Analyzing Narrative: Discourse and Sociolinguistic Perspectives*. Cambridge and New York, NY: Cambridge University Press.

Dewey, J. (1910) *How We Think*. Lexington, MA: D. C. Heath.

DiMarco, N. (2018) Nyle DiMarco opens up about having to leave *Black Panther* because he's deaf. *Teen Vogue*, February 23. Retrieved May 7, 2020 from www.teenvogue.com/story/nyle-dimarco-opens-up-about-leaving-black-panther-because-hes-deaf.

Dwyer, M. K. (2015) 8 reasons to catch the Fresh Off the Boat premiere tonight. *8Asians*, February 4. Retrieved May 7, 2020 from www.8asians.com/2015/02/04/8-reasons-to-catch-the-fresh-off-the-boat-premiere-tonight/.

Eckert, P. (2008) Variation and the indexical field. *Journal of Sociolinguistics*, 12(4), 453–476.

(2012) Three waves of variation study: The emergence of meaning in the study of sociolinguistic variation. *Annual Review of Anthropology*, 41, 87–100.

Education Week (2018) Hate in schools: An in-depth look. *Education Week*, August 6. Retrieved May 7, 2020 from www.edweek.org/ew/projects/hate-in-schools.html.

Figueroa, A. M. (2011) Citizenship and education in the homework completion routine. *Anthropology & Education Quarterly*, 42(3), 263–280.

Flege, J. E. (1980) Phonetic approximation in second language acquisition. *Language Learning*, 30, 117–134.

FoldIt (n.d.) The Science behind FoldIt. Retrieved May 7, 2020 from https://fold.it/portal/info/about.

Garfinkel, H (1976) *Studies in Ethnomethodology*. Cambridge, UK: Polity Press.

Geertz, C. (1973) Thick description: Toward an interpretive theory of culture. In *The Interpretation of Cultures: Selected Essays*, pp. 3–30. New York, NY: Basic Books.

Giddens, A. (1991) *Modernity and Self-Identity: Self and Society in the Late Modern Age*. Stanford, CA: Stanford University Press.

Goffman, A. (2014) *On the Run: Fugitive Life in an American City*. Chicago, IL: Chicago University Press.

Goffman, E. (1964) The neglected situation. *American Anthropologist*, 66(6), 133–136.

Goffman, E. (1981) *Interaction Ritual: Essays on Face-to-Face Behavior*. New York, NY: Pantheon.

(1981) *Forms of Talk*. Pennsylvania, PA: University of Pennsylvania.

Gumperz, J. J. (1982 [1976]) *Discourse Strategies*. Cambridge, UK: Cambridge University Press.

(2001) Interactional sociolinguistics: A personal perspective. In D. Schiffrin, D. Tannen, and H. E. Hamilton (eds.), *The Handbook of Discourse Analysis*, pp. 215–228. Malden, MA: Blackwell.

Heller, M. and Duchêne, A. (2012) Pride and profit: Changing discourses of language, capital, and nation-state. In A. Duchêne and M. Heller (eds.), *Language in Late Capitalism: Pride and Profit*, pp. 1–21. New York, NY: Routledge.

Herring, S. C. (2013) Discourse in Web 2.0: Familiar, reconfigured, and emergent. In D. Tannen and A. M. Trester (eds.), *Discourse 2.0. Language and New Media*, pp. 47–71. Washington, DC: Georgetown University Press.

Himanen, P. (2001) *The Hacker Ethic and the Spirit of the Information Age*. New York, NY: Random House.

Isin, E. (2008) Theorizing acts of citizenship. In E. F. Isin and G. M. Nielson (eds.), *Acts of Citizenship*, pp. 15–43. London and New York, NY: Zed Books.

Jacewicz, E., Fox, R. A., and Salmons, J. (2007) Vowel duration in three American English dialects. *American Speech*, 82(4), 367–385. doi:10.1215/00031283-2007-024.

Jenkins, H. (2006) *Convergence Culture: Where Old and New Media Collide*. New York, NY: New York University Press.

Jenkins, H., Ford, S., and Green, J. (2014) *Spreadable Media: Creating Value and Meaning in a Networked Culture*. New York, NY and London: New York University Press.

Johnson, S. (1751) *The Rambler, No. 103* (March 12, 1751).

Johnstone, B. (2004) Place, globalization and linguistic variation. In C. Fought (ed.), *Sociolinguistic Variation: Critical Reflections*. New York, NY: Oxford University Press.

Katz, J. and W. Andrews (2013) How y'all, youse and you guys talk: What does the way you speak say about where you're from? Answer all the questions below to see your personal dialect map. *New York Times*, December 21. Retrieved November 2, 2015 from www.nytimes.com/interactive/2013/12/20/sunday-review/dialect-quiz-map.html?_r=0.

Kimmel, A. (2017) Litigating bullying cases: Holding school districts and officials accountable. Public Justice Bullying Litigation Primer, Fall 2017. Retrieved May 4, 2020 from www.publicjustice.net/wp-content/uploads/2016/02/Bullying-Litigation-Primer-Fall-2017-Update-FINAL.pdf.

Knight, C. (2012) A brief history of citizen science. *Science 2.0*. Retrieved July 10, 2014 from www.science20.com/anthrophysis/brief_history_citizen_science-93317.

Kroskrity, P.V. (2016) Language ideologies: Emergence, elaboration, and application. In Bonvillain, N. (ed.), *The Routledge Handbook of Linguistic Anthropology*, pp. 95–108. New York, NY: Routledge.

Labov, W. (1966 [2006]) *The Social Stratification of English in New York City*. Cambridge: Cambridge University Press.

(1979 [2013]) *The Language of Life and Death: The Transformation of Experience in Oral Narrative*. Cambridge and New York, NY: Cambridge University Press.

Labov, W. and J. Waletzky (1967) W., Ash, S., and Boberg, C. (2006) *Atlas of North American English: Phonetics, Phonology and Sound Change* (package edition). Berlin: Mouton De Gruyter.

Larson, S. (2014) What do y'All, yinz, and yix call stretchy office supplies? *The New Yorker*, January 2. Retrieved August 26, 2019 from www.newyorker.com/humor/daily-shouts/what-do-yall-yinz-and-yix-call-stretchy-office-supplies.

LeBlanc, R.J. (2019) Institutional rituals as interpersonal verbal rituals as interactional resources in classroom talk. In M. Juzwik, J. Stone, D. Davila, & K. Burke (Eds.), Legacies of Christian languages and literacies in US education (p. 51–66). New York: Routledge.

Lee, Chang-rae (1995) *Native Speaker*. Grand Haven, MI: Brilliance Corp.

Lewis-Kraus, G. (2016) The Trials of Alice Goffman. *New York Times Magazine*, January 17. Retrieved August 30, 2019 from www.nytimes.com/2016/01/17/magazine/the-trials-of-alice-goffman.html.

Leemann, A., Kolly, M.-J., and Britain, D. (2018) The English Dialects app: The creation of a crowdsourced dialect corpus. *Ampersand*, 5, 1–17. doi:10.1016/j.amper.2017.11.001.

Leone-Pizzighella, A. and Rymes, B. (2017) Gathering everyday metacommentary: A methodology to counteract institutional erasure. *Language and Communication*, 59, 53–65.

LifeTracking (2012) Philly Accent Challenge. Retrieved 6 September 2013 from www.youtube.com/watch?v=1_LTYGx_2fE.

Lippmann, W. (1922 [1991]) *Public Opinion*. New Brunswick, NJ and London: Transaction Publishers.

Lorente, B. P. (2018) *Scripts of Servitude: Language, Labor Migration, and Transnational Domestic Work*. Bristol: Multilingual Matters.

LovingLanguage (2014) Do robots love language? Bias and Google Translate. *Loving Language* [Blog], May 4. Retrieved May 7, 2020 from https://lovinglanguage.wordpress.com/2014/05/04/do-robots-love-language/.

Marcuse, H. (1978) *The Aesthetic Dimension: Toward a Critique of Marxist Aesthetics*. Boston, MA: Beacon Press.

Marian, V. (2018) The US needs to embrace multilingual education – our children will benefit from it. *The Hill*. Retrieved May 7, 2020 from https://thehill.com/opinion/education/378691-the-us-needs-to-embrace-multilingual-education-our-children-will-benefit.

Mishler, E. G. (1999) *Storylines: Craftartists' Narratives of Identity*. Cambridge, MA: Harvard University Press.

Moore, R. (2011) "If I actually talked like that, I'd pull a gun on myself": Accent, avoidance, and moral panic in Irish English. *Anthropological Quarterly*, 84(1), 41–64.

Nijhuis, M. (2007) Teaming up with Thoreau. *Smithsonian Magazine*, October 2017. Retrieved August 24, 2019 from www.smithsonianmag.com/science-nature/teaming-up-with-thoreau-163861621/.

Nosowitz, D. (2015) How capicola became gabagool: The Italian New Jersey accent, explained. *Atlas Obscura*, November 5. Retrieved May 7, 2020 from www.atlasobscura.com/articles/how-capicola-became-gabagool-the-italian-new-jersey-accent-explained.

Nunberg, G. (2015) Don't you dare use comprised of on Wikipedia. *Fresh Air*, March 12. Retrieved August 31, 2019 from www.npr.org/2015/03/12/392568604/dont-you-dare-use-comprised-of-on-wikipedia-one-editor-will-take-it-out.

Ochs, E. and Capps, L. (2001) *Living Narrative: Creating Lives in Everyday Storytelling*. Cambridge, MA: Harvard University Press.

O'Neil, C. (2016) *Weapons of Math Destruction: How Big Data Increases Inequality and Threatens Democracy*. New York, NY: Broadway Books.

O'Reilly, T. (2005) What is Web 2.0. Design patterns and business models for the next generation of software. *O'Reilly.com*, September 30. Retrieved May 7, 2020 from www.oreilly.com/pub/a/web2/archive/what-is-web-20.html.

Passyunk Post (n.d.) Write for us. *Passyunk Post*. Retrieved May 7, 2020 from www.passyunkpost.com/write-for-us/.

Pinker, S. (1994) *The Language Instinct*. New York, NY: Perennial.

Preston, D. (2011) Methods in (applied) folk linguistics: Getting into the minds of the folk. *AILA Review*, 24, 15–39.

Rushkoff, D. (2006) Douglas Rushkoff, in J. Brockman (ed.). What We Believe but Cannot Prove (pp. 7–8). New York: Harper Collins.

Rymes, B. (1997) Second language socialization: A new approach to second language acquisition research. *Journal of Intensive English Studies*, 11, 143–155.

(2014) *Communicating beyond Language: Everyday Encounters with Diversity*. New York, NY and London: Routledge.

Sacks, H. (1974) An analysis of the course of a joke's telling in conversation. In R. Bauman and J. F. Sherzer (eds.), *Explorations in the Ethnography of Speaking*, pp. 337–353. Cambridge: Cambridge University Press.

Schilling-Estes, N. (2008) Stylistic variation and the sociolinguistic interview: A reconsideration. In R. Monroy and A. Sánchez (eds.) *25 años de lingüística aplicada en España: hitos y retos* (25 years of applied linguistics in Spain: Milestones and challenges; proceedings from AESLA 25). Murcia: Servicio de Publicaciones de la Universidad de Murcia.

Shankar, S. (2015) Asian Americans, they're just like us. *Pacific Standard*, February 10. Retrieved May 7, 2020 from www.psmag.com/books-and-culture/asian-americans-theyre-just-like-us-fresh-off-the-boat-eddie-huang.

Silverstein, M. (1992) The uses and utility of ideology: Some reflections. *Pragmatics*, 2(3), 311–323.

Slee, M. (2012) *Flight of the Butterflies* [Documentary]. Canada: SK Films.

Steinem, G. (2015) *My Life on the Road*. New York, NY: Random House.

Stein, N. L. and M. Policastro. (1984) The concept of a story: A comparison between children's and teachers' viewpoints. In H. Mandl, N. L. Stein, and T. Trabasso (eds.), *Learning and Comprehension of Text*, pp. 113–155. Hillsdale, NJ: Erlbaum.

Tannen, D. and A. M. Trester (eds.) (2013) *Discourse 2.0: Language and New Media*. Washington, DC: Georgetown University Press.

Tantris (2006) February 11, 1941. *Ghost of Philly* [Blog], June 18. Retrieved May 7, 2020 from http://ghostofsouthphilly.blogspot.com/2006/06/.

Thethugyone (2015) Philly Accent Challenge. Retrieved September 6, 2013 from www.youtube.com/watch?v=1_LTYGx_2fE.

Tom, A. (2014) "Fresh Off the Boat": Smart or a soy sorry joke? *Huffington Post*, April 2. Retrieved August 30, 2019 from www.huffingtonpost.com/pamela-tom/fresh-off-the-boat-smart-_b_6588044.html.

Vaux, B. and Golder, S. (2003) Welcome to the Dialect Survey. Retrieved November 3, 2015 from http://dialect.redlog.net/.

Walls, L. D. (2017) *Henry David Thoreau: A Life*. Chicago, IL: University of Chicago Press.

Wee, L. (2018) *The Singlish Controversy: Language, Culture and Identity in a Globalizing World*. Cambridge: Cambridge University Press.

Wortham, S. (2001) *Narratives in Action: A Strategy for Research and Analysis*. New York, NY: Teachers College Press.

(2005) Socialization beyond the speech event. *Journal of Linguistic Anthropology*, 15(1), 95–112.

Xue, K. (2014) In the Internet era, research moves from professionals' labs to amateurs' homes, *Harvard Magazine*, January to February. Retrieved August 26, 2019 from http://harvardmagazine.com/2014/01/popular-science.

Zimmerman, J. (2019) Speaking English on campus is actually important: What the shaming of Duke's Megan Neely got wrong. *New York Daily News*, January 28. Retrieved September 2, 2019 from www.nydailynews.com/opinion/ny-oped-speaking-english-on-campus-is-actually-important-20190128-story.html.

Index

acAme. *See* Acme
Ac-a-me. *See* Acme
accent challenge, 159–164, *See* accent tag
accent tag, 80–82, 101, 135, 136
Acme, 136, 166
acts of citizen sociolinguistics, 6, 8, 10, 14, 16, 26, 27, 99, 143, 170, 172, 174, 179, 182, 183, 192
American Enterprise Institute, 51, 54
American Sign Language, 83–86
answerability, 26, 170, 183, 184
Australia, 77

Bakhtin, Mikhail, 95, 96, 183, 193
big data, 19
Black Panther, 84, 85, 86
Black Twitter, 139
Boseman, Chadwick, 88
Brooklyn, 110, 111
Bruner, Jerome, 151, 154, 157, 158, 193
bullying, verbal, 27, 185, 187
bureaucratic control of language, 175–176

call centers, 15
Cameron, Deborah, 172
capicola. *See* gabagool usage
censorship, 49, 50, 51, 182
Charlie Bit My Finger, 132, 137, 171
Chicago, 72
Chinese language, 22, 26, 121, 122, 123, 126, 142, 143, 144, 145, 146, 147, 171, 172, 175, 190, 191
Cho, Margaret, 122, 123
citizen science, 3–5
  and citizen sociolinguistics, 5
  and monarch butterflies, 4
  and possum behavior, 4
  and Thoreau, Henry David, 3
citizen sociolinguistic arrests, 29–33, 55, 56, 59, 63, 66, 68, 82, 146, 171, 187
citizen sociolinguistic wonderment, 66–68, 82, 171, 187

citizenship grade, 35
coke. *See* pop
comprised of, 1–2
Concord, Massachusetts, 3
context collapse. *See* cross-posting
contextualiztion cues, 116
convergence culture, 21, 155, 158, 174, 195
conversational inferencing, 63
conversational narrative, 154
creativity, 16, 22, 23, 82, 129, 139
croissant pronunciation, 70–73
cross talk, 63
cross-posting, 119, 120, 121, 124, 146, 149, 152, 174
crowd sourcing, 18–21
custard, frozen, 101
cwtch, 137, 138

data sharing, 115–116
Davis, Mike, 181, 194
Dewey, John, 33, 48, 54–56, 64, 194
dialect surveys, 100, 101, 156, 157, 158, 160, 166
DiMarco, Nyle, 83–86
Discourse Strategies (Gumperz), 63
DIY methods, 100
Double Rainbow, 90–91
Double Rainbow All the Way, 68, 92
Duke University language controversy, 143–147

Eckert, Penelope, 159, 160, 194
English-only boarding schools, 148
Ethnomethodology, 25, 34, 62–63
eye-dialect, 116–118

feedback loops, 26, 128, 129, 130, 132, 135, 138, 139, 140, 141, 143, 144, 145, 149, 151, 152, 178, 181
  of fear, 181
finna, 94, 95
Florida, 165, 180

199

folk linguistics, 57–59
French language, 72
Fresh off the Boat, 123

gabagool usage, 73–76
Garfinkel, Harold, 62–63
gender neutral pronouns, 22, 176, 177, 178, 180, 181
Geno's Cheesesteaks, 9–11
gentrification, 96–97
German language, 160
Goffman, Alice, 124
Goffman, Erving, 86, 87, 89, 124, 150, 194, 196
Google Translate, 103–106
Greenwich (street), 6, 7, 8, 9, 10, 13, 55, 58, 64, 67, 171
Gumperz, John, 63, 116, 195

hacks, 103, 105, 108, 174
Harvard Dialect Survey, 18, 156
hate speech, 186, 187
hoagie, 67, 68, 171, 191
Holland, Tom, 72
How We Think (Dewey), 55

idioms, 104
indexical biography, 160
indexical field, 159, 160, 194
irregardless, 113–115
Isin, Engin F., 170

Japanese language, 82
jawn, 94, 95, 171
Jenkins, Henry, 21, 22, 153, 155, 159, 174, 195
Johnstone, Barbara, 159, 160, 195

Koe No Katachi, 83
Konglish, 80, 81, 82, 84, 100, 101, 132, 134, 135, 137, 138, 140, 171, 176
Konglishee. *See* Konglish
Kurath, Hans, 100

Labov, William, 110, 111, 127, 154, 155, 158, 195, 196
language awareness, 7, 14, 27, 67, 81, 92, 108, 124, 126, 142, 143, 147, 172, 187, 188, 190
language education, 27, 67, 75, 142, 190
language ideology, 34, 57, 60
language mavens, 57, 59
language pies, 106–108
language policing, 26, 146, 148, 149, 171, 172, 173, 174
Language quizzes, 100–103

Laugh tracks, 121–123
Let It Go, 105
Linguistic Anthropology, 25, 34, 57, 110, 195, 198
linguistic gentrification, 88, 93, 94, 95, 97, 174, 182
linguistic gentrification., 93–95
linguistic Taylorism, 15
Lippman, Walter, 50, 51, 53, 54, 55, 56, 64
Los Angeles, 29, 30, 37, 48, 181
Los Angeles Times, 40

Mangual Figueroa, Ariana, 34–36
Marcuse, Herbert, 23
members' meanings, 89, 90, 92, 93, 94, 95
Memes, 88–93
micro-aggression, 142
microtargeting, 140, 141
monolingualism, 145, 148, 149
Moyamensing (street), 7
multilingualism, 145
  and google translate, 104, 106
  and language pies, 107

narrative logic, 151, 157
narrative ways of knowing, 151
National Education Association, 186
neglected situation. *See* Neglected Situation, The
Neglected Situation, The, 86, 194
New York Times Dialect Quiz, 17
Noah, Trevor, 66

O'Neil, Cathy, 19, 140, 197
Oklahoma City, 78
On the Run (Goffman), 124
open source, 116
outtakes
  citizen sociolinguistic, 111
  in animation, 109
  in movies, 109
  in research, 110
  in school projects, 109

participatory spectacle, 160
Pashunk. *See* Passyunk (avenue)
Passyunk (avenue), 11, 12, 13, 14, 23, 55, 57, 58, 67, 69, 171
Passyunk Post, The, 8–9
Pennsylvania, Southwestern, 34, 36, 40, 46
Pepe the Frog, 42, 43, 51, 52
Peters, Russel, 122
Philadelphia street names, 176
Phillytawk, 80, 118
pill bug. *See* roly poly

Index

Pittsburghese, 159, 160
pop, 17, 19, 37, 39, 156
propaganda, 50, 51, 141
Proposition 187, 30
Public Opinion (Lippman), 50

quackson. *See croissant* pronunciation

raciolinguistics, 173
research gap, 99
retweet, 130, 147
roly poly, 156

Scripts of Servitude (Lorente), 15
Sexism, 142, 172, 173
  and Google Translate, 103, 129
shaved ice. *See* water ice
Shit Academics Say, 25, 87
Shit Girls Say, 87, 90
Singlish, 80, 84, 198
small stories, 151, 155, 156, 167, 169
soda. *See* pop
soft-serve ice-cream. *See* custard, frozen
Sopranos, 73, 74, 75
South Philadelphia, 8, 10, 12, 14, 21, 22, 54, 57, 64, 136, 164, 165
South Philly, 8, 9, 10, 11, 12, 13, 15, 64, 80, 127, 136, 138, 161, 164, 165, 166
South Philly Accent Challenge, 80
sow bug. *See* roly poly
Spanish. *See* Spanish Language
Spanish language, 29, 30
spreadability, 153, 156, 157, 167, 168
standardized ways of speaking
  and linguistic Taylorism, 15
  and scripts of servitude, 15
  resistance to, 9, 14
Steinem, Gloria, 130, 197
Steve K., 110, 111
succinct pronunciation, 76–80
Switched at Birth, 83

talk
  as a shield, 187
  as an invitation, 187, 188
talk moves, 131, 139
technological affordances, 168
technological determinism, 167
Texan, 15, 81, 159, 160
The Language Instinct (Pinker), 59
thick description, 74
Thoreau, Henry David, 3, 5, 7, 16, 27, 196, 198
tone-deaf, 141–143, 189
transcription, 71, 90, 117, 118, 119
  citizen, 117
trolls, 22, 54, 176, 179, 181, 182

unintended consequences, 145, 146, 147, 149, 149, 171, 175
upmost respect. *See* utmost respect
Urban Dictionary. *See* UrbanDictionary.com
urbandictionary.com, 44, 113
Urquhart, Fred, 4, 5, 16
utmost respect, 146

Verbal Hygiene (Cameron), 57, 60
verisimilitude, 157
Vietnamese language, 105

Wakanda Forever, 68, 85, 89
Wakandan language, 84
water. *See* wooder
water ice, 67, 68, 69, 165, 171
Web 1.0, 151, 158
Web 2.0, 151, 152, 155, 156, 158, 159, 167, 195
weg, 112, 113, 171
Welsh language, 80, 137, 138, 140, 168, 171, 176, 177, 180
West Philadelphia, 179, 180
wooder, 165, 166, 172
World's Sexiest Accents, The, 66

y'all, 81, 156, 159, 195
Yale University, 120
yinz, 159, 196
Yosemitebear62, 90

Lightning Source UK Ltd.
Milton Keynes UK
UKHW020238221020
371822UK00013B/155